The Grass Arena

The last thing John Healy needs is a tidy snippet of blurb from the likes of me which is a good thing because economy defeats me; I don't know how to be moderate or concise in praise of his startling autobiography *The Grass Arena*. So economy I'll leave to him, a master storyteller with an ear, an eye and a voice that should be the envy of many men with weightier reputations. There is no perceptible distance between the words, which seem to have chosen themselves and the experiences from which they blossomed like a garden of wild flowers. Armed to the teeth with his wit and self-knowledge he takes us to that other place, his grass arena, the one which we pass how many times in any given day, averting our eyes? The one into whose violent clutches we might descend more easily than we dare to contemplate. He is our jaunty, gleeful tour guide and messenger from hell. His fellow combatants, exuberant, murderous and sentimental, by turns touchingly loyal, vengeful and treacherous seem to have sprung from the same bloodlines as Falstaff, Pistol, Nell and their fellows. They pitch their tents in the same refuse-filled shadows as their forebears; a confederacy of the dispossessed. Healy's life, were it not for an astonishing turn of events, seems predestined to be a short one.

As in Knut Hamsun's mighty book *Hunger*, we are utterly compelled both by the power of Healy's story and his great power in the telling of it, no matter how bleak the outlook, to stay by his side until the last word is writ.

Daniel Day-Lewis
August 2008

Born in London to poor Irish parents, hardened on the streets by the age of seven, out of school at fourteen, John Healey casts himself neither as hero nor victim as he recalls the downward spiral of his teenage years, overwhelmed by alcoholism, isolated on the edge of society.

Pressed into the army, bruised by military prison and the boxing ring, dependent on drink, he ends up in the grass arena – the terrifying world ruled by psychopaths and peopled by beggars, con-men, thieves, prostitutes and killers, where the law is enforced with the broken bottle, the boot and the knife. A sordid early death seems inevitable until, in prison, he learns to play chess. His single-minded devotion to the game combines with a remarkable natural ability: he becomes a tournament champion, he plays grand masters; his brilliances are reported in the national press. One addiction is abandoned for another and his life is transformed. Peace, however, remains elusive and the quest continues.

John Healy has written an astonishing autobiography. By turns lyrical and brutal, *The Grass Arena* scalds the reader with the harsh intensity of its vision. See www.thegrassarena.net for more.

JOHN HEALY

The Grass Arena
An Autobiography

with an Afterword by Colin MacCabe

PENGUIN BOOKS

PENGUIN CLASSICS

Published by the Penguin Group
Penguin Books Ltd, 80 Strand, London WC2R ORL, England
Penguin Group (USA) Inc., 375 Hudson Street, New York, New York 10014, USA
Penguin Group (Canada), 90 Eglinton Avenue East, Suite 700, Toronto, Ontario, Canada M4P 2Y3
(a division of Pearson Penguin Canada Inc.)
Penguin Ireland, 25 St Stephen's Green, Dublin 2, Ireland (a division of Penguin Books Ltd)
Penguin Group (Australia), 250 Camberwell Road,
Camberwell, Victoria 3124, Australia (a division of Pearson Australia Group Pty Ltd)
Penguin Books India Pvt Ltd, 11 Community Centre,
Panchsheel Park, New Delhi – 110 017, India
Penguin Group (NZ), 67 Apollo Drive, Rosedale, North Shore 0632, New Zealand
(a division of Pearson New Zealand Ltd)
Penguin Books (South Africa) (Pty) Ltd, 24 Sturdee Avenue,
Rosebank, Johannesburg 2196, South Africa

Penguin Books Ltd, Registered Offices: 80 Strand, London WC2R ORL, England

www.penguin.com

First published Faber and Faber 1988
Published in Penguin Classics with revisions 2008

6

Copyright © John Healy, 1988, 2008
All rights reserved

The moral right of the author has been asserted

Printed in Great Britain by Clays Ltd, St Ives plc

978-0-141-18959-8

www.greenpenguin.co.uk

To my mother

Acknowledgements

I wish to thank:

Yana Stajna for her energy and encouragement
Frank McAllan for typing *The Grass Arena*
Clive Soley for aiding my escape from the grass arena

I

My father didn't look like he would harm anyone. He was of average height and build, jet-black hair, a handsome, weather-beaten face from working outdoors. He had nice brown eyes, and when he laughed you could see all his perfect teeth. He never laughed with me, though; instead, whatever I did or said, he would tell me to shut my mouth. When he got into a temper his eyes seemed to turn backwards in his head, going a dark muddy colour, and he would lash out with his fist or foot. He would not stop until I was bleeding or until my mother got in between us; even then he would take a long time to calm down, and he would still keep shouting abuse and threats for a good while after.

One cold winter's night, it started to snow. My father quickened his pace, forcing myself and the puppy he held on a lead to run to keep up. As we reached the old railway bridge in Kentish Town, the snow began to fall heavier causing us to take shelter under it. A few minutes later a policeman came by, his helmet and tunic white with snowflakes. Seeing us huddled against the wall, he made as if to stop, changed his mind, nodded at my father and walked smartly on. I looked up at my father's face. I thought he looked worried. At six years of age it's difficult to know what adults are thinking, so I asked, 'Haven't you got a dog licence, Dad?'

His eyes turned back in his head as he punched me in the

face, knocking me to the ground. The pain and the shock made me cry. He dragged me back to my feet, shouting all the while that I was a tyrant. Pushing a hanky into my face he started to wipe the blood and snot from my nose, saying, 'Be quiet, or I'll tell your mother what a tyrant you are.' I didn't know what a tyrant was, nor how I had become one.

My father and mother were Irish immigrants. They came from small farms within twenty miles of each other. They met in London in the 1930s at a dance and got married. We lived in the top two rooms of an old house in Kentish Town, a three-storey decrepit pile of bricks, the surrounding houses only a little better. Our neighbours on both sides were Londoners and, being immigrants, we were treated as lepers. Our backyards, separated by low walls, backed on to each other forming a large T-shape where they met. The Hams made up the cross-section of the T, while Mr and Mrs Somers and ourselves formed the stem. Looking back now I realize Mr Ham was henpecked by his formidable-looking wife, for when any of our family called a greeting over the wall, his eyes would roll towards heaven as if trying to convey the futility of words and, palming the air with his hand, he would draw a loud and laboured breath, his face in a tortured grimace throughout.

Mr Somers looked like a tough guy – cigarette hanging from his lips, hair greased back, always walking very fast as if he had somewhere important to go even when he was only going to the dustbin. I don't think Mr Somers had time to speak, but Mrs Somers made up for that. She walked very slowly and deliberately, her hips moving with a cute little motion – first one side would jut out, then the other; perhaps it was her skirts, they were skin-tight, and her slip never showed at the bottom like the other women's did. I liked watching her:

she would linger at the dustbin, saying, 'How's my sweetheart today?' Then wiggling and wobbling, like a clockwork doll, she'd go back to her door, stop, turn her head slowly and wink at me.

My mother needed to go to work so, from the age of two and a half, I was put in a nursery situated on top of a block of flats. One entered from the balcony through an iron door. I didn't like it; there was a slide, and from the top I could see my house and wanted to go home. One day I managed to open the door and was found wandering the streets by the police, who took me back to the police station, giving me tea and sandwiches until my mother, frantic with worry, came to collect me. Some time passed and I broke out again! After that a lock and chain were put on the door.

My mother was a kindly and attractive woman – the gestures of her hands were gentle and her body was wonderfully slender – but you were not supposed to show your feelings to her or for her. She would defend me physically with her own life, but she would recoil if I tried to cuddle or kiss her. She considered that people who gave each other kisses on the cheek as a greeting or a goodbye were false. She was fond of saying that the more they start kissing and touching, the quicker love goes out of the window. She was also a deeply religious woman, a devout Catholic, and never missed Mass. Apart from this, she was noble and sincere, and would try to stop my father when he attacked me with fist or boot, but he would have the damage done before her intervention could save me. Then he would stop for a while, but he would keep on at me verbally. It became impossible to find the wavelength on which I could gain his approval and, I hoped, his affection. If I was ill, my mother would do anything for me.

It was a tough area of London. The locals had no time for

foreigners, and although I was born in London and mixed and played with children of my own age, I was considered alien. I could hold my own with my own age group, but their elder brothers (sometimes by six or seven years) would verbally and physically attack me. Sometimes their mothers and fathers would make insulting remarks to me about immigrants, and I had to smile and bear it or be prevented from playing with my friends, their sons. I became a bit timid and hesitant to speak or voice an opinion in company.

My mother longed to move to a nicer area, but poverty destroyed such fond hopes. Of course it would be pointless to go home after being beaten up, so I'd hang about round the corner. One Sunday afternoon, standing on the corner with kids my own age, playing and larking about, one of the big fuckers, George Chilt, told me to fuck off.

'Why should I? Why not all of us? Why just me?' I stood my ground, but he was years older.

He caught the back of my neck – 'You fucking Irish cunt,' and crashing his knee into my face smashed my nose.

I became very tense. I could never be sure when they would carry out their threats: at least once a week the older boys would beat me up, but my desire for company and fun always overcame fear, and I would be back the next day. Eventually this treatment had its effect. I started to suffer from tension in the upper back and neck, which gradually caused me to walk hunched up. My mum used to chide me, for my own good, telling me to pull back my shoulders, throw my chest out and breathe deeply – but it was impossible. One day at school, in a mass X-ray, they found I had developed a shadow or something on my lung from being hunched over my chest. No one knew about my beatings on the street or thought about tension and I never told anyone.

It was decided to send me to school at Margate, where I would stay for six months. I was overjoyed living there. We were taken for walks every day on the beach and in the surrounding countryside, and as there were only kids, i.e. boys and girls of my own age, I had lots of friends and no trouble. It was heaven. At night I could see the ships with their lights passing way out to sea from the dormitory window. To a boy from the city it was bliss. My mum used to come every Sunday to visit and bring me some small toy or other.

Six months flew by and one morning a bunch of us frail-looking but possibly healthier kids were loaded into a coach and driven to London to be unloaded amid welcoming cries from parents at County Hall. I looked and looked for my mother but she was not there. I waited, watching all my new friends being greeted as if they had just returned from a perilous adventure rather than the cosy convalescent home. My mother was very late. Women were always late; at least, the women who had anything to do with me were. My aunts were always late, making me wait alone for hours on platforms looking after cases. Eventually, my mother came rushing round the corner, but, always in the process of being left by a woman, I did not rush to meet her.

I was back home and facing the big bastards on the streets once more. Then another problem arose. Sometimes the big cunts would beat me up too much. One evening I came in off the street with my eye cut, my nose bleeding and two front teeth knocked out. My father had just got in from the pub. He flew into a temper, shouting, 'How is it they only beat *you* up? It must be your own fault!' As he could hardly hit me in the state I was in, things took a new turn. 'You're not religious enough,' he roared. 'You've no respect for God, that's your trouble. I'll see that you get religious; yes, I'll see that you get religious all right. It's my duty, I'm your father!'

5

That was my last free evening. Every evening after that, I can't remember for how long, I would be bent over the Catechism – 'I believe in the Immaculate Conception . . . I believe in the Holy Ghost . . .' and on and on. I believed in anything just to get to bed. Six questions had to be learnt each night; to get one wrong resulted in a good beating. I should have been a priest!

One night I forgot all the answers to the questions. I just couldn't remember a thing. My father's eyes started to narrow. I tried to explain, making some excuse or other. He interrupted, imitating my London accent. It was making his temper boil. I wasn't sure how to react. Better to stay silent, I thought.

'What are you sulking about?' he demanded, drawing back his fists as if to strike. Putting my hands over my head, I covered up, backing away. This happened a few more times. Then, one night, as he threatened to strike, I just stood in front of him without flinching. I don't remember what I thought – maybe that the threats were becoming worse than the execution. Whatever it was though, he went berserk: 'You bloody young pup,' he roared, smashing me to the ground with his fists. 'I'll teach you to defy me. I'm your father, God blast you to hell!' After that night, whenever he hit me, I felt only physical pain, whereas before I would agonize over how I could gain his approval. I sensed that if he did not allow you the choice of standing up straight against a threat, then there was no honour in him.

One day at school assembly a kid called Peter Farr was missing. No one moved into his place, it was just left empty. Then the teacher got up on the stage and said: 'We are going to offer prayers up this morning for the soul of Peter Farr's father, who has just passed away.' Everybody lowered their heads and seemed very sad. I thought Peter Farr was very lucky. I wished my father would die, then I could get rid of this scared feeling and I'd be happy.

2

There's a sort of calmness that seems to come out of the grass and the ditches and the mossy banks. Lonely mists that suddenly spread over the fields give an old feeling, cosy and warm. Always a lot of work to be done everywhere. The bogs are very ancient. The people, especially the women with their delicate skin, soft as the misty climate, give the warmest welcome to friend and stranger alike. Each time I returned these feelings became stronger. It was nice to be on a farm: the world is contained within it. Animals, relations, the weekly jaunt to church or the shop; things to occupy the days ... Of course, I didn't experience any difference there between myself and the people around me, everybody was friendly, everybody knew me. I did not have to prove anything.

Leaving Ireland was always a wrench. Each time an aunt would be sent with instructions to bring me back to London. I'd manage to avoid this at first by being near hysterical every time the matter was mentioned. They'd return without me. Then sterner methods would be employed. I would be dragged kicking and screaming up the hill and on to the back road to catch the once-a-day bus for town, in tears all the way back to London. Later on an aunt would only have to arrive at the farm and I'd run away or hide on the day we were supposed to leave. They had to devise ever more tricks and traps to entice me to go with them, so by the time I realized the trick it would be too late! The journey itself was not without fears for me. It was the waiting that worried me most. It seemed I was always waiting; I waited and watched the luggage. My aunts would go off and sometimes not return for an hour, one time it was three – running out of money in Dublin they left me looking after luggage while they went off to another aunt's house (a fifty-mile journey or so) to borrow some more.

From the age of two I would be brought over to Ireland from time to time and left with my grandmother and her sons and daughters. She had altogether three boys and eleven girls, including my mother. My first recollection of Ireland was when I was about four years old – playing in green fields, surrounded by animals, loved by my uncles, grandmother, grandfather and especially by young aunties, who seemed to be Love itself. No matter what I did my uncles would not punish me.

My grandmother was tall, six feet tall. The only trouble was she never reached that height when I was a child; she'd bent into an upside-down L-shape. She'd had fourteen children and I suppose with all the bending and washing, lifting cooking-pots, wood, laundry, carrying buckets to feed calves, fetching water, cooking over an open fire, she never bothered to straighten up. She was, however, not a pushover, and from time to time would give me a slap with a willow rod. I remember one instance of her wrath. The neighbouring family farm was owned by a couple called Coyle, who had four young children, all boys. Their mother, Mrs Coyle, was a highly educated woman having had the benefit of a university education, unusual for a country woman in a deep, rural community. She was very fond of me and tended to cosset me a little too much, preventing me sometimes from playing with any of the other lads, telling me they were too rough for me and that I should stay by her big, open fire, drink tea, eat sweet cakes and talk with her. She had a donkey that was too old for work and was full of lice; she let me ride it and treat it as my own. I loved that ass and dreamed of it each night. My grandmother had warned me that I was not to bring it on to her land as it was so verminous. One afternoon I begged Mrs Coyle to let me ride it back home. She agreed if I would stay a little longer with her and her husband and take some tea. I seldom took tea off her as her husband had bad lungs and could sometimes only get his breath by squatting on his haunches holding his head between his hands; retching and coughing, he would bring up a lot of phlegm which he would spit in the direction of the fire, usually missing. It would land with a crackling hiss on the side of the frying-pan or kettle. This day I readily agreed and after finishing the tea she caught up the ass and gave me the rope. I proudly led him away home, and put him in the old stable without being seen. Then it dawned on me, the ass was no good if I couldn't show him off.

'Granny, I've got something to show you. You won't be cross, will you?'

Well, she was cross. In fact, she went berserk, grabbed me by the scruff of the neck and beat me on the legs with a sally-rod. I made a run for the open window, got my head and shoulders out, hands touching the ground ready to balance me through, when down came the window trapping me, and down came the sally-rod on my trapped bum. After, she was sorry, started to pet me up, could not do enough for me. I took full advantage of the situation and demanded that she let me keep the ass, which she did, promising never to beat me in future. Both promises she kept.

After I'd been staying with my grandmother for some months, the authorities said I'd have to attend school. So one fine morning my granny packed some sandwiches for me and I headed off towards the gate by the sand road, where it was arranged that the Coyle boys would take me to school. There were four of them, three older than myself; the youngest, Sean, was about my age but a lot bigger. We set off along the road. None of us wore any shoes. None of the kids wore shoes in the summer months, saving them for winter as money was scarce. One of the lessons consisted of learning to speak Gaelic. I could not understand it at all. What use was the Irish language to me? So I never tried. Then Miss Barnes, our old Infants' teacher, asked me to stand up and read some Gaelic words to the rest of the class. I just stood there. 'Come out here,' she said. 'You're as thick as Conner's ass.' She walloped me with a ruler – not too hard so I didn't really mind. Besides, I liked the place.

One Saturday everyone seemed very busy on my uncle's farm. My uncles and grandfather rounded up two young bullocks and tied them by their heads to the posts in the cowhouse. It seemed funny to be milking at that time of the day – round noon – so I watched them. They tied ropes around the animals' back legs, and pulled them tight up to the front stalls so they could not kick back. Everybody was talking as if something different was going to happen, when a tall man came down the lane on a bike. Getting off his bike, he shook hands with everybody, then bent down and made a big fuss of me. They all went into the cow-house. The tall man pulled a package from his coat pocket and took out a cut-throat razor like my grandfather used to shave with . . . Suddenly he bent down behind the nearest bullock and catching what seemed to be his privates, he ran the razor slowly down the bullock's long ball bag. The bullock did not seem to notice. He did it again and the bag split open. I could see red and white meat inside; the blood started flowing out; the bullock was lifting his back legs with pain and trying to kick out, but was held tight by the ropes. I got scared. I felt shy, but mostly I got very angry. I could not see why they should do such a terrible thing, the most evil thing I had ever seen. I was so confused that I could not speak. My uncle told me to go and get a jam jar of Jeyes' fluid from my granny. I did not move, I would not go, I would not help them hurt this bullock any more. My uncle put his arm round me but I started screaming at them for cutting the calf. They said it had to be done or he would ruin the cows. Did I want the cows to be ruined? 'No.' Then they said they had to do it. 'No,' I screamed. They said he would not only ruin *our* cows but would jump over the ditch into Casey's land and ruin his cows. My grandfather came back with the jar of Jeyes' fluid and Mr Farrel shoved the jar up between the calf's legs and rinsed it round. They untied him and drove him out. He tried to run but his back legs were too stiff after what they'd taken out of him and he staggered along in a giddy sort of way. I went away into the house crying. My granny gave me some sweets and sat me by the fire.

After a while the men came in. I was still mad at them and would not speak to them. My uncle put his hands round me and picked me up. Kidding me to make me laugh, he said, 'Shall we take one out of little Johnny?' I knew they were only fooling but I would not look at him or at any of them. I could not see how the bullocks would ruin the cows. They were all friends in the fields. I had seen them playing together, and the bullock would put his two front feet up on to the cow's back and try to get a piggy-back off her. What harm had he ever done?

We used to finish school at 3 p.m. in the summer, and as well as the Coyles, the Farrel kids used to walk our way. Two boys older than me and a girl called Mary. One day coming home from school I found out that the Farrel kids' father was the man who had cut our calves. I kept quiet until we reached the county crossroads, then I started screaming at them: 'Your father is a pig . . . he cut our calves!'

The Farrel boys started laughing and tried to make me shut

up but I went on. So they picked up stones and started throwing them at me, shouting, 'You English cur! Go back to England!' The row had arisen. I went for one of the boys. We punched each other in the face. Then Mary and her brother went for me, but the Coyle boys pulled them off, separating us, warning the Farrels to keep going on in front quick-like. They kept shouting back, 'You English black and tan swine!' I kept shouting that their father, mother and all belonging to them were evil calf cutters. After this I refused to attend school. So my uncle asked if I would go if he took me in the horse and trap. I said I would if he made the horse gallop past the Farrels. And that's how I went to school for a few weeks. But me and the Farrels were always fighting, and the others started siding with them, saying, 'Go back to England, John Bull.'

'Calf cutters!' I'd shout back. Then we'd start throwing stones at each other. Fair play to the Coyle boys, they'd always take my part.

After a while it got out of hand and I refused to go to school at all or be near the Farrels. So I was taken back to England.

I placed my head between my hands, my elbows resting on the chair that I was kneeling in front of. When the rest of my family began to close their eyes, whether through tiredness or devotion, I would pull the chair closer to my stomach and lean back on my heels: I'd found that this was the most comfortable position to get through the half-hour rosary sessions my father insisted on lately.

When we were all kneeling facing a picture of Our Lady of the Rosary, we began, my father's strong voice recalling the terrible sufferings of the Madonna, who was looking up, arms raised towards the figure of her Son's agony on the cross, her tight-fitting bodice suggesting sex more than sorrow. My father's voice fell silent as we replied with words which, apart from being strange, seemed to be forcing me to think that suffering was nicer than looking at women. And the girls at my school, who were beginning to swell inside their blouses, how would they work it? Would they be able to have kids without letting a bloke have a fuck? The words didn't seem right in our back room ... virgins ... fornicating ... agony ... ecstasy ... damnation ... lustful. Don't have sex, pluck out your eye instead. Amen.

I'd go down to the corner to play. Some of the older boys would start putting on an Irish accent and take the mickey out of me. One guy, Ronnie, would never let up; he was about five years older than me and twice my size; no chance. He could not lose. All his mouthy family were behind him too. I was playing with his brother and a few other kids one day when he came up.

'Top of the morning to you, Paddy,' he said.

All the happiness went out of me but I pretended to smile. 'What you laughing at, you Irish cunt?'

'Nothing,' I said.

'You better not be laughing at me, you cunt,' and grabbing me by the collar he kneed me in the bollocks. I went down holding my privates, tears coming out of my eyes, but I was not crying.

Some of the kids laughed and his young brother said, 'Leave him, Ron, he's not laughing at you.'

'He'd better not be.'

I got off the ground but did not go – he'd not hit me again that day. Besides, I had nowhere else to play.

It seemed that the world was made up of punishment and suffering, especially when you looked at the religious pictures that hung on the walls of our home and at school. In every one a man or a woman was in bad trouble, especially God's own son, who hung crucified from the cross, thorns in his head, spears in his side and daggers dripping blood plunged to the hilt in his heart while his mother, eyes raised in anguish, reaching, stretching, bodice straining to the point of incest, clasps him to her bosom. Just when you thought you might have seen it all you discovered a fresh agony – there was that lovely French girl getting roasted in her armour! Floggings, flailings and not even an armed angel in sight to stop the perpetual torment. Not content with making us look, we had to read, study and contemplate it as well. It makes one a better, happier and more noble person, I was told with enthusiasm whenever I sullenly asked.

But we doubted that and even to doubt was an enormous sin in itself. So we begged, borrowed or stole. Bolts and ball bearings from scrap yards, timber from outside shops to make scooters, decorating the front with coloured beer-bottle tops to make them look sharp.

From waste dumps we sorted out parts of discarded bicycle wheels, knocking out the spokes to stretch a piece of sacking tight as a drum round the rim. Three pieces of string tied the lot together and they in turn were knotted on to a long rope. This contraption we lowered down into the canal and dragged along the bottom, where the glistening sticklebacks lay. We loved to peer down into this reflective world where those slippery fish hid from us to try and see what other secrets it contained. But it was an offence even to walk there, never mind fish from the canal bank. And if brought to the attention of my father it would have warranted a wallop along with an early night. But being sent to bed early sometimes held its own amazement. Though sleep swollen, lying silently in the dark, my limbs would sometimes tremble in anticipation when the boards creaked on the landing outside the bedroom door. No longer limp with sleep you stiffened, as an aunt would come quietly in with her latest purchase. A new skirt, a blouse or perhaps a more intimate garment. Suddenly the room would be swimming with light. Then I would realize that everywhere was full of things waiting to be seen. Startled by this sudden exposure the room would change shape as one of them, private and mysterious in the chipped silvery scales of the wardrobe mirror, softly removed their dress to reveal a pink slip of which the transparent folds never quite concealed. When they raised their bare arms to push the slippery straps from their slender shoulders, the slip, with one silken, shimmering swish would slither slowly all the way down their body to the floor. So smooth, you could feel yourself shiver, you knew how it felt without having to touch. Though you had not raised your eyes to look in any particular direction, the world would have appeared a duller place if suspender belts and stocking tops had not imposed their glitter. At such times it was easy to forget, to become lost as the mirror prepared to reveal more in a nylon dream.

In the summer some of us kids would meet early in the morning and head off to Hampstead Heath. We'd mess about in the ponds, fishing, swimming and tadpoling. In autumn we'd go scrumping fruit off the trees in the posh gardens. In the winter we would chop wood, bundle it up and sell it to the old women in the surrounding streets. When we'd made enough, we would share it out, then go to the pictures to see the latest swashbuckler with Errol Flynn. Afterwards we'd start imitation sword-fights with bits of wood, using dustbin lids for shields. We'd be cowboys, Indians, knights in armour, whatever the current film . . . We would all want to be the hero and act out all the scenes.

Once when a local cinema showed *Ivanhoe*, a bigger kid called

Billy took us up to his house. We painted beards and moustaches on to our faces, got his mother's saucepans and pots, put them on to our heads and painted helmcrests on the front. Armed with long sticks for broadswords, we were ready. Down into the street we went. There were about six of us. Everyone wanted to be Ivanhoe. But Billy said he was going to be Ivanhoe as it was his gear. So I had to be the bad black knight, and we started a mock battle. Ivanhoe was supposed to beat me up, but I hit Billy on the knees first and over went Ivanhoe. When he got up, I was trying to swordfence another kid and Billy tripped me up. We all went down in a heap, grazing our knees and foreheads, but we loved it.

Another money-maker for us kids was to collect old newspapers and take them round to the scrap-dealer. Once I badly wanted to go to the pictures but my papers were not heavy enough. So I put a little bit of metal between them. The scrap-dealer never suspected it, and I got enough for sweets as well as the pictures.

When I was about eleven years old, my father made my young brother Terry and me join a Sunday School class at our regular school – more catechism classes! The teacher would always come in late but we did not mind. One Sunday we started playing around with a bigger kid called Joe MacGinley, throwing chalk at each other. Heavier stuff came to hand like the empty earthenware ink pots. It got out of hand when my brother threw a chair and ran out of the room with Joe after us in a flaming temper. We shot into another classroom and I shut the door (which was all glass at the top) and crouching down behind it, held the handle fast so Joe could not get in. He tried the handle a couple of times and then let out a shout and smashed his fist right through the glass. I heard my brother scream and jumped to comfort him. I did not know what he was screaming for. Then I heard Joe crying and holding his hand up. It was spilling blood so I said to Terry, 'Fuck him, don't get scared, the bastard can't hurt you now.'

'It's my eye,' said Terry.

'What?'

'I think the glass is gone in my eye.'

'No, Ter, let me look, it couldn't have.'

I was scared to even think about it. His eye was streaming tears, I could see nothing, so I said, 'It's OK now, Ter, yeah, it's all right I think.' Just then the teacher came up with the caretaker. They were shocked at the sight of Joe's hand and the caretaker ran off to phone an ambulance. We were sent home. On the way we met my father who was going to twelve o'clock Mass. I thought I'd better tell him, although my brother seemed to be all right by then. I explained what happened, leaving out earlier playing about in the rooms.

'Here's a couple of bob. Catch a bus home and tell your mother. I can see nothing in your eye, Terry,' said my father.

We walked home and bought sweets with the money. My mother was very concerned and took Terry to Moorfields Eye Hospital. When they reached the hospital, Terry was put on a stretcher, examined and wheeled into the operating theatre. The doctor came up to my mum and told her, 'We can save the eye, but we can't save the sight.' My mother cried all the way home. I was as sad as hell and felt like taking some kind of revenge on Joe, but he was off school for a month with his arm. My brother was in hospital for six months, and it all blew over. I was glad no one blamed me for anything.

One day Terry came home with my mother. We were all surprised and happy to see him. His eye looked normal and moved like his good one, but the sight was gone. He never mentioned it and neither did I. One good thing came out of it; we never had to go to Sunday School again!

My father used to pass the local boxing club each week on

his way home from work. I suppose that gave him the idea. He sent me and my brother out one evening to join it. One look at the place, the smell of sweat, the noise of the punch balls rocking back and forth, and the tough-looking blokes punching fuck out of each other in the rings, was more than enough to put us right off the idea. We managed to kid him each week that the secretary was away, and that he was the only person that could let us join. This worked for a while, but one evening our Dad surprised us when he told us he was going to come down to the club and find out when the secretary would be there. We had no way out and became members that same night. After the first week I loved it, and was always willing to go into the ring to spar with lads bigger than myself for the experience. It was a joy, just the two of us, no insults about race, no mates to back my opponent up against me. I would get stuck right in, landing punches and taking them in return. My brother Terry was a brave little fucker and would fight well, but he would get backed up into a corner and smashed on his blind side. But the little bugger never complained. After two weeks though, the trainers realized he could not see out of one eye, and they barred him from going into the ring. Then he used to just punch the bag and do some skipping, and after a while he got bored and gave it up.

There was a small grocer's shop on the corner near our house. It was owned by an old woman called Mrs Payne and she kept an old man as a lodger.

There was a metal grid on the floor at the entrance and when you stepped on it, it produced a loud rattling sound that alerted Mrs Payne. She always dozed in the armchair in a back room with a window looking into the shop. My mother used to send me to the shop for things. One day I stepped over the grid and stood silently in the shop. I moved over to the door window: Mrs Payne was reading the paper, the lodger was looking at a book. I bent down and crouched past the door and in behind the counter – Jesus, I was just by the till. My heart was in my mouth, my breathing was tight, and my mind went very still, no thoughts, just a sort of sexy fear, like when I cuddled one of the girls in class. The till was broken, the drawer was half-open, packed with money. I quietly took out one half-crown, and made my way round past the door, back into the middle of the shop just as Mrs Payne got up, seeing me, opened the door and came in.

'Yes, Johnny?'

'A sliced loaf, Mrs Payne, please.' My voice was hoarse and trembling.

'Help yourself, there's a good boy.'

I took a loaf, paid her and left. Jesus, I was now a thief! What did the Catholic Church say about thieves? We would burn in everlasting fire. Still, there would be lots burning with me. I wouldn't be on my own. Some blokes were 'thieves and despoilers of women'; first they stole a bloke's wife, then they fucked with her. Christ, whatever you did it was against the Ten Commandments. I wished I never knew about them. I could not stop myself nicking from that till. It was nearly like magic – so beautiful, terrifying and dangerous. If I ever got caught, I was dead. My dad would kill me, my mum would stop loving me, Mrs Payne would hate me, and God (if he was there) knew already even before I did it, so I was fucked with him. Anyhow, according to the rules of the Catholic Church, I was going to hell when I died. But I could not see myself dying for a long time yet, and maybe I could talk my way out of it. It did not matter, I could not stop. I got bolder and took more money. The only thing I could not guard against was someone coming into the shop while I was behind the counter.

I'd just taken the money out of the till one day, when a girl came in. She looked at me. We stood staring at each other from either side of the situation. I walked past the room door and, sliding round to the customers' side, I called Mrs Payne. As she opened the door I said, 'There's a girl here, Mrs Payne,' and pointed to show that it was true.

She served her. Then I bought a loaf and left. It was close. I kept on nicking out of the till for about another year, then I told a mate called Charlie, whose sister was pretty. We both started doing it together, but one day Charlie went on his own and fucked it up. Somehow he never told me the truth of what happened, but after that Mrs Payne put up a wooden door between the shop and the other side. I wished his sister had been ugly!

3

One Sunday morning on my way to church I met a kid called Albert.

'Where you going, Johnny?'

'For a walk.' I didn't want to tell anybody I had to go to church.

'Fancy a game of darts?'

'Where?'

'In the pub.' Off we went to the pub. He was bigger than me and a bit older and seemed used to going in the pub. I felt a bit strange as if everyone was going to turn on me and throw me out or something. We pushed through to the bar, and when the bartender came over I was sure we would not be allowed to stay. But Albert said, 'Two brown ales, mate.' The bartender put them on the counter, Albert paid him and asked for a set of arrows. We went over to the dartboard. I could not count up the scores but I could throw a bit. We played against two older men. After a while we finished our drinks and I gave Albert the church collection money to go and get more browns as he thought I might look too young to get served. The time flew round and when we came out at closing time I felt a bit giddy. It was a terrific feeling and my back and neck were not playing me up. I'm going to have some more of this, I thought.

I was playing truant from school a lot that year and I got in a bit of bother over it now and then. Funny thing was, I liked school in one way because it got me near different people from my old man; but I hated it in another, because I could not keep my mind on lessons and was always falling asleep at my desk. I used to be happy on Wednesday afternoons. That was when we had art class. The art teacher was a nice-looking woman. She was kinder and a lot curvier than the other teachers and she had lovely long legs. Sometimes she would sit on the front of her desk with her legs crossed and her slip would show. Then the boys would look, staring out of their own surprise, paying very strict attention indeed! One day, sitting on the desk, wiping chalk dust from her hands, her dress rode up on one side; the top of her stocking was showing. Because it was something that happened in spite of yourself, I could not take my eyes away; everything disappeared – no sounds, no noise, no nothing – except Miss Golon's shapely legs. Then I heard the other kids giggling: I was caught, Miss Golon was looking right at me. She called me to the front of the class. Jesus! I went all red, standing out beside her like that. The rest of the class had stopped giggling now, so as to extract the most from what was about to happen. It was totally silent as she straightened a clip that pinned her hair before thoughtfully moistening her lips. 'If you kids don't know how the mechanics of life work', she began and she tapped with her fingers on my arm, 'it's about time you found out.' She had a foreign accent, and it sounded really serious and sexy at the same time. Then she placed her hand on my shoulder and said, 'Your father's got an organ and your mother receives it into her organ.' I couldn't keep my mind on it – out in front of the class like that, it had no shape. After a while she stopped talking and dismissed the class. Then when everybody had gone she pushed back her hair, turned to me and said, 'Will you do something for me?' I was afraid I would die from fear and excitement, my mind stopped, my voice went hoarse.

'What?' I asked.

'Take the palettes to the cloakroom and wash them all nice and clean for me.' Then with a smile of sweet forgiveness she went over to the door and called out to a kid in the corridor named Green to help me. We had to use the girls' cloakroom. Two girls were on monitor duty. They kept coming round us giggling. So after we'd washed up, we started to chase them round the coat stands. After we caught them we gave them a kiss and a cuddle. One of the girls used to let us feel her tits through her cardigan on which the buttons strained to keep them contained, and I think she was brave enough to let us feel elsewhere too. But I was too shy to put my hand anywhere else, and we would stop and start giggling. They were the best days at school. I can remember that girl. Her name was Ann. She was very pretty and friendly.

Benediction was compulsory every Wednesday evening. The whole of St Dominick's school would file out into the massive priory next door while the organ played softly, longingly inviting, imploring what isn't there to appear, for the invisible to become present. I'd kneel, gazing up at the ornate ceiling, the stained-glass windows and the curved pulpit, wondering what it was all about. Until the ringing of a bell announced the entrance of an altar boy, swinging a crucible billowing thick incense smoke, and walking slowly in front of a priest, who with hands clasped in supplication would, after murmuring a few 'Aves' and 'Paters', solemnly encourage us to lose our wicked thoughts in ador-ation of a statue of the Virgin Mary. She had a little crucifix dangling from her neck that would jump around and tap her marble breasts every time a tram juddered past. Her stone stare suddenly expanded and the immaculate lips parted one more time in vibration and her ecstasy would have been complete but the tram had gone. And now your chest began to heave as the organ music rose up with a rush in your throat and gushed out:

'*The saints are high in glory on golden thrones above – but brighter still is Mary upon her throne of light.*' You were deterred momentarily from thinking as the whole church was vibrating with the Virgin's name. Sound became longing, you began to feel passion, you began to feel pain, in fact you wanted to weep at the sound of her name. The effect was strangely beautiful and in that moment waves of sadness would all but overwhelm me until the voices of the clear-skinned girls, mounting in unison vowing purity and modesty, would send a surge of desire racing through me. As if straining to hear some inner voice everybody's head would bow in devotion. Even the rouged imps and smirking cherubs adorning the marble pulpit seemed to suddenly become grave as the priest held up the chalice to show that Christ had risen. You could feel it in the girls' voices and in the throbbing of your blood. With embarrassment and guilt I would try to check my thoughts from destroying the sacredness around me by viewing the girls as saintly. Unfortunately, regardless of the vows they had just uttered so modestly, the kneeling position the girls adopted made their bums jut out so wickedly that, in spite of a desire to worship, an urge to fuck all of them, starting with the Virgin Mary herself, would grip me until I got out of that church.

What with playing truant and falling asleep during lessons, I never learned much from going to school, so after I left I didn't have much luck finding a job until my mate Frankie spoke to the governor of the builders' merchants where he was working. The work consisted of unloading and loading hundredweight bags of cement, shovelling sand out of railway trucks and stacking bricks. It was heavy work and the governor on the railway sidings did not think I would be able for it, but Frankie told him I was very strong. I'm sure the guv was trying not to laugh as I looked anything but strong, but he decided to give me the job anyway.

It was smashing there. Frankie and I used to muck about all the time even though the work was hard. A lot of tough kids used to come round that wharf and when the horseplay got out of hand there would be fights. But I was quite happy and could hold my own against kids two stone heavier. I had developed a strong punch in either hand.

My father got less violent now that I was getting older, but I still felt as if there was a lump riding across my shoulders and neck; the only time I got rid of it was when I went to sleep or had a drink. In those days the kids used to meet on the corners of the street. They got the nickname 'corner boys'. The boys would watch the girls go by, and one girl called Janet was very pretty, tall and slim, with blonde hair. Most of the boys fancied her but, if anyone said they liked her, everyone would take the piss out of them, saying she was too skinny. I didn't mind. She was my dream girl, so I would try to bump into her and her mate Rita every chance I could. One night I got up the courage to go round to her house and ask for a date. Trouble was, I got the courage up in the pub, and when I got round to Janet's flat there was another guy there called Mickey Jordan, who was also a boxer. The trouble with Mickey was that he was quite good-looking; I was jealous, I suppose, and a bit drunk. I managed to land a fast left and avoided a murderous right, but fell on to a left upper-cut which split my lower lip in two. It never healed properly, and the scar's still there to this day. Needless to say I was sad as hell losing a fight to Jordan, losing Janet and losing my pride, so I stayed in, licking my wound, for the next week. On the Saturday evening there was a knock on my door. I was a bit worried in case it was Jordan coming to finish me off. What a shock I got on opening the door to find Janet and her friend Rita standing there. We went round to Frankie's house. Was he surprised – and I had a girl for him too! I was soon going steady with Janet and I was as happy as a sandboy. But the invisible lump of spiteful pain would not go away. It was becoming such a nuisance that I found it difficult to talk, and I was getting exhausted just being in anyone's company.

There was a kid called Billy. He had thick black hair greased back and cut in a Tony Curtis style – not bad-looking with plenty of chat. I had been staying in for a while, hoping the tension would go away. When I went on the corner again, Billy was standing with Janet. After a while, she came over and asked me where I'd been. I told her I'd been ill and asked her if Billy was her boyfriend now. She said they were just friends. I wasn't feeling too good so I walked away and went into the pub. I was drinking a bit more now; it was the only way I could shift the pain. That always reminded me of how fucked up I was!

I did not have enough money to get much drink with, so I started to go to a professional boxing gym at Warren Street called the Olympic Gym. It was situated in a basement and some of the best boxers in the country used to train there including Terry Downes. I used to spar for thirty shillings for a few rounds with some of the best bantams and lightweights in the country. I was as proud as Punch to be on first names with them all. I started trying to copy some of the champion boxers of the time. Floyd Patterson was the heavyweight champion of the world; only trouble was, he wasn't a natural heavyweight so he built up his shoulders and chest. He used to hold his hands high and looked like a bunny rabbit bobbing up and down. I found that a cute way of avoiding punches. Then there was Willie Pastrano, a real favourite of mine, a swarthy, good-looking Italian-American, he was the light-heavyweight champion of the world at twelve stone six pounds. Pastrano was the fastest, classiest boxer I had ever seen, so I copied from him to improve my style. There are a few other things that you need to help you win in the ring like skipping, running, punching heavy sandbags, plenty of good food and sparring practice. I never bothered with any of it except sparring. One of the older trainers used to tell us, 'Lads, keep away from women.' Like it was the secret of secrets. His warning was a bit wasted on me; I thought chance would be a fine thing!

I enjoyed boxing and within a year had managed to win a few amateur titles. I got some good write-ups in the paper. I might have done well in the ring except for two things, drink and tension: I took one to relieve the other. The leading manager at the time (unaware that I was under-age) offered me a six-month trial period, after which I would get a licence to fight professionally, but my increasing appearances at the gym, obviously the worse for drink, caused him to reconsider and he left me one night with the choice: 'Either give up drink or stay out of the ring.' After that I pawned all my silver boxing cups for drink. Some nights I would be too drunk to get home, waking up stiff and frozen in doorways or somebody's garden. By this time my parents were sick of my drinking. I could see no way of stopping. So no one was too worried when I left home. I used to doss down in old cars: the streets in those days were littered with old bangers. I had nowhere else to go.

One day I was wasting time sitting in a café that was run by a spiv called Jack. Although only in his early twenties, he had gone completely grey owing to the fact, it was said, that he had just missed the rope one time for murder. He served me a cup of tea with hands that shook, but this was due more to the fact that he'd overdone it in the saloon bar of the Old Eagle the night before rather than to any last-minute death cell reprieve. As I was sipping the tea, this tall, slim woman came in with an Alsatian dog. She sat down and ordered a cup of coffee. You could see how the night had bruised her.

I went over and started talking to the dog, then I got chatting to her. The eyes of the builders lingered on her momentarily.

She was good-looking in a wasted kind of way. When she'd finished her coffee, she invited me round to her house which was only a couple of blocks away. I went with her. As we entered her front room, the smell that came at me was sickening. Then I noticed this old guy, just skin and bone, lying in the armchair. His eyes followed me as I sat down; he said nothing and did not seem surprised to see me with the woman.

'This is my husband,' she said.

'Hello, guv'nor.'

He just stared at the wall. The room was dimly lit and filthy but it would do me. The woman seemed to sense my thought and said, 'You can stay here, sleep in the chair, you'll be warm there.'

'Thanks, lady.' And that was that.

I never asked her name and she never told me. Every night when I'd come in drunk, she'd be in the bedroom with a different bloke. They seemed to be mostly seafaring gentlemen. I could hear them moaning and wrestling about on nights when I wasn't too drunk. Those old tars were certainly very serious in their efforts but she seemed to be quite playful and when squeezed in a certain way would let out a little shriek. Although the door of the bedroom was not locked, I never went into it, I just didn't want to know. She had a handsome face, but I didn't fancy her, so we got on OK. She used to tell the blokes I was her son. I didn't mind what she told them, so long as I could kip free in the armchair.

Sometimes I didn't get in till dawn, my face scratched and bruised, an eye just turning black from brawling in the clubs with navvies and seamen. Flopping into an armchair exhausted from my overnight efforts to become world lightweight champion of the clubs and pubs, I'd just be peacefully dozing off when she would kneel down beside the chair and start cuddling and stroking my head, sobbing quietly. Now and again between sobs she'd let out an actress's tortured sigh, moaning, 'My poor pussycat, where have you been? What have they done to you?' Poor cow! Just as I would be thinking of responding and taking her in my arms, the old boy would look over with his haunting eyes . . . I'd remember my bruised ribs and turn away.

I couldn't relax without a drink. In a way I was like Siamese twins with my invisible lump joined on to my neck and back. I don't know if twins give each other any pain, but my fucking twin lump was murdering me and I couldn't get away from the bastard.

I had to get money for drink, but I could not keep a job. Too drunk or sick from drink, I could not earn money in the boxing ring either. There was only one way left: thieving and shop-lifting. One morning I woke up on the floor, with the lingering echo of a scream in my ears. Everything was smashed to pieces around the room. I could not remember what happened the night before. I looked over at the old boy. I knew he was dead. Funny how you can tell. I wasn't really worried that he was dead, but I was beginning to get worried about what made him dead. Anyway, first things first: I needed a drink. Moving over towards him, I was just about to search his pockets when the bedroom door swung open. This big bloke followed by the woman came through. I could not make out what they were saying, he was mumbling and growling, and she started screeching, but in a sedate kind of way, saying that he and I had been fighting the night before and the shock had killed her beloved husband. Her beloved husband! Some smelly old man in a bed. I really needed a drink. I didn't like the way she was putting things. The guy roared at her to shut up, and she went all weepy and left the room. He asked me if I'd go for a bottle of wine and gave me some money. I was out of that house like a shot. 'Fuck the wine.' I kept going until I reached the Cider House pub at Kentish Town.

I drank all day, deciding after closing time to keep away from the manor for a while. I caught a tube to Burnt Oak. As I got out, the drink began to catch up with me. I tried to get into a car for a kip; it was locked, fuck it! They were all locked. I kept trying to find one open.

'What are you doing here? Who are you?'

I didn't know what I was doing there or who I was. Two big plain-clothes coppers grabbed hold of me. I could hear the static crackling of their car radio: 'We got a young sus here.'

'OK, van's on the way.'

I was as sleepy as hell. Everything seemed blurred. A police van pulled up beside us. I was bundled into the back. I rolled over and went to sleep. I was woken, dragged into the cop shop, fingerprinted, charged on sus – trying car door handles – and thrown in a cell. It was nice and warm. I fell asleep. Next day in court I was remanded to Brixton Prison for a week. I had a bath, got fed, slept most of the days, all the nights. When I got back to court I was feeling good. Looking round the courtroom I was surprised to see my mother. I got off with two years' probation. I walked out of court with my mum. After promising her I'd never drink again, we went home. She was really worried. I felt sad for her. She was very fond of me, always trying to help; but it never seemed to work. Whatever anyone did for me, gave me, told me, threatened, pleaded, promised, I would still end up on the drink. Perhaps this time would be different.

Ironically, my parents were running a pub now. I got a job working sub-contract for the railway six days a week, which included Sunday (double time). The work was hard, lifting out sixty-foot railway lines and replacing them with new ones; unloading truckloads of sleepers, sand, ballast, etc. I kept my drinking to weekends. This way I managed to save up the deposit for a new car. I was under age, so I forged my father's signature, paid the deposit and drove away. One night after the pubs closed, I took Maureen, the young barmaid, for a drive out to a transport café. It had a juke box with all the latest rock 'n' roll hits. As we sped along Hendon Way, breasting a hill, too late I saw a new roundabout that was in the process of being built. We hit the concrete blocks at sixty m.p.h., the front of the car just caved in. The passenger door was ripped clean off and the windscreen disintegrated. The front wheels were wedged up in the air by the concrete blocks. We were thrown back against the seats with such force, I was stunned. I looked over at Maureen. She was out cold. I was really worried. Get away from the wreck, say nothing, I thought. I shook Maureen gently. There was no response. Going round to her side where the door was ripped off, I reached in and got her on to my back, gripped her tightly and staggered off up the road; I was glad she was slim! Laying her down on the side of the road I saw her eyes opening. She had only fainted. She sat up slowly, clearly shocked. I explained I was going to leave the motor and say nothing about the crash to anyone. She was great, promised she would never tell. We got a lift back to London and forgot about it.

Trouble was the car sales people did not forget about it, and the insurance and finance detectives came after me. Lucky they didn't know me by sight. I was drinking at the bar in my father's pub when they came in. They ordered a drink off Maureen and started to quiz her about me. She told them I was a big six-foot bloke with blond hair and that I'd moved down to Cornwall. I really admired her for that. In the end it got too hot and I left home again.

It was spring. My life consisted of stealing, drinking and finding somewhere to sleep. By summer the probation officer made it clear that if I did not get and keep a regular job or join the army, he would take me back to court and recommend a stiff prison sentence. I went into the army recruitment office and was sent out to the country to a training barracks. They were awaiting a full contingent so all I had to do was hang around and wait. I was tapping the squaddies for money and drink. When I got my first week's wages, I put on my civvy clothes, climbed over the wire fence and jumped a train back to London.

4

Life was becoming more complicated. I was back in the old routine: stealing, drinking, fighting. I was also on the trot from the army, my probation order, the car insurance detectives. I was pulling so many strokes for drink that I could not remember what I was doing, so I decided to get out of the way by joining the army again. Back in another recruitment office, I joined the Royal Fusiliers and was sent to the Tower of London, where burly Beefeaters manned the main gate and scarlet grenadiers stood there for splendour. Billeted in the White Tower, surrounded by moat and wall, I realized I might not be able to escape from this mob so easily. As the training got more intense, the weeks sped by and I found myself becoming quite fit. With only one night a week to get drunk I became quite human too! At the end of our training a boxing tournament was held. I managed to stop my opponent in the first round. After that the lads were a bit more tolerant of my increased drinking sprees. We were sent to join up with our battalion HQ at Colchester Barracks. The battalion was full of London boys, most of them doing National Service. I still had my Siamese twin on my back, only now he was spreading himself around my body more. Drink was the only way I could get away from him and there was plenty of that here. I was always in some kind of trouble through it.

One day the Company Commander, Major Lains-Markham,

sent for me. He was tall and hard-looking in a posh kind of way. He had a lovely-looking wife. I was sent round to their house once to deliver a message. I had to wait for a reply so she invited me in and gave me a cup of tea. Lains-Markham told me the boxing season was starting and that I should pull myself together and volunteer to fight for the company. I would be looked after, excused all duties, given best steaks to eat, put in a separate training block and allowed to come and go more or less as I pleased. I volunteered immediately, and we shook hands on it.

There were eight other boxers, and we were supposed to train all day, running, skipping, punching the heavy bags and sparring. What a laugh! Big Scotty came in as our heavyweight hope! I was happy as a sandboy. Fuck the training. Me and Scott were in the boozer from opening till closing, rolling into bed pissed out of our minds each night. One morning I woke up and couldn't believe my eyes. Scotty had a bird in bed with him. He was a fucking genius. How did he do it? It was beyond me. I really admired him. I helped smuggle her out the back way later on, and we went off drinking for the day. The trainer never said anything to me, but I got the feeling that if we lost our first fight we were going to pay for all this. Five companies made up the battalion's full strength: A, B, C, and D were combat units, 'HQ' was administration staff. We were to have one fight each against the other companies; if you won all three fights you challenged the current battalion champions in HQ for the title.

It was November when C Company, which I represented, fought A Company. The massive gym was full; officers and wives in the ringside seats, non-coms in the middle, other ranks with their birds at the back. The gypo was a nutter; all the nurses down the town said so; everybody kept out of his way when he was drinking. He tried to burn the Motor Transport shed down one time and kicked the guard that caught him to fuck. He was representing A Company; he was my opponent this night. I stayed in the dressing-room smoking a fag. I wasn't worried. I just didn't want all the company's happy attention in case I let them down.

'Put that fucking fag out, Healy, you're on, let's go!'

On the way to the ring we passed the last two boxers coming back, their faces bloody and bruised.

'Go on, Healy, I'll buy you a drink if you win, son.'

'Go on, Johnny.'

Girls' voices. I didn't know any girls. I climbed through the ropes. The MC was making the announcements as we were being gloved up. I looked over at the gypo. He looked heavier built around the chest and shoulders than me, not that I was worried strengthwise. It's just that I thought if I was heavier built, then I might get a good-looking bird. The ref called us to the middle of the ring: 'Fight clean.' The bell sounded and I slid into position. The gypo looked good. He came at me all crouched and tiger-like, spitting out his breath with a loud sound as he threw a punch. I touched him with a soft left. He rushed me, hands going like a windmill. I sidestepped smashing a right into his jaw and over he went. He jumped straight up going berserk. He was hitting air. I picked him off with lefts, then I caught him with two hard rights. He went down and stayed there. It was easy. I could see everyone shouting and clapping as I was putting my dressing-gown on and climbing down.

Lains-Markham said, 'Well done, lad.' What a thrill! His beautiful wife gave me a terrific smile. The next two went about the same way. Everybody seemed to know my name now that I could do something besides getting drunk.

Then the big night arrived: the Battalion Championships. Scotty had lost his first fight and was out. At 6 p.m. we left for the gym but ended up in the pub. There was a nice barmaid serving. After a few Scotches, Scotty told her I was fighting later on. She was really surprised because she'd never seen a boxer smoking and drinking before he got into the ring. We eventually left. When we got to the gym, I felt really happy, but a little giddy. My opponent was the camp cobbler. He'd been champion for three years running. The sergeant came up. 'Come on, lad, you're on, put that fag out.'

'Bollocks.'

'What?'

'Bollocks, you cunt.'

'You're fucking pissed, how'd you get like that? Come on, son, don't fuck about.'

He linked me down the aisle to the ring. I couldn't give a fuck about the lot of them. Everyone was shouting, insults or cheers. The noise was deafening. It scared me a bit.

'I've forgot my dressing-gown!' I yelled.

'Pull yourself together, lad, don't do anything stupid tonight. Don't let him catch you, he's got a murderous punch.'

'Fuck him.'

'Keep your voice down. All the officers and their wives can hear you.' I looked down: Lains-Markham was there with his wife. She was lovely. I'd rather be with her than fucking about here, I thought.

The bell went. The cobbler lumbered over. I stayed where I was, let him do all the walking. He shot out a left. I swayed back out of reach, then pushed three fast lefts into his face, sidestepped round him and moved out into the centre of the ring. I felt good. Bang!!! Lights exploded in my head as he caught me with his right ... I grabbed him and hung on, laying all my weight on him. The bastard, he was trying to punch low. I ran the lace of my right glove across his eye. The ref pulled us apart. The cobbler, fuming at what I'd done, tried to rush me; I spun around him, clubbed him with a right, shot a hard left into his eye and moving away I saw blood. Now all I had to do was work on the eye. The bell went for end of round 1. They patched the eye up but it was no good. I kept on at it till he was splashing blood. I was getting really tired; he was very strong. My breath was coming painfully in short gasps, but I kept on at that fucking eye.

The ref stopped it just before the end of the third. Everybody from C Company was cheering. Next a fucking general got in the ring and all the other boxers were called in too. The general shook all our hands. He stopped by me and said: 'Anyone who can fight like that will never get in trouble in the army.' It was all bullshit but I was too happy to care. I was in for an easy ride! I was the *new battalion champion*! As I climbed out through the ropes, Lains-Markham stood up and shook hands with me. He was saying something, but I was looking at his wife. She saw me, then she burst out laughing; so did I. Lains-Markham started laughing too; fuck knows what we were laughing at.

The day after, the Regimental Sergeant Major took all the boxers into the mess and bought us a drink. Then he told Scotty and me to pack our kit. We were being transferred to HQ Company and would be placed on the provost staff (military police). I was about to protest when Scotty nudged me and whispered that it would be a great dodge, no more parades or drills, prisoners to clean our kit. Something about it I did not like, but I kept quiet. I now wore white gaiters and belt and carried a swagger stick. We checked passes, controlled traffic, guarded prisoners, kept order in queues, etc. I began to hate going on duty. I thought the white belt and gaiters made me look smart but Scotty told me the women in the Naafi thought I looked like a schoolboy playing at toy soldiers and, 'You don't look stern enough'.

'What?'

'You don't look fucking hard enough. You'll have to stop

laughing. Be more serious.' I went away to the pub. It was OK for Scotty. He was six foot two, fourteen stone and he didn't get drunk like I did. He could always pull nice birds. The fucking times I'd helped him sneak them out next morning, I should know. It was a mystery to me, birds used to be very friendly with me, even invite me in and give me tea. But they did all their fucking with Scotty or someone else. Fuck him.

I was beginning to get really sad when he came up with a clever stroke. All men confined to barracks reported to the duty copper every four hours, then at 11 p.m. they had to appear on parade in best kit, immaculate for inspection. Their names were in the defaulters' book in the guardroom, but the Duty Officer was usually a bit pissed and did not know who was who by that time of night. So we would let defaulters home for the weekend for £2. Scotty made a few quid the first weekend. Then it was my turn. There were twenty defaulters. I let six go home. Just my fucking luck, Lieutenant Court-Davies, a real right bastard, was duty officer and he demanded to see the book. 'Twenty?'

'Yes, sir.'

'Carry on, Staff.'

'Yes, sir.'

I went into the pub and got pissed. Then it hit me. I shot out and up to B Company. There were ten squaddies lying on their beds: 'You're all nicked.'

'What for, Staff?'

'Shut up, get your best kit on.' I came back in half an hour and took the smartest six. 'I'll give you £1 each and there'll be no charges if you appear on defaulters' parade tonight.' I put their names in the book. It worked. What a relief. I was getting sick of it all. The old monkey on my back, the drink, the army, never pulling a classy bird, fighting. I got mad one day when they were beating up a prisoner in the guardroom because he had a speck of dust on his boots. I called them all poofs. They jumped me and slung me in a cell, giving me a few bangs for good measure. Next morning I was up before the Regimental Sergeant Major who dismissed me from the provost staff.

The sanitary vehicle collected the camp refuse every day. When it was full, it would be driven to a tip in the country. No one liked working on the shit truck; they gave the job to me. The shit stank; I sat among it, loaded it, unloaded it, then into the pub till three. Came out, drove back to camp, simple! Everything went fine for a week. Then a new bloke joined us – Scotty!

'How did you swing it?'

'Bribed the company clerk!' What a laugh! It was great fun for a few weeks. Then Scotty decided we should sell the swill to a pig farmer in Chelmsford whom he just happened to know. Things got better and better. We got drunker and drunker. We had loads of laughs, it was great.

One morning I awoke handcuffed to the hot-water pipe on the floor in the guardroom. There were twelve other blokes cuffed up too, including Borthwed – a bit of a rogue from D Company. I had a terrible hangover, with not the slightest memory of the night before.

'Shut the noise, you horrible cunts, answer your names.'

Jackson, the duty copper, was standing in front of us. He read out our names from the charge sheet in his hand. After we'd been checked, he took off our handcuffs, ordering us to be in best battle dress and on commanding officer's orders by twelve noon to answer charges. We were all lined up rigidly at attention under the flag but the duty bugler did not sound noon taps today. Instead, two drummers of the Provost's Piquet stood directly in front of us. Dressed to the nines in full ceremonials they came to the ready, drumsticks raised above their heads. We all stood staring in the quivering, aching silence. Then the sticks came down as each one was doubled in between two coppers, another was doubled out under escort to the guardroom. I was charged with being drunk and fighting with the military police, sentenced to twenty-one days' detention, then doubled out and made to double on the spot: 'Knees up to your fucking chin, lad, we're going to smarten you up.'

'Double forward.'

'Stand still.'

'Open the guardroom door.'

'Double in, you horrible bastard. What you waiting for? Christmas?'

'Get them knees up. I won't tell you again.'

Provost Sergeant Roberts was six foot five, sixteen stone of hard muscle with a scar across his nose and down his left cheek. He was an evil bastard, but in this place he was God.

There were six other prisoners doubling on the spot, we were all wearing full kit, overcoats, knapsacks on our backs with our large kit bags on the floor beside us.

'Halt, stand still, pick up them kit bags and lay them over shoulders and hold them in position, now move it!'

I was ready to drop with the extra weight. Roberts entered us in the book while Staff Bond, who had a bull neck and shoulders like a barn door, doubled us into the holding cell. There were six blocks of wood, three on each side which served as beds. As first kit inspection was at 6.30 a.m. each day, we slept on the floor beside them with our kit laid out immaculately on the boards. There were a number of rules which had to be learned as fast as possible or the provost staff would be likely to batter you into the middle of next week. These included:

The police will be called Staff at all times.

Prisoners move at the double at all times.

Prisoners will stand to attention when the provost staff enter the cells.

Prisoners will not stand still at any time except when urinating.

(While sitting on the toilet, depending on the duty copper, we had to mark time with our boots.)

Prisoners will not talk except when addressed by the provost staff.

Prisoners must not have tobacco or matches.

We were allowed two cigarettes a day, one at midday, one at tea-time. The duty copper would hand each prisoner a fag then blow a whistle. We would smoke. After a few minutes the whistle would go. We would put out our smoke and hand the ends back to the copper who would tick our names off in a book. They seemed to be kinky about tobacco and anyone caught with even a dog-end would get a good beating coupled with extra drill.

Lights went out at 9 p.m.

There was a window so that the coppers could look in at us from the guardroom. We were like goldfish in a bowl.

'Healy?'

'Yeah.'

'How long you get?'

'Twenty-one days.'

'Your ribs hurt?'

'Yeah, what happened?'

'Don't you remember anything? The Redcaps brought you in.'

'What happened?'

'You was kicking and struggling; they got you cuffed to the pipes, you spat at them, they gave you a few kicks in the ribs. Bastards.'

'Yeah.'

'How long you get, Borth?'

'Fourteen days.'

'What for?'

'Fucking Lains-Markham's wife.'

'Bollocks,' I growled at the blank ceiling.

'No, it's not. You were round her house, what happened?'

'Nothing happened. She made me some tea and told me about her garden.'

'You cunt. If I had gotten in, that would have been it!'

'Yeah, what would you have done?'

'First, I would have took all her clothes off, slowly, then I would have kissed her pussy, then I would've fucked her, then . . .'

'No kiddin', Borth . . .,' I said, and almost laughed. I had a good imagination too in those days but somehow I couldn't see Borthwed tucked up in bed with the Commandant's wife!

'Look, H, if they invite you in you got to get hold of them. They ain't going to take your hand and do it for you.'

'She seems too nice.'

'Too nice! What you think she's got up there, something different than a cunt?'

'Shut that fucking noise in there.' We all went silent.

Borthwed was sort of good-looking, with big shoulders and chest. He had a different girl every week. He made a bottle of light ale last an hour in a pub, never got drunk: and at closing time would go back to the girls' places. He could do something I couldn't, I admired him. I also liked drinking with him because when he walked into a pub all the girls looked at him and anyone that was with him got looked at too!

My sleep was shattered by voices roaring and swearing. The blankets were ripped off us by the duty coppers.

'Hands off cocks, put on socks, you shower of gungy bastards, move yourselves.' And for those that were slow about it the coppers moved in with their swagger sticks and speedily woke them up.

We dressed quickly, washed and shaved, then it was first kit inspection. Roberts, flanked by two coppers, went berserk: he threw all our kit around the cell despite the effort that went into cleaning it, into polishing floors and walls and dusting bed spaces. Some of the others came unstuck; some received punches and kicks, Yates worst of all. Yates was awaiting a court martial for desertion. That morning he was suspected of hiding a fag behind the toilet cistern, the worst sin of all. Roberts beat the living daylights out of him. The rest of us had to stay at attention while it happened; it made me want to cry; at the same time I wanted to jump Roberts and sink my teeth into his jugular vein. I did neither. That made me feel worse. Then they were gone as suddenly as they had appeared. Breakfast was brought in. It consisted of a plate of porridge, a slice of dry bread, and a mug of tea. After breakfast we were assembled outside and double marched up to the square. We spent the morning doing bunny hops, drills and press-ups. By dinner time we were all fit to drop, no one could eat. Ten days passed. I could hardly remember when it all started. Heavy rain had caused a draining ditch to collapse near the officers' married quarters. We were given shovels and taken over to dig the muck clear. It was heavy work. Every time we shovelled a load out, the slimy wet muck would slide back into the drain. The coppers were in a treacherous mood; they had to stand with the rain pouring down on them while we worked.

'Everybody's doing time,' whispered Borthwed. We were covered in muck. After an hour the rain stopped, the sun came out and dried the muck into us. Borthwed nudged me. Two young officers' wives were passing. I was looking at them. Suddenly Staff Corporal Mace was standing in front of me.

'You're nicked, Healy.'

'What for, Staff?'

'Refusing labour. Staff Jackson.'

'Staff Mace.'

'Take this one back to the guardroom. He's nicked.'

'Yes, Staff.'

'Right, you, double away. Left, right, left, right. Get them up, get them up. Halt, inside, move it.'

I was allowed a shower and changed into dry clean denims. Locked in the cell, I sat on the floor pretending to clean my kit. Well, out of one load of shit and into another, I thought.

Smash, crash, wallop, the door opened. In came Borthwed, doubling his knees up to his chin, between two staffs. As soon as they left, I asked, 'What happened, Borth?'

'I refused labour too, fuck it. Can't leave you on your own. No telling what you might get up to.'

'Bollocks.'

'Ha, ha, ha.'

We were both given three days' extra field punishment. Borthwed is a very brave bloke. It's hard not to be charmed.

The following night, loud sucking noises and heavy breathing coming from Borth after lights out.

'Borth, give us a drag of that smoke.' No answer. 'Borth, come on, I'm dying.'

'Keep your voice down, you want to get us all nicked.'

Yatesy still pleaded but in a whisper. He kept on and on. Borthwed told him to put his hand under the bed. As their hands touched all hell broke loose. Yates screamed with rage, shaking his hand now covered with wet slimy phlegm, or was it a more intimate fluid? We never did find out. The duty coppers burst in with pickaxe handles to separate Yates and Borth. Anyone that was foolish enough to try and get off the floor got quickly clobbered down. Staff Mace was a greedy bastard; when our dinner was brought in each day in two big pots, he would beat us back with his pace stick, fill his own mess tin with half of our rations and walk off laughing and eating. One day he was

slow coming in. Before we could stop him Borthwed hacked
and spat into the dinners and mixed them around. We all went
hungry, but it was a thrill to see Mace eating Borth's spit. Some
things here were funny, some not. If the staffs got to dislike
some poor cunt, they gave him a bit of No. 1 drill: simply
put, they drilled the prisoner until he couldn't stand, then they
woke him at all hours of the night. It was murderous. They
brought in an interesting guy one day. He'd escaped from that
guardroom four times and been AWOL twenty-six times. He
had a baby face; he was also a good laugh. Borth heard one
of the staffs say Babyface was in for No. 1 drill. I was glad to
finish my time and rejoin my company.

A few weeks later, we were flown out to Cyprus for
manoeuvres. After a few hours' flight we landed at Limassol;
it was evening. Coming down from the plane, I was surprised
how warm the air was; it carried a lovely smell of what seemed
like perfume, but must have been flowers or fruit or something.
We were taken in trucks to the camp; tents laid out in rows
which seemed to stretch for miles. We played at war most of
the days. What a waste of time! The sea was blue and inviting,
the sun hot and bright. We could see people on the beaches,
mothers with kids, pretty girls with sugar-daddies. We sweated
and climbed more hills. I wished I was a sugar-daddy. The days
went slowly by, a mixture of long marches and mock battles.
During the evenings we were allowed out with a pass if our
uniforms were immaculate; we were inspected by the duty
sergeant, a slight mark on your uniform meant having your
pass taken away.

The main pastime there was drinking. A bottle of brandy
was very cheap so nearly everybody got pissed. Only two nights
I didn't touch a drink; I'd found a little tea shop where the
waitress was very pretty and friendly! Her name was Maria.
Many others soon found it too, so the shop would fill up with

soldiers all calling for crumpets and tea; but none of us seemed to be getting near the crumpet we were really after.

The Redcaps picked myself, Scott, Borthwed and some other guys up for drunk one night. We were given an extra weekend guard duty. We were awoken at four in the morning and bundled into a truck which took us out to the ammunition dump. We had twenty-four hours' guard before us and needed to be immaculate and on parade by 6.30 a.m. for duty officer's inspection. I spent my periods of guard on top of a hill overlooking the sea. All through the day people were enjoying themselves on the beach and I could hear the laughter of the girls as they played in the sea. A girl's laugh is a very happy sound.

Eventually, we returned to England; it was now September. I decided to desert on the Friday night. The lads bought me a good drink down the town. I said goodbye to Scotty and Borthwed. I felt sad as hell. We knew we would probably never meet again. If caught I could be sentenced to two years in the penal companies at a military prison.

I'd been thinking about going on the trot for a long time, deciding that my uncle's in Ireland would be the safest place to stay. Two big Redcaps with an Alsatian dog standing watchfully by the barrier at Holyhead sobered me a little as I passed through on the way to the boat. The wind howled. It was going to be rough crossing the Channel tonight.

5

It was 1960. I caught the boat from Holyhead, drinking and sleeping all the way. I eventually reached the small town of Boyle in County Sligo. I got off the train; the one cab driver didn't think I was worth it with no luggage. I went into a pub on a bridge overlooking the fairly fast-flowing Boyle river. It felt really cosy and relaxed. Everything seemed to have slowed down. The barmaid served me a pint, a lovely healthy-looking country girl with a nice brogue. The men standing at the bar nodded politely to the stranger in their midst. I drank a few pints and was told that the bus left at 7 p.m. I caught it and fell asleep till the driver woke me at the county crossroads. I thanked him and got off.

I reached my uncle's gate, walked down the hill to the house. Dogs barked in the distance, my uncle's dog took up the cry as I reached the door. I knocked, opened it, walked in. My grandfather was sitting at the big open fire, my uncle at the table fixing a bridle. He jumped up to greet me after they got over the surprise. Vincent made me tea. I told him I was on the trot from the army. 'That's fine, you'll be OK here.' Old Dad (I'd called my grandfather that as a kid) looked old now: at times he would talk sensible, at others not so sensible. He was raving a little, his mind wandering between the past and the present. He would ask if I were Tommy from the village. My uncle would tell him gently that I wasn't. There was only the two of them left now – Grandmother dead, the rest scattered. Vincent and I talked well into the night.

Next morning I got up late. I was sober, free, happy, everything was interesting: animal smells, stunted trees, dark outhouses, chickens with different-coloured feathers, Bronzo the black and white collie. I walked through green rushy fields, avoiding wet marshy spots, to look at the cattle, twelve in-calf heifers, 'the first due any time now, Seanee' (he used the Irish for Johnny).

'Are the Clancys still alive?'

'They are indeed, and younger they're behaving. Why Michael's only ninety-one and Mrs Clancy's eighty-nine.'

'They're great, Vince.'

'Yes. And I want you to take them up a wee drop of fresh milk every day.' We were walking out the back of the hills. 'There's the house now.' We knocked and entered. 'God bless all of this house,' said Vincent.

'Who have you with you?'

''Tis Seanee Healy.' We were all pleased to see each other, handshakes all round. Then the kettle went on for tea.

My uncle took advantage of the cheap labour, leaving me to look after Old Dad and the farm while he got a job on the local council. I dug the potatoes, cleared drains and built ditches, cleaned and cooked for us all, brought milk up to the Clancys each evening and got their supplies twice a week from the shop, went to Mass on Sundays – no choice, *mandatory*. I got two packets of Woodbines a week and a couple of pints of Guinness on the way home from Mass on Sundays. Something would have to be done.

They say young cows are like young women: they have a hard time getting their first calf. I assisted each one by tying a rope around the stuck calf's foot, passing it behind my back, tying it again to the calf's other little foot; as the cow heaved, I pulled. The method worked, the cows and myself delivered each calf safely. My uncle was pleased and gave me the price of two pints for every calf. Big Pat in the pub had no spuds that year. I told him I'd drop him a hundredweight bag each week for ten shillings. I dug them in the day and along with the milk fired the bag up on my back under cover of darkness.

It wasn't enough. I not only had the monkey on my back, but also the fucking painful lump: I had to have more drink.

The Clancys supplied it; they got their supplies on three-monthly credit. The money my uncle gave me for my own supplies I now kept and charged it to the Clancys' account . . . simple!

Everything was going fine. Going for a loaf one day, I ended up in the pub. I only had the price of two pints, but the place was packed with men coming from the fair. Everyone bought me a pint. I left at 3 p.m. – I was too drunk to ride the bike, and weaving from one side of the road to the other reached the ditch at the back of our place. I must have fallen down on the grass verge and gone to sleep. I woke to find about ten or twelve high-school girls standing around me giggling and laughing.

'Hello, girls.'

'Well, well, well, Seanee. Have you been drinking?'

'No. I been working so hard I fell down asleep. Help me up.'

'Aw, go on Agnes.'

'You help us too, Mary.'

I gave them my hands. They tried to pull me up. I pulled them down in a heap on top of me; we were all rolling around and the screams and laughs must have been heard for miles. After a bit more kidding and fooling, they got on their bikes and waved me out of sight. After that, any time I met them on the road they would get off their bikes and indulge in some mild horseplay.

One night after I gave them their milk, the Clancys asked me if I'd seen any fox around. I'd have to be careful. These country people talk in riddles. They're all a load of cunning buggers! It was a laugh, though. I was getting the drink, a bit of fun. I was free and happy. My uncle tackled the horse up to the cart and we went to the bog for turf. At dinner time, we went down to Jimmy Corfton's to brew up. He was the local blacksmith. He was nowhere around. My uncle found him hanging in the forge. Dead. He whispered an act of contrition into his ear, then went into town to report his death. Jimmy had been in the local nut-house for killing two cows with an axe and firing their bodies into a bog last year. I made some tea and fell asleep in the armchair for the afternoon. The months went quickly by. It was May already. Along with the usual work I did little chores like splitting logs with a mallet and metal wedges. Fetching water from the well, if I met anyone we'd sit down talking for up to an hour. I was becoming a right swede basher! Everywhere was so green. I used to walk about slowly. In Sligo everything goes at a much easier pace. My back still pained me but not nearly so much as in the city.

On Monday nights I listened to the Irish Top Ten on the radio: 'Devil Woman', 'Bobby's Girl', 'Spanish Lace', 'Ginny Come Lately' ... great! I can't sing, but Old Dad thought I could. So I sang for him some nights. He was a nice old man. I liked him a lot. People often used to drop in. Two young girls called one night with a message for my uncle who was out. I made them tea and we started teasing each other, then throwing things about. I chased them up into the room and we rolled around kissing and cuddling on the bed. Old Dad lost his temper with the three of us, started lashing out with his stick, saying it was sinful and wicked. He's off his head sometimes. I took the girls out the back of the hill to the tar road where they left their bikes and kissed them goodnight. They promised to call again.

When Tommy the Dummy called, I'd give him some tea. Old Dad would give him a couple of coppers, and he'd go off as happy as could be. One morning my uncle left me an envelope with £20 for the priest who called in a brand new car later that day. Just as I was trying to shave Old Dad outside the door, he got out of the car and gave me a stern gaze: 'Who are you?'

'It's no concern of yours who I am. Vincent left you this.'

'Who is Vincent?'

'He's the poor farmer who's just given you that money!'

I turned my back on him. He got in the car and drove off, scattering the hens and sending plumes of dust into the air.

Some days I heard a banging noise coming from Joe's place.

'What's that banging, Old Dad?' I asked.

'Oh, that's poor Tommy. Joe ties him by the neck with a chain to the hayshed.'

'That's terrible.'

'Oh, sure he has to do it. Joe delivers the milk to the creamery and Tommy would get into mischief on his own. The chain is long enough for him to walk around and get under the shed if it rains.'

As time went by, the banging seemed to get louder. Funny, they reckon you're blessed here if one of the family becomes a priest. Three of Tommy's sisters were nuns and two of his brothers priests.

Our house lay in a little hollow about a quarter of a mile from the front gate. Not far from the gate, there was a well of clear fresh spring water. People from the surrounding farms came there with buckets to draw water. I met big Mike Brady there one day. Mike was nearly seven foot and built like a barn door. He was about sixty, lived with his brother and had never married. He was a great laugh. I gave him a cigarette and we sat down for a smoke when a girl called Annie Teresa called out as she went by the road. She was a fine sort of a girl, keeping house for her father and brother and helping on the farm since her mother's death when she was a child.

'Hey, Annie Teresa, what's your hurry?' I called back.

'Come over here and help me carry this heavy bucket.' Stopping, she leaned her arms over the gate. 'Well, well, well, isn't it easy for you men?' she said, her voice full of mock annoyance.

'Have ye all the hay cut yet, Annie?' asked Mike, as I got on my feet and moved toward the gate.

'Not yet, Mike,' she called back as a strong breeze suddenly lifted her dress. What a mischievous breeze! Such legs! I gave a wolf-whistle. She looked so appealing, blushing, embarrassed as she attempted to keep the dress from billowing. I put my arm through the gate, catching her slim waist. 'Let go of me, you young devil,' she squealed, but I held her tight. She stopped struggling. I put my free hand on her cheek. Holding her like that I could feel it all the way down into my toes.

'Give me a kiss, Annie,' I whispered.

'Will you have sense, Seanee, big Mike is watching you,' she replied, shaking her head like a frisky filly.

'What night are you taking me out?' I asked smiling.

She looked cross. 'Is that how they speak to girls in England?' Her annoyance was real.

Taking my hands away from her, I said, 'No, Annie Teresa, I'm only teasing,' adding softly, 'Will you come out with me one night?'

She gave me a serious look. 'How long will you be here, Seanee?'

'Oh, I'll be here for a long time yet,' trying to sound certain about it.

'Well,' she replied, smiling at me truthfully, 'if you're sure you're going to be staying for so long, what's your hurry? If you're here after the hay's taken in, I'll go out with you. Now I have a bus to catch into town. Bye, bye, Seanee.' She moved off, waving to Mike.

'Well, Healy,' said Mike, 'my mother used to walk ten miles into town with a big bag of spuds, fire them on the scales, get some food for us and walk home again.'

'Well, that's great, Mike, but did she have as nice legs as Annie Teresa?'

'God blast it to hell, nice legs indeed. Is that all you be thinking of? Sure the women nowadays are too lazy to make their own piss,' and he jumped up and walked off. I couldn't help laughing out loud. Mike kept looking back muttering to himself. As I walked back towards the house, a tinker in a horse and trap pulled on to our land. He reached the house in two minutes. What a beautiful horse!

'Hello, mate.'

'Good day to you, lad. You're not from around here, are you?'

'No, I'm from England.'

'How are they all over yonder?' he said, shaking my hand. 'Could you spare a sup of milk and some sugar?' I gave him some milk and sugar. 'The blessing of God on you.'

As he was about to leave I remembered our horse had some kind of sore on his jaw; I asked the tinker about it. 'If you put a little sulphur in its food every day, it will heal up nicely,' he assured me, and off he went. He looked terrific in his horse and trap. I wished I was a tinker with a lovely horse and trap. When I went inside, Old Dad was gone. I looked all over calling him, then I saw him making his way out the hill. I ran after him and when I caught up with him he looked as if he did not know me.

'Come on, Daddy.' I tried to link him back, but he struggled and started crying that he was going back to Mary's house where he was born (once a man, twice a child). I kept promising to take him there.

'First we have to put our Sunday clothes on, Daddy.'

'All right, young fellow.' He didn't even remember me. Back at the house I changed and washed him. He'd dirtied his trousers, his bowels were weak.

A few days later, the horse's sore had nearly healed. I tackled her up to the cart and went to the bog for a load of turf. A slow old plod took us there – a wide open area with turf stacked all over in little piles, deep bog holes filled with murky black water. The wind was strong, blowing turf dust everywhere. I had to keep my eyes squinted while filling the cart. No one else was there. It's a wild, lonely place and I was glad when the cart was full. The girls passed us out on the road, holding their bikes with one hand, waving the other, shouting and cheering. They disappeared round the bend. The widow Conlan waved from her door. I waved back. Her dog chased after us yelping at the horse's heels. She took no notice. Then something caught the dog's interest in a field and he raced away towards it. Sitting on top of the turf, I could see for miles around. Different shades of green; white cottages dotted among it; small mountains seem blue in the distance; close by you can see rushes in the fields. Rushes only grow on good land, they say; or wet land perhaps? It's always raining in Ireland. There's a lot of rushes.

Sunday morning, my uncle got up early, milked the cows, then cycled to first Mass. When he returned, I left for second Mass. That way one of us was always with Old Dad. It also allowed me to go to the pub after church. The pub was a small room serving groceries at one end, drink at the other.

Everybody seemed to know everyone else; they greeted each other in a most friendly manner. They were friendly towards me too, but I wasn't really a part of the community, so I was more or less treated as a poor visitor. There may also have been some suspicion regarding my longish stay.

Annalee, the landlady's seventeen-year-old daughter, used to get up on a stool to reach packages on the top shelf. One time Joe Riley (who kept the breeding bull) gave a longing look at her shapely legs, then turned to me and winked. I whispered, 'She's streamlined.' He burst out laughing; later he sent me over a pint.

I drank a lot of pints that evening. By closing time I was drunk. On the way home I kept wobbling from one side of the road to the other. The last thing I remember as I approached the county crossroads with MacQuin's forge on one side and Sarah Barnes's thatched cottage on the other was a large triangular road sign proclaiming in Irish Gaelic a warning only made understandable to me by bold letters at the bottom of the sign: 'YIELD!' I must have done, because I woke up shivering with cold in the ditch looking up at that sign, the bicycle lying flat on the wet grass a few feet further on. I got home before dawn, being sick outside the door. (The week before I was sick inside the door. My uncle was pleased with the difference.)

Towards the end of June the weather became dry and warm. In the long sunny days my uncle asked Mike Crine to cut our hay. He arrived on the Monday with the tractor. I pulled the bushes clear of the gap, letting him into the meadow. He went round about in ever-decreasing circles, the blades of the cutter slicing through the tall yellow grass, which fell flat on the meadow to wait while the sun's heat turned it into hay, which would feed the cattle through the winter. At dinner time I made cheese sandwiches and a large pot of strong tea and brought them to the meadow. Old Dad joined us and the three of us soon wolfed the lot. Then it was back to the grind, Mike cutting, me following with a pitchfork to clear away if the grass became bunched on the cutter blades.

On the second day, my aunt Noreen arrived with her husband from England. Noreen's husband Mickey was supposed to be smart. I thought he was a chicken's head. He'd got a new car and he fucked off sightseeing every day, leaving Noreen to help with the work. She took some of the pressure off me with the cooking and looking after Old Dad. She also helped with the hay. She was nice-looking – seemed more a girl than a woman. As we sat down for a rest, her dress rode up around her thighs showing all that long leg. Sod the bloodline, I'd have loved to fuck her right there in the hay! As Mike came over she pulled her dress down. Fuck Mike, I thought, he's going to tell us a wild story; it better be as interesting as Noreen's legs!

'Joe Finn had an old crow tied by the leg to a stone outside his house,' he started.

'How did he catch it, Mike?' asked Noreen.

'He boiled an egg, ate half and put the shell on the ground, the crow came down and with its beak and eyes inside the shell eating, never saw Joe creep up and grab him.'

That evening Noreen gave me £1. I couldn't get to the pub quick enough. I got drink from everyone, the crack was good, I never remembered getting home. I had a sick head in the meadow next day when we had to put the hay into cocks ready to pull into the shed.

Then we started dragging in the cocks. A lot of neighbours came to help out. Noreen stayed in the house cooking for the men. I was pulling in the cocks from the meadow with a horse. The lads built a rick in the shed; we all worked at a good pace to get it finished in one day. I had to lead the horse up to a cock, put a long chain around it, hooking the two ends to the trace chains, attach them to the horse's collar, then pull away. We had a good laugh at dinner time. The lads all liked Noreen's cooking. I think they liked Noreen too!

We finished at 11 p.m. that evening and as soon as I hit the pillow I was gone.

Old Dad and myself were a bit sad. Noreen and her old man left; the house seemed empty without a woman. I tidied the place up, boiled some spuds for dinner, and was back to being head cook again.

I went to the pub that evening. There was a big nosy guy called Hughes who drank there. He'd been putting it about that I might be on the run from the British Army; fuck knows how he'd come up with that. Anyway, he wasn't there that night. I'd been thinking how I could get his mind off me, so I left the pub early and cycled to his place. I put my shoulders against his massive heavy iron gate, wrenched it out of its sockets and up across my back. Then I staggered about a quarter of a mile up the road with it and fired it into the ditch, went back for the bike and rode home to bed.

Two evenings later my uncle came home with a wild tale about how the two strongest lads in the area had got something against Hughes, and they stole his gate! Hughes was worried for the next few weeks. He seemed to have forgotten all about me.

Supposedly of modest means, my uncle had one extravagance in the form of a quarter-blood horse. As a young man he'd bought a half-blood mare, she'd left a foal and Molly, the mare I was gazing at in the lower pasture, was the granddaughter. Of course the pure bloodline of the old stallion was strongly diluted by now, but she was still a beauty: black as midnight all over except for a small white star on her forehead. She could pull any load. Calm enough under a cart, she was none the less given to moods of skittishness and boldness when her blood was up. Only used now and again for cart work, she was not accustomed to a man on her back.

Every day I would go out to the field to look at her and talk to her. If I had something for her she would stop cropping the grass and saunter over, letting me stroke her and run my fingers through her long, black mane. We would be good friends for a day or two but just when I'd think she was getting fond of me, she would throw back her ears in annoyance at my approach, turn her head and slowly move away, making it plain that she didn't want to know that day.

Getting out of bed one cold bright sunshiny morning, I got this terrific urge to catch that half-wild, beautiful mare and ride her into the wind. I didn't know much about horses, but the odd question here and there to my uncle led me to understand that a horse fed on oats would have fire in its veins and one with a small strain of a bloodline would be buck leaping. I washed and dressed slowly. My mind seemed to have stopped thinking as I gathered up the bridle and a bucket. Coming into the field I hid the bridle in the ditch – the mare would run if she caught a glimpse of it! I was beginning to get a little nervous as I drew near her. Then she sensed me, made to move off, saw the bucket, whinnied affectionately and came up to me. As she was eating, I put my hand in her mane, holding her tightly. Up close like this she really was beautiful, trembling at my touch and pawing the ground, her warm body throbbing with energy and power from the handfuls of oats I had been giving her each day for the last month.

Standing so close to her I forgot all my previous plans. Before I knew it, I had vaulted on to her back, gripping her tightly with my knees and holding her mane in a vice-like grip. Lifting her head, outraged with surprise, she reared up on her hind legs in a fury while I tried to soothe and coax her, whispering, 'Good girl, Molly, take it easy, Moll.' She sprang forward, I tightened my hold on her mane, gripped her sides fiercely with my legs and with my heart in my mouth we thundered towards the hill. We raced through field after field, onwards and upwards, with the wind and her mane whipping my face. She took that hill in leaps and bounds. We sped through a gap in a line of alder trees; then out into the green fields beyond, approaching at breakneck speed the ditch that separated our land from the county road. My stomach tightened as we closed on the ditch. At the last second she suddenly swerved left, but my grip held and I stayed with her. Then, without breaking her stride, that crafty mare leaned in against the ditch. Jesus, my right knee seemed like it was being ripped from the socket. I felt myself flying through the air, and then I smashed face down into the field. Bruised and winded I climbed to my feet to see the big mare further on rearing up on her hind legs by Casey's meadow.

One night I was cycling home from the pub without any lights when a car shot past, braking suddenly in front of me. I jumped off the bike just as two big Irish coppers climbed out of the car. There was a little stream running alongside the road flanked by a tall thick hedge which blocked the way on to a field beyond. Realizing I could not afford to be nicked even on such a silly charge as 'no lights', I picked up the heavy, old bike and fired it on to the hedge. It created an escape route. Jumping over the stream, I clambered over the bike into the field beyond. Turning quickly, I pulled the bike off the hedge which sprang back up just as the law came up to it, cursing and shouting at me to come back. I started off across the field to the minor sand road that led home. The law, seeing my intention but unable to get through the hedge, jumped back into their car and sped off in the direction of the crossroads to cut me off. I thought they had the advantage in the game until it dawned on me that if they kept their lights on I could follow their moves but they could not follow mine: I turned back, threw the bike back on to the hedge, crawled across it, pulled it after me and cycled off up the road after the car. When I reached the crossroads I could see them and the car waiting a few hundred yards up the sand road, expecting to catch me coming out of the field. I continued on up the main county road stopping and hiding from every car that came behind me. It took me hours to reach the back way to my uncle's. Coppers never seem to consider more than one plan.

It was August. With the hay in and the work all finished for another year, my uncle seemed to be finding a lot of faults, especially with my visits to the pub. One night he gave me my fare to England and £5 to spend – not much for a year's work. I said goodbye to Old Dad. He was crying. So I fucked off quick in case I started crying too. Arriving in town with an hour to spare before my train, I got six pints down me, bought half a bottle of Scotch, and went up to the station just as the train was pulling in. I got in with a bloke in the buffet. We drank all the way to Dublin. By the time I got on the boat I was a bit pissed and fell asleep on the deck. Drinking and sleeping I eventually reached London.

6

The noise from the London traffic seemed very loud and for a while the fumes seemed choking.

I went around to a friend's house. He said I could stay there for a few nights. After a while a couple of mates from the boxing gym got me into a job in Covent Garden taking fruit and veg off the lorries and delivering it to the warehouses. I used to sleep in the back of one of the firm's vans, take any stuff I found lying around and sell it in the market. I finished work at 1 p.m., passing the rest of the day and night drinking.

Any afternoon I was sober, or more correctly too sick from drink to drink, I used to go home to visit my mum. She was consoled when I told her that I wasn't drinking so much and had a nice room.

Drinking a cup of tea with her one afternoon, we were both startled by a loud knock on the door. I went and opened the door to two very big guys dressed in sharp double-breasted suits with very short haircuts and square, determined chins. I suppose I had always been expecting them, though I hadn't thought so soon, well not today. But here they were standing shoulder to shoulder, solid as a pair of brick shithouses, outside my mum's front door.

'Are you John Healy?' one asked.

'No.'

'Who are you then?' he said, while his mate's eyes searched for clues. They were obviously performing a familiar duty.

'I'm Terry. John's at work. Who the fuck are you?' I spoke with some defiance. If I was Terry I would not be intimidated by those looking for another.

Looking down at the photo in his hand, he placed his flat foot quickly against the door. 'We are the SIB.'

'What?'

'Special Investigation Branch. Royal Military Police.'

'So?' I enquired as casually as I could, but I was already breathing too fast.

'So we think you are John Healy, and you have been absent without official leave from your battalion for a year.' For a moment we stood looking at one another. Their clipped hair was very taut. Up to this point they had been satisfied to ask questions, but now considering their obligations they had noticeably stiffened.

Some dark memory of a fetish or a drill performed and polished above and beyond human perfection caused me to try to jump out the door between them. With one it might have worked but their reflexes were marvellous, their timing perfect. I got caught with a rabbit punch on the back of the neck and went down. They put the cuffs on me. My mum came out, pleading with them to let me go. But these were not the guys to listen to a mother's plea.

'He's ours and we're keeping him,' said one, very sharp and sure. 'We're taking him to Chelsea Barracks to await escort to his unit.' They lifted me up between them and carried me downstairs to the jeep, shoved me in the back, and jumped in the front, their wide-boned shoulders stiff and blunt. Then when the armed service vehicle was turned round we took off so fast my stomach shot into my mouth.

After three days in a cell the escort finally arrived to take me to Sutton Coldfield. There I was put in another cell in another guardroom. Next morning, I was brought before the officer commanding, who was good enough to inform me in a tone of pained regret that I was in breach of Article 503, subsection so-and-so, contrary to paragraph 9 – was it? – amendment 12 or some such. He was immaculately pressed, the pips glittered on his epaulets. 'And since you cannot be relied upon to stay where you are put we shall have to keep you under lock and key.' I began to sag in my ruffled fatigues while he sat there, perpetually upright eyes fixed on some distant banner of bravery, loyalty and honour. Then his brows darkened as he picked up the authorizing stamp and brought the Crown seal down on my committal form so hard it made me jump. 'Close arrest, pending court martial,' he said at the top of his voice.

While awaiting trial I got friendly with another guy who was doing fourteen days for insubordination. Although he was only nineteen he was considered an old soldier, a barrack room lawyer, since he knew a thing or two. At least he knew I wanted to go on the trot again and told me that since my regiment was stationed in Germany now it might be months before they got round to sending an escort for me. So my best chance would be to bolt from here. 'Because they have special escorts for those in transit'. 'Why?' I was naive enough to ask. 'They don't like to look along the line a second time and find it wanting.' He laughed. 'So, they're armed and sometimes bring along a fucking dog.' 'No,' I moaned. ''Fraid so,' he grinned, 'but the best thing about going on the trot from here is that if they catch you they send you straight to Colchester or even Shepton Mallet and they try you there, then you don't get messed around so much and allowing for the findings and according to the judgement of the court martial you could end up doing all your time here.' One night, after his release from the guardroom, just as I was about to start saying my prayers, he stood under my window quietly calling my name.

I pulled myself up on the bars. 'Cop this.' He passed up a bottle of Scotch and offered advice which I did not listen to.

Not long after the bottle was empty and I could hardly stand up. I began laughing, singing and shouting abuse at the provost staff.

'Cut the noise.'

'Bollocks.'

Bang, crash, wallop, they didn't mess about. I awoke on the floor next morning. I was still too sick to care about them, and at nine-thirty I was hauled up before the adjutant. I decided to brazen it out. I told him I intended to desert and as soon as the chance arose, I would be off again. Summary Courts Martial are very expensive: a deserter at heart, and coupled with the drink, they decided that I would never make a gallant soldier. In fact, I would never make any kind of soldier. I was more trouble than I was worth; two days later they gave me a dishonourable discharge. Though officially drummed out, I was demob happy. To celebrate I got drunk on the train back to London. I went on the drink heavy for a week and lost my job in the market, but with the few quid I had coming I decided to try and straighten myself out a bit.

I knew a guy who was working in Eastbourne, so I went down there. He got me fixed up with lodgings and a job digging holes in fields for telegraph poles. Heavy work! Drinking each night, digging each day. I got alcoholic poisoning in some cuts on my hands. I got in a fight with a big gypo in the pub; others joined in; got my eye badly damaged so I couldn't see, couldn't work, just kept drinking in my room, getting drunk and going to sleep. My face was a mess. After a week the landlord told me to go. I got drunk the next day, then jumped the London train.

I was back to shoplifting, drinking, sleeping in derelict houses. I got nicked with a Jock for burglary and sentenced to fifteen months. I was just settling down in Wandsworth Prison, sharing a cell with a guy who was in for doping greyhounds, when the fuckers transferred me to Albany on the Isle of Wight. Things were a bit stricter on the island and I was put breaking the ground with a pickaxe along with nine other cons. They were in for anything from armed robbery, assault and fraud to murder. They were aggressively confident, taking no bullshit off the screws; their voices menacing, slow and arrogant. Every one of them had distinguished himself in some spectacularly violent manner against the prison staff. I was the only one without credentials; I had the feeling I would not be accepted until I proved myself.

I didn't have long to wait. One morning a screw from another work party came over, pointing to a builder's truck that was loaded with bricks. He told me to start unloading it. I refused outright. Calling another screw they frogmarched me inside along the landing to the chief officer's room. He was sitting behind a desk, the biggest bloke I'd ever seen: I was surprised that a man could be so huge and still be a human being. As the escort screw was telling him of my crime – refusing an order – I was wondering if this was the same Scouse chief that was supposed to have beaten up a certain top gangster so bad that he was now in a wheelchair. The escort screw finished speaking and the freak said, 'Is that so?' in a broad Scouse accent. With an exaggerated calmness he took off his gold-braided peaked cap, stared right into my eyes with a barely controlled fury and in a voice so low I could just hear him, he said, 'Now, lad, you are stepping very, very close to the thin red line.' He glared at his watch. 'It's almost dinner time, so after dinner you will be taken out and you will unload that truck fast, RIGHT?' he suddenly roared, making me jump.

Well, here was my chance to get out of this mess. My mouth went dry, I was scared. I heard a voice – it sounded like mine – saying, 'No.' Everything went completely still. The big freak and I stared at each other. That one little word seemed to have totally stunned him. For a split second I thought I might escape my fate, but suddenly my arms were pinned to my sides by the escort screws and, with surprising agility for a man of his size, the chief sprang up from the chair and reached me in one bound. I lowered my chin just as he threw a right which caught me too high on the head to knock me down but still with enough force to stagger me. The screws released their hold on me and with a swift blow to the guts he dropped me. The last thing I remember was a boot coming at me. Then I got it in the head.

I knew I was in the punishment block even without opening my eyes: a weird silence hangs over the place. I was a bit sore round the ribs and my head felt like a balloon. There was no bed or mattress – nothing, just the bare cell. I went back to sleep. The grinding of drawn bolts, coupled with the rattling of keys, jolted me awake. The door swung open. Two of the heavy mob stood there, one holding a plastic plate of food and a mug of tea. He shoved these into my hands, then stepped back briskly. Without a word they left, slamming the door. Out of habit I started to look round for somewhere to sit before sitting back down on the floor. A small piece of cheese, two slices of bread, a teaspoonful of jam and a mug of cold tea made up the evening meal. Hindered by a swollen jaw, I slowly and carefully chewed each mouthful after first softening it with tea. Just before lights out I was allowed to fetch my bed into the cell. Each morning I had to place it back outside (such a thing as too much comfort, you know). After two days I appeared before the Assistant Governor – a hard-looking Jock. He never looked up as he sentenced me to fourteen days' solitary confinement and loss of privileges. For the first few days I was on the alert for the slightest sound, always associating it with someone coming to visit me. When I realized how wearing this was on the nerves, I gave it up.

Sometimes I would lie flat on the floor going deeper and deeper into myself until I could feel my breath coming and going, in and out, slower and slower, till it became so fine as to be hardly noticeable. Then mind and thoughts became still. At other times I passed the hours by pacing up and down, to and fro. Sometimes I found myself sitting on the floor, staring at the wall. As my eyes became heavy and closed, the quietness gave me a calm and peaceful feeling which could last for a couple of hours or more; a scream from a nearby cell might break the spell as the screws did someone over. I'd hear the door clang shut. The sound of their boots coming along the landing would give me a nervous twinge in my stomach as they neared my door. They'd go past and I'd relax. Sometimes I daydreamed about becoming a famous boxer – I'd have had no drinks for months, no longing for it. All I would have to do when I was released from this dump was to get a room, train hard, get fit, give a false age, get a licence to fight and I'd be there. Other times I was going to be a smart confidence trickster and con royalty, business moguls, governments and councils. I might even visit this nick disguised as a government health inspector and fuck these screws about. Yes, and I'd have nice suits and shirts and attractive women to cuddle up to at night, and I'd not touch a drink! Never mind that I didn't have the brains or the fine chat to be a con man, I used to get really carried away and pass hours dreaming about the possibility. Of course,

I might not go straight into boxing or confidence tricking . . . if I just managed to get a room and a job on a building site, drinking a few pints only at weekends, I'd be content enough too, I thought.

In the end, though, whichever way you handled it, you were just staring at a wall. A concrete wall reinforced by time and silence. Then I would console myself with the thought of the welcome I would receive from the lads when I rejoined them for work. The day came for my release. I was taken before the block screw who informed me that I was not being put back with my former gang! Instead, I was to work in the prison overall shop . . . Was I gutted! Had it all been for nothing? Some con man . . . For now the most pressing thing was to get a smoke.

Eventually I finished my sentence and was released. I got drunk on the train with another con. We got in a fight over a bird and the police dragged us off the train at London. When they found out we had just come out they let us go.

My parents had given up the pub and moved back to the old council house in Kentish Town. My father took a job in the country and could only come home once or twice a month. In an effort to stop me drinking my mother suggested that I come back to live with the family.

I got a labouring job on a building site at Hampstead. A week passed, then another without touching a drink. I was doing all right. At dinner time each day instead of going into a pub I went to a café. Afterwards I would sit on a bench near the posh houses. They all seemed to employ au pair girls who would pass by me either going for the shopping or coming back. Every day one girl stopped for a rest beside me on the bench; her name was Teresa. She was French, very friendly, very attractive. We began talking to each other.

Sometimes, unable to find the correct word for something, she would get cross with herself; her mannerisms became very endearing.

I asked her out one night. We went to the pictures. Afterwards I walked her home. We kissed goodnight, arranging to meet again the following evening. We met outside the tube and headed off in the direction of a coffee bar, but before reaching it there was a pub. I took Teresa in. We sat at the bar; she sipped lemonade, I drank beer. I felt less anxious after a few pints. We laughed and talked, time passed quickly. She put some money in the juke box. The place started to fill up. 'Will you love me tomorrow?' asked the record in the juke box. Teresa swayed her body in time with the music. 'Let's dance, John,' she said.

'Later, when I've had a drink,' I answered.

'Oh, John, you 'ave 'ad many drinks alreadee!'

I got up and ordered us more drinks. I felt OK buying drink. A young bloke came over and asked Teresa to dance. They danced in the middle of the floor, moving faster and faster to the rock music. Other couples joined them; the girls looked delicious, full of energy, excited. I sat watching and drinking with my back against the wall. I felt safe.

A building site can be really cold in winter, especially if you're hung over from drink. The wind howls, blowing rain or sleet into your face; you shiver and shake and think of the rent, then the tension starts to crease you up. To me life without a drink was death and, as I wasn't interested in anything but drink, being a builder's labourer was a very difficult business. Monday mornings, hail, rain or shine would find me ankle-deep in muck, mixing concrete, carrying bricks, unloading hundred-weight bags of cement. Home each night to a warm house and a welcoming dinner from my mother, who about Thursday night would really be beginning to have faith in my promise to stop drinking. In fact, I'd be beginning to believe it myself until the sickness from the previous weekend's binge cleared out of my system and that insane urge gripped me to have just one. Friday dinner times we got our wages and I couldn't wait to get into the pub. That would be the end of the job for me: I'd roll home Saturday morning, not a clue where I'd been and not enough wages left to pay my rent. About Sunday evening I'd sober up enough to promise my mother it wouldn't happen again; Monday would find me out looking for another job and Tuesday I'd start work again.

I woke up with one of my worst hangovers; I was fully dressed – shoes and all – in the bed. I crawled out. My body was sore all over. I dragged myself down the stairs one at a time gently so as my head wouldn't explode. I opened the kitchen door. My mother sat at the table; she was glueing and fixing what seemed to be toys. I sat down. Neither of us spoke. After a while my mother looked over at me. 'Why did you break all my little holy statues?' she asked, her voice calm and low.

I didn't know what to say, I couldn't remember a thing. 'I'm sorry, Mum, if I did that, I'm sorry.'

'*If you did it* . . . who else do you think would do a thing like that? God will punish you if you don't stop drinking. You're getting more violent, something will have to be done; none of us can put up with it much longer. You'll end up killing someone, or someone in them low pubs you drink in will kill you.'

I felt rotten about upsetting her. 'Mum,' I said, 'I don't mean to get drunk, it just creeps up on me, but I'm going to stop; I'm not going to touch it again.' And I meant it when I said it.

She looked up at me, her face a mixture of sadness and despair. 'You say that every time and as soon as you get a week's wages you're off worse than before. You're bringing disgrace on the whole family. Dad's disgusted; he's taken a job away from home because of it.'

'Honest, Mum,' I said, 'and I'll buy you a load of new statues when I get another job.'

'Oh, leave me alone, John,' she said shaking her head wearily.

I had been refused service in the better bars and eventually ended up drinking in the Cider House in Kentish Town alongside a dyed blonde with a ravaged face and too much make-up. She had a thin body and was screaming at a big, rough-looking bloke standing at the far end of the bar. The rest of the customers seemed unconcerned by the slanging match; somehow you got the feeling they'd seen it all before. Not the place to get too drunk in, but then with drink in me I'd fight King Kong and most times I had to.

'You whore's bitch!' shouted the big bloke at the blonde.

'You hear that? You hear what he called me?' asked the blonde.

'Leave it out, love, he's pissed,' I said quietly.

'Fuck you,' she screamed at me.

'And fuck you again,' roared the big bloke, coming towards me. He threw a punch at my head, which I easily avoided. My heart wasn't in it, really, but I shot out two fast lefts to his face, crossed with the right and moved back out of range as the blood started trickling from his mashed nose. It went very quiet in that old Cider House ... Yes, I thought, I'll show these cunts, I'll give them an exhibition. I did, too! The bloke came after me, walking right through some of my best punches, to wedge me up against the side of the bar. He started to choke the fucking life out of me, at the same time bouncing my head off the wall. The blonde took a ringside stool, pulled her skirt up, swung her stiletto heels and screamed with laughter.

I awoke in a doorway just as it was beginning to turn light. I was missing a shoe and the rent. Sometimes they let you live if you put up a good show.

7

One morning I woke up in a bombed house in Highbury, not a penny in my pocket, freezing cold and dying for a drink. My legs had gone stiff in the night, so I kept rubbing them to get the circulation back. Then I hit the street. There were two pubs at the old Caledonian Road cattle market, and they used to open for the market workers at 6 a.m. every day. So I brushed myself down, combed my hair as best I could and headed up to the Lamb. It was packed and no one took any notice of me, so I looked around slowly for a friendly face. My world became bright when I spotted an old prison mate from some time back, and it was not long before I had thawed out on the pints he was getting me. He was not a heavy drinker, keeping smart and sober. He had been away for armed robbery; his favourite move was to go into a sub post office near closing time with a mate, who would turn the sign on the door as he pulled out an imitation gun on the staff. He told me that after his last stretch, five years, he had turned that game in and was now at a safer earner known as the Jump Up. He would follow a lorry or van and wait for the driver to pull up to deliver, then a mate and he would grab whatever the guy was delivering from the van when the driver went into the shop. His mate had recently been nicked over another offence and he offered me the job that evening. He took me back to his house and introduced me to his wife. She was a very attractive woman.

I had a bath and he gave me a new suit. His house was like Aladdin's cave – all nicked gear – I was OK for a few months, getting drunk but not too bad. His wife used to try to get me to stop drinking so much; but it was no good.

I began getting memory blackouts far quicker and for much longer stretches. It started to worry me – waking up not knowing what I'd done the day before, who I was with, where I'd been, whether I'd committed a crime. I usually had. But had it been a big or a little one? I also began wetting the bed.

One afternoon, after the pubs closed at 3 p.m., I bought a bottle of Scotch and went into the park to drink it. In about ten minutes I was surrounded by a load of winos and alcoholics. They were the roughest-looking people I had ever seen, and I was no stranger to mangled features. I sent for more drink and one of them brought back a few bottles of wine. I woke up in the park with them the next morning and found about £12 down my sock. They knew where to get a drink even at that early hour and it wasn't long before the party was in full swing again. We all drank fast . . . their conversation coming suddenly in violent bursts, raw and cutting.

One thing that impressed me about these winos was that they did not care what anyone had done in drink or otherwise the day before. They were immune to shock. I remember one instance. A guy called Mills, who they told me was a bit of a psychopath, fell over at the height of the afternoon's drinking and damaged his wrist and ankle. He was lying moaning on the ground when his troubles came to the attention of one of the Scotch blokes. The little Jock was smaller than Mills and, I was told, had been beaten up by him several times in the past. Here was the chance to even the score a little. He did – by kicking most of Mills's front teeth out as he lay writhing in agony. He had further plans for Mills too, but fell down drunk before he could carry them out.

* * *

I woke up next morning – or many mornings later. I could not tell and had lost all track of time. The blackouts were getting even worse. I looked around the place; it seemed to be an old mission hall. Dragging myself up to have a piss, I noticed a hand-written poster on the plaster of the old wall which proclaimed: 'The meek shall inherit the earth.' No doubt it was pasted to the mildewed wall by some Christian-minded person, as encouragement to the parish's poor many years past. I had to smile. The message, it seemed, hadn't exactly got through to the drunks in the place. Lulled, dulled, skulled out of their heads.

I was beginning to feel sorry for myself, thinking about girls I had had crushes on and how I might have been in a nice warm house with them. I wondered how the guys who were no smarter than me used to end up leaving the pub at closing time with a nice bird, while I would be dead drunk. Fuck this line of thought. Better face the fact once and for all – I was a drunk, and in this twilight world of mad men and women you live their way or die. I staggered out on to the street. It was a cold day, empty of laughter, empty of spirit, empty of everything. I asked a bloke if he could help me out with a couple of bob. He shrugged his shoulders and pushed past me. (I was going to have to improve my begging technique fast!) Winos usually have another string to their bow such as shoplifting, thieving, mugging, prostitution – all these acts committed later in the day when you've got some wine down. But begging is the drunk's stock-in-trade. It starts you off. It's got many aspects: it gets your courage up, gets you communicating with normal people – perhaps the only communication many winos ever have. But, most important, it gets the first drink of the day with which to cure the shakes. The day always begins with the shakes, sickness, fear, paranoia, constipation, dry retch and complete loss of memory, which only a drink will cure. So begging a bottle can often turn into demanding with menace, and threatening behaviour into grievous bodily harm. It takes about a week's dry-out before winos show any signs of behaviour that indicate that they might actually be human beings after all. Even then the signs are few!

I owed fines for being drunk and there was a warrant out for me. The law picked me up one afternoon. At court next morning I got a one-month prison sentence. I was sent to Pentonville where all the winos go. Entry into a prison is never a simple matter and I waited many hours. We were all on the one wing and sent to work in the same shop: it was the same company as outside with only one difference – we were all sober! I was put to work in the so-called rag shop. The place was worse than a nut-house. Every wine school was represented by their own table so at one end you had the Waterloo mob, the other the Camden Town mob, etc. Everybody swapped stories, and we all told each other about the money we begged and the amount of wine we had got hold of. We talked about everything, especially giving up drink – soon forgotten on our day of release!

Although these guys looked harmless enough now, devoid of their alcohol, the old rag shop was still not without its danger. Everyone was given a knife to cut up rags with, and some of these guys were clearly raving nutters to say the least. Going to the toilet at the back of the shop was a trial. You had to run the gauntlet of blokes positioned each side of the loo demanding a match or tobacco. Every day there was at least one fight with the heavy mob rushing in and frogmarching the offenders off to the block. One day an old wino called Sully fired a scrubbing brush with all his might. It happened to catch the observation screw (who wasn't observing too good that day) behind his ear. He was streaming blood and roaring blue murder. They never saw Sully do it and nicked some poor nutter, and the more he protested his innocence, the more they battered him out of the shop and over to the block. They had a special round table for the really far gone. We used to call it the Magic Circle! I thought I'd seen it all until I was put in that rag shop. Some of the winos would come out of the loo with their flies undone and their trousers hanging down round their arse, and then they would piss themselves again on the floor of the shop. Some of them went round talking to themselves all day. Others – the skin on their foreheads hardened by falls – used to take shaking fits and kick everything up in the air, fall down and smash their heads. No one took any notice. At first you wondered what was happening; after a while you didn't care. Any bastard that had the misfortune to take a fit in the toilet was always minus his tobacco and matches when he came round.

One day they brought a queer into the shop; he was extremely good-looking. He looked like a pretty girl. They called him Carol. He lasted two days: they hounded him to death every time he went to the loo. In the end he had to sit by the screw, and the screw had to escort him to the loo.

I thought the fuckers were knackered, but it's surprising what a bit of grub and no alcohol can do! I was sharing a cell with two nutters; one of them kept talking and walking up and down all night. I gave the number one a half-ounce of tobacco and he put me on my own in a single cell – what peace! At last I could read.

I only had three days left to do before my discharge and was surprised when the screw came to my cell and told me to pack my kit – I was going out. Then he explained that one of the boys had come up and paid the three days off my fine. This was sort of standard practice. I would now be eligible for a few pounds discharge grant which would buy the wine. The mate who buys you out is onto a good thing – you pay him back out of the grant, he gets half the drink, and you owe him. Sometimes you have only been given seven days' nick and you are just about getting the drink out of your system and begging to get a good sleep and rest, when someone buys you out and you don't want to go. But once the fine is paid you are out on the street again. The fourteen days' lay-down in prison for drunken fines is the only restful bed winos get; saves lives, really.

When I reached the gate I was greeted by Big Con. He's a good guy, about six foot two tall, fifteen stone, hard as nails. He was acting as bouncer on the Valley Club in Caledonian Road. When he heard from one of the lads I was inside, he came straight up. We went back to the club. What an afternoon's drinking! I was quite fit after my short period inside, so I was ready when Con suggested we take two of the girls back to his room.

When they came over drunk and I saw their features in the clearer light, I lost my enthusiasm. The blonde girl had a bottle scar across her nose and running over her cheek towards her left ear. The other girl's nose was broken flat against her face. Can't recall much about anything after that. But sometime later, probably the next day, I was sitting in the park with the Dipper and Cockney Fred, all hung over with the shakes, one bottle of lousy cider between us, no money, no plans, when in walked the Jockey. We were delighted. He was always loaded. He's about five ten, good build, nice-looking honest face, blond hair. He got his name and his money by jumping up on people's backs and mugging them. He pulled out about £200 and sent the Dipper for a carryout – four bottles of Scotch. When he got back, we got stuck right into it and were warming up when the law came in.

'Right, you lot, out of it. Go on, fuck off, or we'll run you in.'

'OK, guv, we're on our way.'

Up the High Street, I hoisted a spin dryer from a shop's display, got a few hundred yards and couldn't move.

'Hurry up, Johnny, everybody's watching.'

'It won't move, Jockey.'

'You cunt, you're pissed. Look!' He pulled out a flick knife, cutting the lead attaching it to the display stand. We sold it to the barrow boys, got well drunk and started fighting among ourselves. Someone got smashed with a bottle – lots of blood. I staggered back to avoid the knife, saw the blur of a car, then blacked out completely. I knew I was in a hospital. I was embarrassed. Someone had had to take all my clothes off: rags full of shit and piss, vomit, stale smell of wine. My leg was bruised all the way down to the shin, my head was covered with bandages. No one expects anything from a guy with his head bandaged. My eyesight was blurred but returned as a young nurse took my pulse; she smelt lovely, not perfume, just young-woman-smell. The plain white uniform, a little too tight, pushed her tits up and out, making her waist appear trim and small. I was surprised, seeing her close up, that she was bigger built than me. I'm sure my pulse was going up as she continued to hold my wrist. I was thrilled and embarrassed by her closeness; even the psychos in the park never got that close to me!

'Are you feeling comfortable?'

'Yes, thanks.'

'You've been hit by a car, not seriously, just a few nasty bruises.'

Then she looked right into my eyes, not sexy, not bold, just nicely. 'You're going to be fine,' she smiled. Jesus, I felt like jumping out of bed and killing ten tigers just for her. But the thought was too much. I blacked out again.

The Dipper looked like something out of Dickens: long overcoat flapping round his ankles, big mop of hair standing up stiff with dirt, wide-open surprised look on his face. He's a good pickpocket, can take a person's watch off their wrist without them feeling a thing. He's fast and quick-witted. Drinking in the park one day with a prostitute called Sheila, who's a bit religious, he laid a trail of peanuts up into her bag. A squirrel came down, gobbled them up, and got into her bag for more. Quick as a flash, the Dip shut it and turned to Sheila.

'Sheila, are you a prostitute?' he asked all innocent like.

She patted him on the head gently. 'No, no, dear, whatever gave you that idea?'

'Sheila?'

'Yes, dear?'

'Give us a fag.'

'Just a minute, dear.' She opened the bag: SWUSH! The squirrel shot up and out in a furry blur. Sheila nearly fainted. A well-dressed bloke came over and joined us. Sheila went out to get a bottle of wine. Dipper nicked the bloke's diamond ring. Later the law picked us up – told us the guy had reported us. They slung us in the back of a squad car with a plain-clothes tec. At the station the guy starts screaming blue murder – 'That's them, that's them!'

Dipper dives at him shouting, 'We are two hard-working blokes, we were just going to our beds to be up early for work in the morning.'

The law pulls him back. 'Turn your pockets out, both of you.'

We emptied the contents on to a table, not 2p between us, and definitely no ring. They searched us; took us in a cell, strip-searched us, sent a copper out to search the car. Nothing! They let us go.

'Blimey, Dipper, how did you do it?'

'Slipped it in the tec's pocket coming over in the car!'

* * *

It was late on a summer's afternoon. Dipper and I jumped the tube to Piccadilly to try and change a prescription he'd found the night before down someone else's pocket. In the chemist the bloke took one look at us and two at the script before going into the back of the shop, where we heard him phoning the law. We shot out and were down the road fast, reaching the tube just as the rush hour was nearing its peak. The number of people waiting for the train to pull in was amazing. Everyone for themselves when it did. We all surged forward. Dip and I wedged in the middle of a crowd of office workers, tight as sardines. When the doors closed I'm smack bang up against this city gent and Dip's crushed right up behind some young blonde secretary type in a pink dress clutching a shoulder bag in front of her. The train sets off, everybody's swaying about, Dip's got his face stuck into the blonde's hair which is giving off a terrific scent of perfume. Well, what with the heat and everything I'm slowly beginning to get some very sexy thoughts about blondes with pink dresses. Suddenly she turns her head and I'm looking right into her very angry blue eyes. 'Jesus, it's mental telepathy,' I thought – until, looking down to avoid her glare, I see Dip's hand fondling her bum. She tried to turn around, only we're packed too tight; it's impossible to move so she pushed her bag round behind her.

We got off next stop. Dip dropped something into the litter bin, then slipped me a couple of quid. 'They're gifts really,' he said. 'Providing you don't grope too obviously, nine times out of ten a young bird will always block with her bag.'

The following day we were wandering about desperate for a drink. We went into an antique shop in Hampstead owned by a young poof. He came round the counter, smooth-skinned, pretty-faced, girlish step. 'No, no, boys. I'm just closing.'

Dipper threw his arms round his neck, kissing him really

passionately. The poof was flustered, his view was blocked.

'You're gorgeous, you're lovely. Do you know what I'd like to do with you?' He didn't wait to be asked.

'Stop it, Paddy, let me go, you naughty man.'

Dipper had got one hand squeezing his arse. I put a beautiful ornate clock under my overcoat, then started to pull Dipper off the poof.

'Come on, don't mess the nice man around, he's got to shut the shop.'

'Yes, yes, boys.' We backed out the shop door and jumped the tube.

Joe Convey is a bit punchy, thick and very violent – drunk or sober. Drink covers his madness a bit . . . just a bit though. The landlady in the pub has got a soft spot for him. We showed him the clock, his eyes lit up. 'Jesus, Johnny, that's Ankle Teak! I'll take it in to Mrs Brady.'

'Get as much as you can, Joe.' He came out clutching a tenner. We got six bottles of wine. I drank one, and half-way down the second I got sick, tried to keep it down, no good – I spewed the lot up all over the street.

'A fucking sinful waste,' said Joe. I agreed.

Some days later a few of us were sitting in the park hunched up with yearning when Convey came in wearing an expensive tailored jacket. He would not say where he got it. In the afternoon the law pulled up in a van, took us all up the nick – separate cells – quizzing us on our whereabouts the previous night. I couldn't remember the previous hour. They done us all for drunk, charged Convey with murdering a guy, knocking him into a pond on Hampstead Heath. It was his jacket Convey was wearing. At the Old Bailey Convey told the court he was with the guy. The guy was a queer, but he'd never killed him intentionally. The judge interrupted him, 'How did you know this man was a homosexual?'

'Because he spoke much like yourself, sir!' replied Convey. He got seven years.

Someone had a go at the toilet attendant once: after that he left the shithouse locked so no strange dossers could sneak a shit. Mad Gerry didn't worry. He just shit on the washroom floor. We look at people with only one thought in mind: how can we get the price of a drink out of them? Even when sick, shuffling along, heads bent, we are always alert, ever aware like half-tamed animals. We cannot switch off.

Woke up feeling terrible – had a fuzziness in my head, everything seemed blurred, out of shape, odd, like looking through wet glass. I could not remember anything about the last few days. That's the trouble with drink, it ruins your brain cells and when that happens regularly you can get a wet brain. Then you're in a horrible fucking position. Mad Rafferty is curled up like a dog in the corner: bearded, straggle-haired, alive with lice, tattered clothes ripped and stained. He's never been the same since the gypos took him into the country working, never paid him, and tied him under a caravan with a chain each night for a week. He wakes up with a sort of alky shrug, enquiring with a roar if there's any drink . . . nothing.

'Fuck it to hell,' he says. 'I wish I knew where there was a good ironmonger's that'd give us a bottle of blue.'[1] We make up the price of a bottle of surgical spirits and head for the chemist. I went in alone. Mad Dog was too dirty, but here it wouldn't have mattered.

The chemist was a German or something. He said, 'Yes, how many bottles you vant?' He's all eyes; you can't nick anything.

We could get no water to mix with it, so we went in the

[1] Methylated spirits.

church and filled a milk bottle out of the holy water font and started slowly to swallow it. But it's hard to get down first thing in the day – any time for that matter. Bastard stuff. It either makes you dead sleepy and fit for nothing, or drives you mad and ready to kill some cunt. We finished the bottle and were trying to open the collection box when this bloke comes in with a camera round his neck and asks Mad Dog if he can take his photo. Well, the only thing that stands between us reaching tomorrow is a drink, so I said we should go out to the porch, we did not want to be disrespectful in God's house. We went into it, and as he was lining the Dog up, I jumped on his back, arms round his neck. We went down in a heap. Mad Dog dropped, and was down his pockets straight away, but he was skint. All the time the bloke was trying to scream and wouldn't keep still. The Dog gave him a few kicks in the head and he went quiet as we were taking the camera off his neck. An old lady came to the door, she blessed herself, said something in a foreign language and fucked off quickly.

We took the camera over to the old Italian, but were shattered when he pointed out that it was broken. Mad Dog pretended to cry, and I begged him for a couple of bob, but the old fence was merciless. He shut the door. His spaghetti was getting cold. We started begging but our hearts weren't in it: the passers-by feel it and don't stop.

It's turned dark and cold all of a sudden. We admit defeat and head off up to the Paul Community to try and get a bowl of soup and thaw out a bit. Supposedly a charitable organization, they receive huge grants to help down-and-outs, give them a bed for the night, that sort of thing. What a laugh! Where does the money go? They never let any winos sleep there in case they see too much. You're OK with them if you've got a wet brain or you're a perv that don't drink. The place is run by young middle-class types. They're nice when they first come to work, but the heads soon get them trained to be hard by sending them out with a different old dosser every day. After watching his antics for a few weeks, they wouldn't give their own mother a drink of water if she were dying.

Though singing the saving hymns tonight, they were none too pleased to see the Dog and me at the door, begging for the crumbs of last week's bread, but eventually they let us in to see the night orderly, a reformed alky named Michael Brennan (or Micky the Monk as we called him now). He goes to Mass every morning of the year, lights so many candles it's lucky he doesn't burn the church down. He's so cured from the drink that the mere sight of a wino is enough to bring him out in the shakes. We gave him a yarn – not that it was really necessary. He could see the state we were in but didn't seem to show too much pity – so close to God's purpose, I suppose, that small things like homelessness and hunger mean nothing to him. 'It will prepare you for a better life to come,' he said. (And we won't have to wait too long for it either, I thought, if we keep this one up much longer.)

'If you were to do a bit more praying and a lot less drinking, you would be much better off,' said he as he wiped the gravy off his chin with the back of his hand. 'Yes,' he continued, looking at us with a mad glint in his eye, 'pray to St Paul and the Virgin Mary.'

'We haven't the strength to pray, we're too fucking tired and hungry. You know the score,' said the Dog, looking angrily back at him. I thought he was going to turn us out after that but to my surprise he let us stay for some soup and a warm on the strict understanding that we would leave afterwards. (Must have recognized a fellow nutcase in the Dog or something.) There was a right crew in here tonight, not a drinker or drug addict among them. A shower of dossers hang around cafés, slobbering over tea all day, never been in the nick in their lives. They'd shit on the floor of the church and wipe their arses with hymns, prayers and bibles, and still have the cheek to go back to Mass next day.

After a while they put us back on the street; we had to leave, there were too many of them. When they shut the door, we went down into the basement coal cellar. It was fucking cold. I just sat against the wall all night shivering, but the Dog dropped off like a baby. Nice to be mad sometimes.

The falling snow, forming a wet slush on the streets, was seeping into my split shoes. I banged my feet on the ground trying to warm them. It was so cold I thought I'd go down the toilets for a warm. Anyway, I hadn't had a clean up for a couple of weeks. It would be something else to do.

The carbolic soap cannot hide the stink down here. Every dosser must be here today. I pity anyone who comes down for a genuine shit; no chance. The fucking tea drinkers from the flop-houses stay in the cubicles for hours on end. There's a couple of nutters arguing in the middle of the floor about fuck all. You'd think it was really important the way they're shouting at each other. Bottle Joe, Humpy Smith and a few more of the gamblers are gathered round one tattered paper trying to pick winners. I pushed through them into the washroom. No one there, no razor, no soap – fuck all.

I get the dry retch, try not to be sick, got nothing to bring up anyway – just pulls your stomach inside out. I knock on the attendant's window to borrow a razor. The bastard says there's to be no shaving in here. He doesn't go as far as to say he wants me out but I get the drift. Can't have a go at him, he'll call the law – too much aggro for my nerves without a bottle. He's only a fucking brown artist, not worth it.

Lot of loud voices, then the door bursts open. In comes Big

Con with the Big Dipper and Mad Gerry ... 'Hello, Johnny, you're looking well' ... the lying cunts, I'm dying. 'Here' – hands me a bottle of jake.[1]

'Oh, fuck that, Gerry, I'm too sick.' He grabs it back and takes a big swallow – nearly makes me spew, just watching him, face all chewed up on one side where a police dog got him one time. I bend to tie my shoe. Gerry lets out a roar, making all our nerves jump as he misfired, singeing his nose trying to light a dog end.

Big Con starts to shave. We're having a laugh till he's finished. Then he gives me the razor. It feels funny taking my coat off. I feel as light as a feather. After I've shaved and washed, I'm surprised to see my own eyes looking back at me from the big mirror. I ain't seen my face for a couple of weeks. It don't look too bad. If I had new clothes on I could walk in anywhere. No way anyone could see I was a drunk. Makes me feel brave again. What with the heat and the company, I feel I could nick anything today. Big Con asks me if I heard about the guardsman Blake. 'No.' He got five years for killing Boylan, a fellow vagrant, in a skipper[2] over a bottle of wine. He got the charge down to manslaughter – not a bad result really.

I liked Blake. You could see he'd been good-looking once in a military kind of way, but his face had become all sort of ravaged and wrinkled from the drink. He used to clean himself up now and then, put on a posh accent and con someone that he was a Guards officer in the Queen's 29th or something; you had to laugh.

'What we going to do?' I asked.

'Let's go up to Jim's for a tea,' says Mad Gerry.

We all burst out laughing at that. Jim's is the dirtiest dosser's

---

[1] Surgical spirits.
[2] Somewhere – anywhere – to spend the night, e.g. a derelict house.

café in the country, but it's too posh for us. We're all barred. We're barred everywhere – pubs, off-licences, cafés, doss-houses, flop-houses, toilets, betting shops, stations, parks, hospitals, the only place they'll take us is the nick. I'm slowly becoming unhappy again. I thought at first these lads would have some wine or money but nothing's come up yet. The attendant gets pissed off and leaves; nothing to nick here anyway.

Mad Gerry's drinking the jake and frothing at the mouth, talking about fucking the priest and the nuns in Regent's Park convent. I don't care what he does so long as I get a fucking drink out of it – don't know whether he's a religious maniac, a pervert and degenerate, plain mad or all three! We must have been down there about two hours now. No one's making a move.

Pill-head comes in. I think I'll take a walk. Pill-head slides some pills into my hand. I give him a wink, swallow them with a drop of water, then sit on the floor till I get the buzz. Everybody's talking at once. It's OK.

Think I'll have a crap. Funny how they make you relaxed. I could sit here all day now. Kilroy was here too. That's always on the door. I read a book in the nick about Ancient Rome; it said that, under the arena, written on the walls of the gladiators' cells were the words '*Subachias hic.*' It's supposed to mean Kilroy was here. Funny. Some things never change. Read about this guy, got done for striking his cohort officer; sentenced to the arena to die. He had over 300 fights, winning every one of them. When they offered him his freedom, he said, 'You must be mad. I've got gold-trimmed armour, slaves to clean it for me, all the wine I can drink, and beautiful women throw themselves at me.' He came from a remote part of the country. His name was Flama. He was supposed to be uneducated, but he did all right. Wish I was a gladiator. It's like being in the arena down the park. Sometimes you might get a drop of wine if you win. Never had any beautiful women throwing themselves at me, though.

I must have blacked out, because when I came to I was sitting by the telephone boxes in the tube station. It had turned dark. I felt as weak as a cat. I jumped the tube to Euston but didn't bother to look in the park to see if there was any drink. I felt really ill. I picked up a few dog ends and fucked off into the skipper. There's no mattress there, so I put rolled-up paper between my hip bone and the floor.

Rolling a smoke, I thought, Well, it's Sunday night. I realized I'd got through another week without falling down any stairs. It seems to be a major cause of death round here. Scotch Billy was found dead in a police cell on Monday. Seems he fell down the stairs.

After finishing a month for 'trespassing on railway property', I'd just started on my first bottle in the park when in walked Rabbiting Jock, his face all grimed with dirt. He gave me a world-weary look that missed nothing. 'All right, Johnny?' he said. 'The lads said you were away. Where did you get done?'

'Over on the station.'

'What happened?'

Now the only way to stop his troubles pouring out was to pour mine out instead, so I gave it to him. 'I was blind drunk; it was raining, raining very hard; I could avoid the rain when I moved my head from side to side. Not for long though . . . just as I'd relax another gush would suddenly find my face, forcing my head back. I soon became sober enough to make out two black shapes, silver badges gleaming on their helmets, laughing as they trained a hose on me. They'd got me handcuffed to that old iron refuse container in the yard at the back of the station and my wrist was rubbed raw where the cuff had bit into it.'

'Bastards!' he said.

'Yeah, well, when they'd had enough fun they slung me out on the street. Trouble is, after their free shower they don't supply a free towel, so I'm down the tube trying to dry out a bit when this posh-looking bird comes along carrying a violin case. She stops at the bottom of the escalator, takes out the violin and after poncing about with it for a while starts playing in earnest.'

'What was she playing? Schubert or something?' asked Jock.

'Fuck knows. I'm just watching the expression on her face every time she hits a high note . . . it comes over all sort of painfully happy like she's having a bunk-up or something. Was she giving that violin one! I just got my comb out to try and comb the water out of my hair when I see the same two coppers that gave me the wet earlier on coming down the escalator.'

'Sod that, Johnny, what did you do?' His words were slurred; I glanced at the bottle, it was nearly empty. I grabbed it and took a swig.

'What could I do? You know, there's no other way out except by train so I pulled out a piece of toilet paper that I keep in my pocket in case of emergency when I'm on the cider, wrapped it round the comb, stood over beside the violinist and began to accompany her on my makeshift mouth organ . . . The coppers are right beside us now, but they don't seem to notice me 'cause the girl's playing really well and I'm going through the motions: pretending to blow, shaking my head and giving it all that, as if this classical stuff's really sending me. Well, with my eyes shut I don't know anything until this old lady's voice whispers in my ear as she drops a coin in front of us: "Oh, Mozart is so stylish!" Then she lets out a shriek when water from my hair hits her in the face as I shake my head. The coppers had just gone past, but hearing the screech they spun round. I made a dash for the stairs but they grabbed me. As they're bundling me up the escalator, the violinist (fair play to her), grasps the situation and shouts out, "Excuse me, officers, why are you arresting my accompanist?" For a second I thought it might work until the shorter of the two shouted back: "We don't care whether he's your accompanist or an infant prodigy – he's nicked!"'

Memory goes and returns. Meantime the weather got warmer. It was one of those few very hot days that we sometimes get in summer. I was weak and tired from a month's non-stop drinking, and the glare of the sun reflecting from the cars, shop windows and other shiny objects was doing my eyes up and jangling my nerves. I was so weak I'd been reduced to waiting and watching the park for a friendly face with a drink. Not that anyone was around with a bottle. I could see at least half a dozen people from where I stood, but they were all whores, and they become mighty brave when they are all together like that. Their memories become short too, about good deeds rendered in the past. So, to avoid sharing a bottle, they con any man brave enough, or perhaps foolish enough, who tries for a drink. He finds his nerves shattered rather than cured by their violent screams of abuse about crimes real or made up that he has done to one or all of them in the past.

I must have blinked or looked away because when I next gazed over a man was actually standing in front of the women. I waited for the banshee's wail, but the only wail I heard was that of a passing police car – the coppers late for their tea break again! I thought the sun was playing tricks: one of the women handed the guy the bottle! As he put it to his mouth I suddenly understood. It was Macglaccan. I walked over. As I came up to him he stuck out his hand holding the bottle; whether by accident or intention it caught me a jarring knock in the belly. 'Hello, Johnny,' he said. My heart lifted when I saw his face: one eye was completely closed and over the eyebrow was a deep open gash, congealed blood forming thick brown layers around it. Things were turning out OK, I might get to enjoy a good drink in peace today. Still, he was very unpredictable; you couldn't be too careful.

'OK, Mac?' I smiled. 'Jesus, what happened?'

The good eye flashed, he leant towards me and growled, 'You got us both slung out of the George the other night.' He was well built, carried his left shoulder higher than the right and had a way of lowering his head to one side as if to allow his face and eyes quick protection should anyone throw a sudden punch. 'And to top it all, Johnny lad, we had to leave a load of drink on the counter.'

He was playing the law-abiding citizen, so I said, 'Sorry about that, Mac.' He didn't answer. Then I realized I shouldn't have said that. An apology was a sign of weakness. It's the sort of thing you end up saying without thinking, so while I had the bottle in my hand I took another good swig and as I passed it back to him Mac gave me a powerful slap on the back that served as sign of renewed friendship and a reminder of his strength.

Still, I was on my guard with Mac, trying to have a laugh with the women and drinking a bit too fast. The heat and glare from the sun forced me to sit down on the grass. I must have dozed off. When I opened my eyes the sun had gone in and Big Simon, the seaman, had joined the group. Mac was sitting near me, his hand around a bottle of wine. You never can judge when wine will hit you – no wonder the Yanks call it 'sneaky Pete'!

I was trying to roll a smoke when the throbbing in my head started up. I'd been getting headaches in the morning ever since a brawl over on the station a few weeks back when someone had caught me on the side of the head with a cider bottle. I was looking at the antics of Mac. He hadn't shaved and his black stubble looked like dirt; half drunk he was, pulling up fistfuls of grass, mumbling, 'A fucking shower of cunts. My sister would beat the lot of them. My father was as straight as a rush at eighty years of age and drinking raw poteen.' No one said a word; he looked like a mad ape. Trying to light a fag I didn't realize he was talking to me. 'That big bastard's cunt-struck,' he said. It was true: Big Simon was a seaman and they're all cunt-struck or boy-struck or both. But what had that got to do with me?

The conversation was taking a dodgy turn, so I said, 'He's dead fit though.' But that didn't sound right either.

Mac gave a humourless laugh: 'How's he keep so fit then, sleeping under the trees and giving it to the whores? Or is it from all those back bends he does when he's picking up dog ends?' And this time he roared with laughter at his wit. I had to laugh at the idea myself and as Mac passed me the bottle I saw the big seaman watching us with an angry glare in his eyes. But a wicked little idea had got into my head – I had visions of Mac, me and the big fellow not with whores but with beautiful secretaries, office girls, classy women, aristocratic ladies, middle-class ladies, au pairs and foreign women, making love like mad, week in week out, trying to see who was the fittest! Mac had his hand round the long, bulbous neck of the bottle, slowly and gently rubbing it up and down like he was really enjoying caressing it that way. His eyes were fixed intently on the big fellow who pretended not to notice. The women had, though, and it felt like a load of uncomfortable vibrations had been released into the group.

A sudden cold blast of wind shook the leaves on the trees; even healthy green ones fluttered to the ground. At that point the big fellow looked over at Mac: 'Don't fuck with me, man.'

Mac ignored him. Looking at me instead, he said, 'Who's doing any fucking round here?' He was talking calmly but his hand round the bottle tightened. 'Jesus,' he continued, 'I wouldn't fuck them with yours.' And he looked right at the big fellow when he said that. It went very quiet; even the birds seemed to stop chattering as the big guy lunged to his feet. He would have had every advantage if only the women had not tried to protect him by holding onto him. Mac sprang to his feet, a knife in his hand.

A swift blow knocked the big fellow back into a sitting position on the seat. The women, screaming, jumped aside as Mac ripped upwards with the blade, slicing open the seaman's face from his chin up the cheek to the eye. It happened in a flash and Mac disappeared amid the screams. As the whores surrounded the big fellow, doing a Florence Nightingale on him, I disappeared quickly too. The next few days were very uncomfortable. What with plain-clothes men suddenly sliding into the parks looking for Mac and uniformed officers scouring Camden Town, it was hard to pull a stroke or relax in our usual haunts with a bottle. No one seemed to know where Mac was until the following week when the Dipper got released from nick. He told us that following the business in the park Mac had started drinking in the back of the Catholic church to avoid capture. This had been fine for a day or so but the funny looks he was attracting from the worshippers prompted him to look round for a more secluded spot. His eye fell on the confessional box. A little drunk, perhaps, and just opening his second bottle of red wine, a woman's voice, seemingly coming from nowhere, startled him, saying, 'Bless me, Father, for I have sinned.'

'Fuck off, you whore,' shouted Mac, more in fear than anger. The poor woman nearly collapsed. It was dark in the cubicle. Had listening to the sins of so many for so long finally driven the priest mad? Or, horror of horrors, had he, in some divine way that only Catholic priests have, glimpsed a future, negative turn in this woman's life? But as she knelt there, stunned,

Mac's next move convinced her – if indeed she had any doubt in her mind – that her troubles were of a more earthly nature. Mac lurched drunkenly to his feet and started to pee, asking, 'Are you still there, you whore?'

The Dipper said Mac's face and body were a mass of cuts and bruises owing to a more than usually vigorous kicking such as the law hand out to winos. We kept hearing rumours that he was doing three years, others had it at five, so we were all surprised when a few months later Mac walked into the park.

As Mad Jerry and I climbed the hill leading to the Convent of the Virgin of the Miracles, I wondered if it was going to be another conversion job. Last week he'd been converted to the Church of England for £2, the week before he'd become a Jew for a cup of tea and packet of fags. 'What's it to be, then?' I asked him.

He grinned. 'Don't worry, act dumb. Don't speak, leave it to me. OK?'

'Yeah.' We arrived at the entrance to the convent and Jerry rang the bell. I looked up over the massive wooden door to where a stone lion wasn't having much luck frightening a praying saint who kept gazing undisturbed towards heaven. What will-power! Kelly gave up praying last winter after the priest refused him a cup of tea.

A middle-aged nun, her face white and unlined, opened the door, beckoning us in with a calm smile that reached all the way up to her eyes. Shutting the door with surprising noiseless ease, she turned towards us: 'Welcome to this house of God. Please wait here while I fetch the duty sister.' She slid through a side door like a shadow. We were standing in a large marble-floored reception area. A life-size statue of the Virgin gazed down on us with such an endearing expression on her face, it caused me a pang of guilt. Out of habit I went to light a cigarette but checked myself before Jerry had time to panic.

The nun seemed to be gone a long time. I looked towards the door she had passed through, and was surprised that I hadn't noticed before that there were three similar doors together, and I couldn't now be sure which one she had used. Looking about I realized that there were also many more statues and stone carvings than my first quick glance had shown. Jerry mistook my roving-eyed awe, whispering out the side of his mouth, 'There's nothing to nick.' I somehow checked laughter. The tinkling of a bell broke the silence, then the singing of the nuns from somewhere inside the convent, 'The Angel of The Lord declared unto Mary . . .' 'The Angelus,' whispered Jerry.

I nodded. 'Where the hell has that nun got to?' I spoke out loud, worried that she might have joined in the singing and forgotten us.

Jerry's eyes flashed with anger. 'Jesus, Johnny, keep your voice down. Better still, keep quiet altogether. You're supposed to be dumb!' He was right of course. I'd agreed to go along with the act so I might as well see it through now. The door opened at last. A young nun stood silently before us covered from head to toe in black with just a little white cloth bordering her face and neck. She was beautiful: smooth delicate skin, lovely brown eyes, perfect white teeth, gorgeous lips. She looked Italian. Jerry started to speak quickly. 'Could you help us, Sister? This is my younger brother,' pointing to me. 'He's just over from Ireland.'

She nodded her lovely head. '*Si.*'

'He cannot speak.' The lovely brown eyes turned towards me full of pity. My heart gave a jump – such a look. Jerry never paused for breath. 'Lost his voice as a child, lost his rosary beads, his luggage, his money, that me poor mother gave him.' She looked at me again, so serious and concerned. I noticed the way her mouth gave a little pout, and the shadow of very fine black hairs over her upper lip added to her beauty. Were there many more like her in the convent? The only men they see are cunts like me and Jerry, winos trying to con them, when they could have the richest and best-looking men in the world. Pretty Lips could anyway. Did she ever think of sex? Did she know she was beautiful? Was it possible that she didn't know she had the power to make better men than me go weak at the knees? Jerry was in full swing. I hoped he wasn't going to blow it. The nun was convinced. 'And the rosary beads, Sister . . .'

'Si.'

'He must have a rosary. I don't want him to lose the faith.'

'Si.'

She disappeared through the door. I started to speak, only to be stopped by the furious shakings of Jerry's head. I was forced to play the dumb younger brother a little longer. The saints in the paintings and stone carvings seemed to look even more pained as if they were all suffering from acute indigestion rather than God's love. I'd seen happier expressions on the faces of lifers in prison.

The beautiful live Virgin returned, rewarding Jerry with a new five-pound note, me with a rosary. 'Thank you, Sister. May God bless you,' said Jerry, nudging me. 'Kiss the holy rosary, Johnny.' They waited expectantly as I brought the beads to my face, brushing my lips on the plastic cross. My eyes met the nun's. She smiled. I don't know if it was the smile or my not being used to the cute way words sound in foreign women's mouths but, when she sweetly asked me if I had thought of visiting Lourdes, my 'No' sounded like thunder. It shot out of my mouth. I gasped, coughed, spluttered, trying to cover it up. The smile froze on her lips. The eyes became sad, confused, questioning. Mad Jerry recovered first, dropping to his knees, arms outstretched, croc tears filling his eyes. He beseeched all the saints, including the young nun, to witness the Virgin's miracle. 'Glory be to Mary, his first words since a child!' Pretty Lips stretched out her arms, walking slowly towards us. We walked backwards, facing her, to the door. Was she joining in praise of the little miracle or shooing two naughty ganders away on some mountain farm in her native Italy? Deftly she opened the door, Jerry still beseeching all the saints in Heaven, me bowing like some demented servant, as she ushered us, without haste, into the street.

Scarface Mick is tall, well built, good-looking in a rough kind of way. He used to be a chauffeur until he got caught in bed with his governor's wife. Now he's got a deep razor scar from ear to chin.

I was begging in the Euston Road. Met him. He was in rags.

'Hello, Johnny. They say you've got charisma. Let's see who can beg the price of a bottle quickest.'

I was clean, shaved and washed. 'OK, Mick.'

A smart-looking secretary-type woman, about fifty, came towards me; stopped, turned her back, faced Mick. 'Do you know where there's a post office?'

'Yes, young woman, straight on, turn first right.'

'Thank you, and thank you for the "young woman" bit. Ha, ha, ha . . .'

'If I had the money I'd take you for a drink, lady.'

'Don't let that stop you, young man. I'll take you.'

They walked off together. I started begging on my own again. Fuck charisma.

Sometime later I did make up the price of a bottle or two and staggered into the park, drunk. Belfast Mary jumped on me from behind. I fell over a park bench; nearly broke my back. She was pilled up. She was also very attractive, with a slim voluptuous figure. At nineteen a real beauty. Only trouble was she'd got a habit of cutting her boyfriends with a razor or broken bottle – she'd already done a couple of stretches for it. She started hugging and wrestling me around on the wet grass. It was maddening, like being mauled by a tigress: if only I was sober I'd have pinned her to the ground and ravished her. Then she slowed down and just as I was getting a good kiss from her, the law came in. They pulled her off and nicked us both for drunk.

On a night when black frost sparkled on the pavements and made rims round the damp patches in the gutters, Dipper and I went begging from everything that moved: men, women, and children . . . Fight a dog for its bone. Dip pulled a smart young bloke: 'Help us with a couple of bob, please, sir.'

'Go to work.'

'Are you working, sir?' asked the Dip in his best illiterate innocent retainer's voice.

It worked. The guy stopped, obviously enjoying the Dip's destitute position. 'Yes, I'm always working.'

'I don't believe you.'

The guy's ego went. With a superior flourish he pulled out a wage packet.

'Wait yet; I can't read quick.' Dip holds the guy's hand; with the other he traces his four fingers along the writing.

'That's what I earn,' happy to explain all the details to stupid homeless vagrants.

'You're a clever man,' said the Dip, forcing the guy's hand with the wage packet back into his inside pocket, loose change jingling as he pats it safely down. 'Jesus, that's great wages, where can I get a job like that?' The guy had had enough fun. Smiling smugly he walked briskly away. 'Run.' We shot down the road and into a pub. 'Two double Scotches, two pints, guv.'

'Here.'

'Thanks.' He handed me a bunch of notes. 'Always keep your thumbnails long, they're handy for opening wage packets!'

The lads reckoned Big Henry was looking for me. He was studying to be a doctor at one time; now he was a fence, smoked dope, a bit weird. I met him later. I was a bit drunk.

'That radio you sold me didn't work.'

'It was working when I had it.'

'Oh well, sod it. Fancy a drink?' he said.

We went back to his flat in Warren Street: a nice place, six floors up, two rooms – a bedroom and a sitting room – two armchairs, a table, a settee. I sat down. He opened a bottle of Scotch, filled my glass to the brim, only half filled his own. We drank for an hour or more. Then his wife came in. She was tasty. She had a darkish brown birthmark running from the corner of her eye to the middle of her cheek, but I didn't notice it when I looked at the rest of her. She wore a tight black costume, black high-heeled shoes; slim shapely legs. She didn't speak to me – just sat on the settee and watched me drink. I could sense that I repelled her. Black with dirt, my clothes crumpled rags, I stank, had no God, stole, cheated, lied, drank. After a while she got up and went into the bedroom. Henry filled my glass; I finished it in two mouthfuls. As I stood up to go for a piss he lunged at me with a knife, ripping my shirt. It sliced down my chest with a sting. I jumped the table, grabbed a chair and threw it at the window, smashing it. He sprang at me. I ran round the table keeping it between us and grabbed another chair. Holding it, legs forward, against my chest, I inched over to the door. His wife came out of the bedroom nude, her eyes wide and staring. Gorgeous body . . . very sexy. Looking at her nearly cost me dearly. I just managed to avoid the bastard's sudden lunge. Now he'd gotten between me and the door. We circled about, trying to think round the fear. None of us spoke. Though my life was on the line I kept sneaking glances at the body, its image continued to flicker forth. It was maddening: the first woman I'd ever seen completely naked and I dare not have a proper look. She watched the sport I was providing for them in a kind of stupor – pilled up to the eyes. I heard the sound of a bus going by in the street below and wished I was on it. Keeping him at bay with the chair, I reached the door, opened it, got out and down the stairs fast. It was close!

A few weeks later Henry thought a young petty thief called Cummings had ripped him off. Luring him back to the flat, he got him drunk and killed him by battering his skull with a hammer. Then he walked into a police station and gave himself up. At his trial it was found that he'd had a couple of brain haemorrhages. He got sent to Broadmoor indefinitely. He'd wait there for a long time, and we'd wait on the streets. You waited, and you waited – for a drink, for jail, the nut-house, the hospital, the doctor, the bus, the tube. I wondered if Henry's wife would wait . . .

A pretty young bird came in the park one day: high cheek-bones, middle-class accent, nicely dressed, she talked sweetly to us for a while, about harmless dainty little things, then asked Jock Lynch if he'd help her with her heavy case. She'd left it in the station. He jumped up with a sly gleam in his eye – she smelt so nice – many fantasies were visualized. She told him she couldn't remember where she had put it down but in the end she found it by the bookstall. Jock picked it up and followed her out to the bus stop. When the bus came she gave him a couple of bob to put it on the bus for her and off she went. About a week later I was in the park when the same bird came in, talked for a while, then asked me if I would help her with her case . . . somewhere over in the station. Her memory seemed really bad because she couldn't even remember what colour it was. I said I'd help if she'd first cure my nerves – give me the price of a bottle. But she didn't want to do that, so I took hold of her and grabbed her bag. She was spitting mad, going to get the law. I told her Jock had been nicked for stealing the other case. She didn't reply . . . just gave me the money for a bottle . . . Going for a bottle! I am already drunk.

Went to see Paddy O'Maly and his wife Claire. They live with their sixteen-year-old daughter Lisa and Scruff the dog in one small room. Claire is very pretty, hair so black in the light it shines blue. She gives out a sort of glow. Every time I meet her I feel like hugging her, stroking and kissing her. Instead desire becomes laughter. She laughs too.

The four of us went to a high street store. Paddy and Claire nicked a few dresses. Lisa and me went back in and exchanged them. The assistant gave us the full price for them. We carried on like that all afternoon until Paddy and I became too drunk to perform. We bought a few bottles of wine and some Guinness and went back to their room to drink. Drank all evening. Last thing I remember seeing before I conked out was Claire standing by the bed.

Someone kissing my face woke me. I opened my eyes. Scruff the dog nuzzled up. I pushed him away and pulled myself out of the armchair where I'd spent the night. Three black heads of hair peeped out from under the sheet covering the bed: Paddy, Claire, Lisa. Women's underclothes on a chair by the bed.

Looking down I could hear the women's breath as it slowly moved their bodies. Scruff startled me as he brushed up against my legs. It was a very sexy scene. Claire's naked body was just a hand's length away. I needed a cure and found a bottle on Paddy's side of the bed. Put it to my lips. Felt the wine trickle down my throat into my stomach, feeding my veins, bringing back the confidence with which to start the new day. Paddy was still fast asleep when Claire woke.

'Good morning, Johnny. How do you feel today?'

'OK, Claire. Shall I go for some milk?'

'Thanks. We'll be up when you come back. I'll have the kettle boiled.'

At the bottom of the stairs I glanced up at the gas meter. Someone had already done it. I took my time coming back, giving them space to get dressed. Paddy was sitting up in bed, Clair was making the tea, Lisa was brushing her hair. Paddy laughed. 'Jesus, I'm dying this morning. Hurry up with that tea, Claire.'

She looked at him. 'Paddy, you're mad. Don't you remember last night?'

'No. What?'

'You caught the governor of the pub by the throat when he wouldn't change a bent cheque for you.'

'Ha, ha, ha . . .'

I gave her the milk. I still had half a bottle of wine. My nerves were bad. So were theirs. I liked them. I shared it with them.

Fred had just finished doing three months. He bought us a good drink. Seems he was eating on the sly. Done a big shit in a shop doorway. Got nicked. In court he said he'd been drinking cider for months and not eating. The big police inspector got up. He wasn't going to let him get away with that. Looking over at the magistrate, he said, 'I don't know about not eating, Your Worship, but by the look of the evidence it took a considerable effort!'

Fred's a good laugh. When he was young he did time in a military glasshouse. On his discharge papers, the Commandant wrote that he was a pathetic delinquent. Fred asked him what that meant.

'It means you are incapable of sustained effort.'

Fred still laughs when he remembers it. 'How is it I have been drinking constantly for twenty years since then; ain't that a sustained effort?'

As he handed over the bottle, I asked him if the nick grub had improved. 'Still the same goulash and porridge then?'

He laughed. 'I don't know. But whatever it was it took away my sense of smell, my sense of taste . . . left me with no fucking sense at all!'

'What are you doing now then, eating by memory?'

'Ha, ha, ha, you cunt, give me that bottle.'

Passing it back, I noticed his clothes. They were a bit smarter than usual, like he'd had first choice at a jumble sale. 'Where did you get those clothes?'

'The welfare woman.'

'Well, you got some sense left,' I told him. 'Dress sense.'

'Bollocks.'

We look at people with only one thought. How can we get the price of a drink out of them. Looking, always looking, even when there is nothing to observe. Though that is not the case today. Sitting between two young whores and drinking a bottle of whisky the big guy was enjoying himself. He might as well, because judging by the look on Freddie's face his happiness might not last. In one way, I suppose, I wished he had gone when he was still sober. The whores had made a few attempts to coax him away. He was too far gone now, though. The drink, which had at first strengthened and stimulated him, was now beginning to enfeeble him, as he lurched to his feet only to fall back with a roar that turned to a drunken laugh. He slid over sideways on to the whore on his left. Squealing with surprise she managed, in spite of her small size, to push him off. This, coupled with renewed efforts from himself, got him to his feet; a few wobbly steps took him over to a wall speckled with yellowish-green weeds. He started to piss. The whores, pretending to be embarrassed, seemed younger still as they began to talk quickly to each other in what sounded from where we sat like schoolgirl slang. I could see the steam rising from his piss and I thought I could smell the whisky off it too, but I suppose that was because I was dying for a drink. Then everything seemed to happen quickly – Freddie standing before the whores, me with the whisky bottle to my lips letting it run down my throat so fast it was trickling out the sides of my mouth, Freddie tipping the seat over, spilling the whores on to the ground, flashes of legs as they scrambled to their feet, screaming back insults as they ran out of the park, leaving the guy cowering in fear, backing up against the wall, helpless, witless and alone, holding a bunch of fivers in his clenched fist, me putting my hand out trying to wrench the money from his grasp, him, face twisted by shock and fear, trying to get away. For a split second I was undecided whether to let him go when Freddie's fist smashed into his face, knocking him to the ground and banging his head against the broken concrete path. Freddie crouched over him trying to prise the money from his hand but, whether through shock or fear, his fist had gone into a death grip round the notes. Flushed with excitement Freddie gave up struggling to open the clenched fist and, bending further over, lowered his head. The guy screamed terribly as Freddie's rotted teeth sank into his flesh. Letting the notes fall loose, he curled up into a ball, moaning with pain. Freddie gathered them up and we hurried away to get a drink. I glanced back: a stray dog, the only witness, trotted over wagging its tail. Passing through the gate Freddie gave me some notes. 'You nearly let him get away back there.'

'I felt sorry for him,' I said.

He glanced sideways at me. 'Sorry! You'll be feeling sorry all right when you're in the nick and anyone that's with you is too. Never let someone get away once you've started on them.' When I thought about that it made sense. I suppose what would be wrong for a man living in a nice warm house might not be too bad for someone living on the streets.

It is very cold. The frost is stiff on the tips of the grass – stabs the eyes if you look too long.

Sitting on a bench in the winter evening as dusk descended. The Dipper, Hogan, Sham, Taffy Ted and myself, wasted from drink, eyes staring out of grey faces, bodies trembling as the shakes take hold – not a drop between us to curb them either when the dry retch turns our guts inside out. Obsessed by the shape things had taken we wrapped our coats more firmly about us. Death has got to be easier than this, I thought as a tall, well-dressed, middle-aged bloke stopped in front of us. In the presence of such a professional figure we all went quiet. Only our teeth kept chattering. He looked straight at us, too, weighing each of us up in turn; we moved uneasily under his careful scrutiny. My eyes met his. I sensed he wasn't a copper though his face looked very tough. 'Well,' he began, 'you lads certainly do look a bit knocked about today.' If he was a copper almost any of us could have been accused.

'Yeah, we're dying, Doc,' replied Hogan, who seemed to know him.

A doctor! I would have liked to look up and seen some sort of sympathy on his face.

'That's very true,' said the Doc in a voice that matched his face. 'And whose fault is it, eh?' Faced with such a professional question no one answered. In the silence that followed we began to count each blade of rigid grass, even the cracks in the concrete path. 'Well,' he went on, smiling gently at our helplessness. 'Do you want to be admitted to the hospital for a week's dry out?' *Did* we? Visions of lovely nurses surrounded by flowers and fruit fluffing up our pillows each night before we dropped off, while the radiators poured out their comforting warmth, floated before me. We were all enthusiastic and so I followed limping along with the rest in the staggeringly cold air as he led the way out of the park down the road to the hospital. In the street we made an effort to hold our heads high and pull our shoulders back in keeping with our new status as patients. In fact the doctor glanced back at us once or twice with what you could only interpret as approval. In the light of the street lamp you could see how his overcoat fitted him perfectly under the armpits. Compared to us scallywags he was indeed a fine figure of a man. He was taking us, it must be remembered, to a place of sympathy and understanding. If I lacked trust it was because I wasn't too keen on his bedside manner.

But we were received for our period of rest and recuperation with warmth and light into an almost empty reception area where we signed our names and were duly entered in the book. Washed and shaved, safe, secure, we slept deeply, the night staff watching over us until morning when slim-hipped nurses, gliding trimly, gently coaxed us out of bed. During the day we watched the telly, after first being given an injection of Antabuse, a harmless enough substance the nurses informed us sweetly, unless challenged in the bloodstream by alcohol, which of course we had promised the lovely nurses (who were full of tenderness for their new patients) never ever to touch again! So we willingly submitted our bare arms to their ministrations, trust had brought us close. I could feel my face filling out as my anxiety dropped away. And the staff invited us to unburden ourselves and give details of why or what prompted us to consume such quantities of alcohol. And they'd noticed also that we sometimes seemed quite fretful. What were our hopes, our joys, our fears? We could only reply that we were short of smokes. But such things could not concern the young nurses, preoccupied by their vocations, who in spite of their desire to comfort slowly turned away. About the fifth day we were all feeling great, glittering and glowing with health. To improve the shining hour I took a walk down to the canteen to beg a smoke. The place was full of cripples and who did I see among them? Fast Eddie. Only now he's not looking so fast – he's on fucking sticks with plasters on his legs. We're both surprised to see each other and he is even more surprised to hear how I'm up with the others suffering more delicately on the alky wing. 'That's where Smithy snuffed it last month,' he warned.

'We all know Smithy died from a heart attack,' I said. He shook his head, 'That fucking quack always puts "Heart Attack" on an alky's death cert when he's pumped full of Antabuse before being force-fed a bottle of Scotch. And it's all legal, 'cause I bet you've already signed a form on admission agreeing to take part in his little aversion treatment "experiments".'

'Bollocks, Eddie,' was all I could come up with because I was less certain than before.

'Is it?' he roared. 'You'll soon fucking find out. Why don't you ask one of them little nurses up there that you all seem so mad about?' And after adjusting his crutches he limped off with the other raspberry ripples laughing to himself.

The laugh convinced me there were limits to what nurses could reveal. I shot down the corridor to the cleaning cupboard, hoping to find an overall to put on over the hospital pyjamas before hitting the street, when a worse thought struck me . . . If our bodies are full of Antabuse, any alcohol taken over the next few days *wherever it's consumed* must have the same result.

Back in the ward Hogan agreed, 'I suppose if we're all going to get fucked we might as well be in the safest place.'

'Yeah,' growled the Sham. 'And after we get over it we'll get out quick before the bastards have a chance to load us up again.' All night long we tossed and turned. It was hard to know which way to be safe.

Ten a.m. in the treatment room next morning, strictness replacing sweetness, the nurses handed each of us a bottle of Scotch while the doctor checked our pulse rates. 'We're going to have a little party,' he said and smiled at us, *like a whore trying to tempt a timid punter*, but no one smiled back. So he watched and he waited along with the nurses who had formed a sort of cordon sanitaire around us eyeing us with detached interest rather than concern. It was obvious, there was no way of avoiding it, the hospital was not going to deviate from its schedule just because a few lousy winos weren't feeling up to it. But we continued to stand there with the bottles in our hand like soldiers waiting for an order which we hoped might never come but eventually it did.

I raised my bottle to my lips sipping, sucking carefully. We all had the same idea. After about twenty minutes, except for a hot, flushed feeling, there seemed to be no bad effects, so we took bolder swallows until all our bottles were empty.

'So much for your fucking Antabuse, Doc,' shouted Dipper as he lurched around the room trying to laugh his sickness off. Sham dropped on to his hands and knees, head down touching the floor, back arching like a dog as he spewed his guts up. Out of the corner of my eye I saw Taffy leaning against the wall vomiting, some sticking to his pyjamas but most splattering the floor. He had grown green and long and sweaty, his teeth were rattling terrible. Hogan staggered forward only to slip in his own spew and lay cursing and roaring, struggling in a sea of vomit. Then my eyes went funny, like looking through a telescope, first everybody was close up and huge, then small and far away. My legs went next as the worst pain I've ever felt hit me in the middle of the spine and everything blurred, uncontrollable vomiting spasms jerking me so hard that my heart started pounding tightly and painfully. I was roaring now, the pain in my spine unbearable. And after receiving a bash in the face from the edge of a table on my way to the floor I too lay writhing in the nearest thing to madness I have ever known.

How long it lasted I don't know. In the end I hadn't the strength, nor did I care to lift my face out of my own steaming vomit. Our former pleasure had lasted but a moment, our greatest pleasure now would have been to die. The last thing I remember before passing out was the thought, 'I will never, ever drink again' . . . and I didn't until the following week back in the park when we all got legless – all except Taffy, that is, who never left the hospital with the rest of us, after we were persuaded we were still alive.

8

You would think some of the lads were related to royalty . . . like Hogan who's been missing for a couple of days, comes back on the street looking like the clerk of the court, clean shirt, clean face, and as usual cleaned out! 'Where you been? Did you have a drink yesterday?' He looks at me slowly, like I've asked him a really stupid question. 'Johnny, you look terrible,' he tells me. 'Why don't you go into the pisshole for a shave?'

'Fuck the looks and the shave. What are you grinning at?' I say.

'And I bet you're loused up too,' he adds. And this from a mate who was ten times worse than me two days before.

'Hogan, it's a drink I'm after, not a lecture on health and cleanliness.'

'I know. That's why you never get into proper company. No one can take you anywhere,' he says, polite and serious, almost like a probation officer. Before I can say anything he takes out a fiver.

'Where did you get that?'

He looks up in the air sort of grandly before replying, 'Lady Margaret.'

'Who?'

'Never mind,' he says. 'Go and get a bottle, I'll wait here.'

I walk over to the off-licence, thinking that it's no use trying to work it out. No one tells the truth round here any more, myself included, but at least I try to tell a bit of the truth, in between the lies.

Long John's always talking about Lord So-and-So. He's a cousin of the Queen, he says, always ending with 'and he was a colonel in my regiment' (not 'I was a private in his regiment'). I must be the only wino left in the park who doesn't have any titled friends. Still it doesn't really impress me. As long as they pull out the money for a drink, I don't care where they got it or who gave it to them. The only blokes that puzzle me are the bird pullers. Even though I don't believe all they tell me, I'm nevertheless impressed. Some of Tony Nolan's tales about the women he's been with make you wonder for days afterwards. Every dolly bird that passed – I'd be thinking I could be in bed with her if only I could say the right words like Nolan does.

And then there's the titled women. Not just any old birds that happen to come up to Nolan when he's skint and sitting around the streets. You know, sounds daft, but I can't help listening to him and there always seems to be some grain of truth in the story, especially when he pulls out a wad of notes and sends me for a bottle or two. Miss World isn't in it with them either. And the higher their titles, the more beautiful and eager to please they seem to be. Of course it's not all plain sailing. And he's sorry to have to spoil any illusions we may have regarding middle-class women, but sometimes it seems those with the poshest voices, best looks and figures, have little kinks, and can only do it with Nolan while their brother or sister or husband or the butler and the cat watch. Still it all sounds like good clean fun, and lots more exciting than drinking meths with Scotch Mary.

Staggering up the road one morning, I wasn't drunk but my knees had gone stiff – not worth thinking what was wrong with them, could be anything – when Big Frank came across the road, roaring like a bull, 'Hello, Johnny. Jesus I'm bad today; come on let's get a bottle!' We soon got one and went into the boneyard to drink it.

There's a narrow entrance between the houses and you're there. It's an old graveyard which has been half-heartedly converted into a park. There's a few trees and a few unkempt flower beds, some grass between the long-forgotten grave-stones. There are only two benches in the whole place and these are taken by the strongest or the ones with the most wine or the most money. During the day everyone else is either squatting or sitting on the ground.

There's no one there this day. We get straight into the wine. We soon get a glow. Frank starts telling me about the time he was on the road with Mad Rafferty in Somerset. They'd been on the cider and they woke up in a field with their mouths stuck together and their throats so dry that they couldn't speak. They needed water really but went into a pub with their last few bob. While Frank ordered two pints, Mad Rafferty, seeing a bowl of water on the counter half-full, put it to his mouth and gulped it down. The noise made the lady turn round just as Rafferty finished the water. She went white and screamed, 'You've just swallowed my Jimmy.'

'Who?'

'Jimmy, my goldfish!'

They both had to leave.

Frank used to get these deep crushes on birds he met when he was drying out in hospital. When he got let out, he broke out on the drink like a madman, smashing pubs and betting shops. I asked him if he was still with June, and he said, 'Ah, fuck the women! I'm not letting my love affairs go above the navel any more!'

The road sweeper came past looking for a woman. Margo, one of the young whores, reckoned he carried a tin can on the side of his barrow and gave the women a couple of quid to pee in it while he watched. You had to laugh. Some of the lads reckoned it was the dirtiest thing in the world. Didn't stop them taking a drink from him though. Would they look if Sophia Loren was doing it? I wondered. Anyway, he ain't such a bad bloke. Gives us a couple of bob for a drink now and then. No such luck this time. He was looking really mean. One of the women must have ripped him off again. They say he's a perv, but he's got a job which he holds down regular, he's got a bed somewhere and he don't drink all the time and carry on crazy like the rest of us. Makes you think. A lot of so-called normal people come into our company in the park. They don't drink the wine, but they're looking for something, and if they hang around long enough they start drinking worse than any of us, like Steed who owned two houses before his missus and kids got burned to death.

We all got nicked for theft one time and were remanded to Brixton. We were all sitting down when Steed started to crack. He went over to the screw ... told him the guard dogs could talk. The screw backed up to the wall, feeling for the alarm. The heavy mob came in just as Steed grabbed the screw. They battered him out of the door. When he appeared in court, he was unfit to plead; they sent him to the nut-house. We only ever saw him in the park a couple of times after that, before he went completely off his head.

It was funny in the boneyard. The other day Finnegan came limping in on crutches. He'd just come out of hospital after having his leg amputated. He'd cut his foot sleeping rough and was unable to keep it clean; gangrene set in. He had no drink, but I had. He came on with the old tear-jerker bit so I gave him a drink and asked him what it felt like to be on one pin now; he looked at me real coy and whispered that he didn't want to talk about it. I told him to fuck off, he was worth a fortune as a beggar. The big cunt started crying so I had to share the bottle with him. I'd get plenty more with a one-legged beggar after he got a cure in him.

Then there was the dentist. He came in looking for his wife who'd run away. He got everyone a drink but when the party got out of hand and he tried to leave they kicked the fuck out of him, then robbed him. Nothing unusual about that. He had them all nicked; they were remanded for the Old Bailey. But in the meantime the dentist came back, murdered one of the whores and fucked off. He could not be found. The case was dropped against the lads.

I got hit by a car and it broke my leg. The driver didn't stop. My leg would not heal properly. Those days you couldn't draw social security unless you had a room, but you couldn't get a room unless you had money, so I stayed in a derelict house for three months. There was a law against that too – 'vagrancy'. Of course the police used it how they liked – putting a bit of lead in your pocket altered it to 'being on enclosed premises to steal'. The criminal charges associated with simple vagrancy were endless. The advantages of this communal life were similar to those enjoyed by a shoal of tiger sharks.

In those three months I never took my clothes off nor had a bath. About ten of us, men and women, slept in that one room because it was the only one in the house that didn't have a leaky roof. We were all getting amphetamines off this quack, washing them down with wine and cider. We were like zombies half of the time. The room was full of filth – lice, human shit and piss, gobs of consumptive phlegm (most of the older guys have TB). In the end I got the horrors. I used to sit there not caring whether I lived or died. I'd start to doze off and some weird furry animal would slink up to my neck and start kissing me, friendly-like. Then spiteful rows of gleaming teeth would sink into my face and lips. I'd jump up with a scream, doze off again, try to be ready for the dreams next time. But they were too crafty. They'd start biting my fingers. A wino is a person in total need of alcohol. No one's going to help you. So I'd drag myself out on to the street and try to hustle up a bottle, get pissed, fall down, maybe injure my leg again. One night the law came and nicked four of us that were there. We got three months each for being on 'enclosed premises'. I was glad in the end – my leg healed up perfectly.

I turned up at the boneyard with a couple of bottles of wine. On the seat were Kelly and Liverpool Lil. They started smiling like a pair of Cheshire cats when they spotted me. They ain't got no drink. Kelly was about twenty-five and Lil was thirty. She was a hustler. Kelly did a day's work every six months; the rest of the time he ponced off Lil. I liked both of them; they always shared a bottle when they had one and they were a great laugh. They were also both illiterate. Kelly's an Irish tinker with a sincere little-boy look and two deep blue honest eyes; he's also one of the crookedest fuckers around. The drink was going fast when One-Eyed Tony joined us. He was no trouble, quiet and inoffensive, but what use was that? He never had any money or drink. He produced a packet of fags, supplied a light and that was it. I thought I'd hate to meet him first thing in the morning if I was bad from the drink. All you'd get out of him would be hard-luck stories: he gambled all his money and always lost. You never heard about his wins. I didn't trust gamblers – fucking non-producers! I was in a very bad mood: the wine all gone, more people arriving and everybody laughing and telling each other fucking lies about the clever strokes they pulled last night, last week, last year. No word about pulling any right *now*. The shower of cunts – they had eyes, they knew what was needed.

'Let's see how much we got between us,' said Lil.

'Nothing,' I moaned.

'That's OK, Johnny, you've given us a good drink.' (Thank fuck they remembered.)

'Who's going to go for it?' Tony volunteered. 'At least he's not a runner; he'll come back,' said Kelly. I watched him go out the gate. Big Patsy and Cork Billy came in a few minutes later. They'd got no drink either, but they had 'a bit of business' to do later on. I thought to myself, you can live on promises down here. The way they talk you'd think they were gangsters or company directors . . . 'business'! Probably get a fucking BI from the labour exchange for the DHSS; get yourself drunk on everybody else's wine, then piss off up the social office, kip there all afternoon and get a voucher for a verminous mattress in a Salvation Army hostel – a shower of lousy bastards!

One-Eye was back at last . . . I won't get a thimbleful out of that bottle, too many here now, everyone acting like Jack the Lad, deep tanking[1] and holding out. Billy and Tony were at it, neither of them any good: a lot of pulling and mauling and noise. The lads got fed up with it after a while and pulled them apart; so much for moments of tenderness with this shower of cunts.

Jock Lynch was talking to me: 'You hear about Little Mo, Johnny?'

'No.'

'They found him dead yesterday in a police cell – fell over . . . banged his head.'

'Leave it out, Jock; you trying to put me into the horrors?'

'Can happen to anyone, police said.' The old law seems to be getting rougher lately.

'Fuck that! Jesus, I'm really sorry about Mo, Jock. What a way to go.'

I wanted a piss; didn't want to lose my seat though. There's

[1] Concealing money deep within your clothing.

about twenty here now: some of us on the bench, the rest on the ground in small groups. I started thinking about the boneyard. You could never really tell the seasons by the trees and greenery in it, unless it was high summer or mid-winter; there didn't seem to be any subtle changes there, like in the books you read in the nick. You know the sort of crap where this ponce turns to his girl and notices how her eyes reflect the subtle changes in the seasons or some bullshit like that. The only change in the boneyard was that it was either freezing cold or boiling hot. Look into any of these women's eyes too deeply and you're likely to get a bottle smashed over your head. 'I think I'm getting a bit pissed,' I told myself. The wind rose up forcing pieces of paper to chase after each other in drunken swirling circles.

The ground was littered with little bits of paper, broken dog-ends, used matches, matchboxes, a couple of empty fag packets, green gob, piss – that reminded me; I left my place and went over to the bushes. The earth around was dead and lifeless from years of being pissed on by winos. The wine was not only polluting bodies and minds but indirectly the earth. It was dotted with little piles of shit; it really stank, made me feel sick – old flaky bits, dry shit, damp shit, wet shit, long bits, small bits, bits like small balls stuck together. I could become a shitman I thought – lead them to a clear spot, when done, lead them out again; take my tea-breaks in wine, holiday in another park . . .

'Fuck this, I'm going up the town to do a bit of hoisting. Anyone coming with me? No, I didn't think you would. Bastards! Stay here safe! I'll bring it back if I don't get caught. If I do, you ain't lost nothing either! It's an easy life – some fuckers just can't lose.'

'Where the fucking hell are you going?' The Dipper's voice pulled me up short. The very man I wanted to see – we both headed off in the direction of the wine shop. The governor of the off-licence was a tall, well-built man with thick silver-grey hair, a high-cheekboned face, thin bloodless lips with a long delicate nose, and skin so fine you could see through it. The lads reckoned it was through in-breeding, that he was a Russian count, and he was queer. The Dipper reckoned he was an ex-copper and he was queer. I reckoned he was just queer.

There was a trap-door in the middle of the floor leading down to the cellar. Dipper and I walked in. It was open. We could hear the Count below. We both had the same idea. Slamming it down, Dip stood on it. I grabbed a handful of notes from the till, and four bottles of Scotch. After putting a few full crates of beer down on the floor against the trap-door, we walked out of the shop.

Alfie the Artist got nicked for vagrancy, failing to maintain himself, failing to comply with the law of 1824, failing this and failing that and so on and so forth. It all sounds like the Articles of War when they read the charge out in court.

Alfie the Artist. That's a laugh. Long before the Mountbatten Report, which led to government establishments becoming security conscious, Alfie used to travel around London museums and art galleries, admiring the paintings. When something in particular took his fancy, he'd pull it off the wall, shove it under the old overcoat he wore winter and summer, and walk casually out. He'd sell it for the price of a bottle of wine, the buyer probably not realizing what he had bought. Sometimes Alfie, unable or maybe unwilling to get a quick sale, would bring a picture into the park, allowing us quick peeps from time to time, the peeps getting slower and longer as the bottle passed around, until eventually we'd be gazing openly at the picture propped brazenly against a park bench. No matter how many times or from what angle you look at a fine painting you always find something new. I remember one picture, a farmyard scene it was. I seem to forget who the painting was by. Still, no need to mention the names of the great, as Alfie used to say. Anyway, it was coming on to dusk in this rural scene, black and white pigs rooting in the dirt, a cockerel and his hens pecking at invisible grains among clumps of grass, and a cow – back arched, tail curled at an angle, making water. When you held the picture in a certain way, you could really see the water pouring out of that cow. Looked at from another angle, and the grains the hens were after could also be seen. Unfortunately after a few more bottles we would be unable to see the frame round the picture unless it were pointed out to us!

Alfie used to drink with a guy called Fingers Knox but Fingers got himself killed when he fell from the top to the bottom of the escalator in the tube. Poor old Fingers, that was some drop – he was a good beggar – lost most of the tops of the fingers of his right hand to the frost, a few winters back. He was a middle-aged Jock, used to travel out on the last tube to Edgware every night to skipper. He'd beg all the way on the tube going out, get a bottle next morning and beg his way back to the park. He was never without a drink. He used to take fits and got mugged often. He got nicked one time and the computer or something showed he was a deserter from the army in 1939! The law handed him over and the army kept him for two days, then threw him out. He used to say it was sad to have to creep and crouch and slink next morning after drink and that was why he always done a bit of late night begging. Someone tried to kill him one night in a skip. That's why he liked to sleep alone. It also kept him free of the stale smell of flop-houses. He had style. He would not keep jumping up at everyone that went past. He would wait. (You learn how to wait . . .) Then when he sensed the best beg, he'd put on his begging smile and beam in. Nine times out of ten it would be a fiver touch.

Begging was like religion to him. Every move worked out – like what you do when some bastard won't give cash, and insists on buying you a meal. He'd convince the beg that he was barred in every café but one where he'd take him. He would say, 'I'm too sick to eat now but if you pay for it I'll eat it when I can.' He had an arrangement with the owner to get half the price of every meal he got someone to order for him.

One thing, we'd never see his wrinkled face in the park again. I remember his old saying . . . Never beg a beggar.

In Britain, begging is a criminal offence punishable by imprisonment. On the third offence, one is charged with being 'an incorrigible rogue'. (Only the Home Office could make asking a bloke for a fag sound worse than shagging your sister.)

An incorrigible rogue! A phrase from a book, but it is a dangerous book, a law book, a firm unyielding statute that condemns vagrants to be tried at a Crown court, where a sentence for this offence (without a trial or jury) now becomes mandatory and ranges from one to three years' imprisonment. The trial moves swiftly on when the judge has determined the sentence beforehand and against that sentence there is no appeal.

I was nicked for begging – my second appearance on this charge. I got three months and warned. I was running out of time on this offence. Locked in the sweat box, driven round London, picking up cons from other courts, we arrived at the prison around 4 p.m. Sat around for hours waiting to be processed, then through reception to the main prison blocks. Started to feel hot and cold, trembling, wanting to vomit. Dry retch. Nothing came up. Withdrawal symptoms. A banging on the door made me jump.

'Coming in with a man, sir.'

Keys jangled as the screw unlocked the metal door. Two coppers with a young boy. 'Where from?'

'Bedford Assizes.'

'Got a body chit?'

'Yes.'

'Thank you, mate.'

'Sign for him. OK.' The police escort left. Everybody went quiet in the room. The chief screw looked at the kid's committal forms . . . mumbled, 'Sex case.' A nonce. The words seemed to hang in the air. Then they sped into all the corners of the room. Frightened, the kid didn't know where to look. There seemed to be something missing in his face and eyes. The cons in the room did not breathe. They just sat or stood – very still now, with expressions of indignation almost like innocent people who had somehow all got in here by mistake. There are three very dangerous words in this world. Grass. Runner. And Nonce. They make the breath come sharp and quick, they act as detonators to the mob, and of the three to be denounced as a nonce is the worst. The screws turned their backs on the agonized creature.

The hunt had begun. He was sent into the bath house. I went next, undressed, given towel and soap. As I reached the door the screw stopped me. A high-pitched scream made me fucking jump. The retarded kid staggered out from the boiling shower. A trustee tripped him up and he fell on the tiles. Three more trustees moved in, breathing hard to show their disapproval, the boot was leaving its mark, too, a spoor of gunge threatened to spill from one corner of what had been his mouth. Since it appeared more formal than spontaneously emotional it gave me a sick feeling, watching somebody being beaten within an inch of his life – with me too scared to do anything about it. And yet the bathhouse officer could have seen it from his office window if he had wanted to or if indeed he had cared to look. Suddenly it ended. The screws picked up the unconscious body, carried it towards the hospital wing while the trustees leaned back against the wall trying to catch their breath, palpitating from their own daring. 'He fell against the door in reception, sir.' Same old bullshit all the time. I got under the shower. Took my time. Two hours later saw the doctor.

'Have you ever had any serious illness?'

'No, but I've got the shakes and I'm going into the horrors from the drink. Can I have some Largactil, please?'

'No, report sick in the morning.'

All night long kept getting the horror dreams. DTs. Wake up shouting at the five-legged rats biting into my guts. Headless chickens. Hot and cold sweats. It lasted four days. After a week I was well enough to read. We were kept locked in our cells one morning. Finally we were opened up. As I passed the No. 1 cell I asked what was wrong. 'Young sex case hanged himself over on the hospital wing early on.'

'All by himself, eh?'

'Yeah. Suppose so. Anything can happen on the hospital wing.'

'Anything can happen on any fucking wing here. Got any good books?'

'Want this one? It's all about wild animals.'

Every two weeks we got to see a film in the chapel. I saw *The Warlord*, all about tenth-century feudalism. I liked it so much I even dreamed about it.

9

The Spiv's missus left him over the drink so Taylor moved in. Taylor's a big bloke, with the shoulders of a bull and a face to match. A bit of a tearaway, he's supposed to be a scrap dealer, only he takes the stuff before it's become scrap. I'd just come out of nick and was having a quiet drink in the Cider House, when he comes in.

'Hello,' he says, shoving up beside me. 'You still drinking that shit? Have a proper pint. Here, luv, give us two pints of best bitter and two large Scotches.' Then he looks at me, smiling – well it looked like a smile – it's hard to tell with Taylor. 'Look at you, you cunt,' he said, shaking his head like he's the chief welfare officer or something, 'you could have been world class if you'd left that shit alone,' pointing at my glass.

'No, it wasn't like that, Joe,' I said. 'I wasn't drinking for fun.'

'What?' he says, looking puzzled.

'No,' I continued, 'it was medicinal, to relieve tension.'

He burst out laughing . . . couldn't stop, bent over, holding his stomach. The barmaid comes up with our drinks, puts them on the counter with a worried frown. Probably hasn't seen Big Taylor laughing before. Neither have I for that matter. 'Have you heard him, Linda?' he asks, tears streaming down his cheeks as he pays her. She's a bit tasty-looking. Except for the till, she's the only thing with a bit of sparkle in here. The blokes are always trying to chat her up. Maybe this is a new line.

'What's he been saying, then?' she asks. 'Hope it's not rude?', sternly wagging a finger at me that seems to include Taylor too.

'Cheers, Joe,' I said, swallowing the Scotch in one mouthful and raising the pint to my mouth as he spoke: 'He doesn't like drinking.'

She gave a mock sigh of horror. 'Well, he gives a good imitation of one who does, larking about and staggering all over the place by closing time every night. God knows what he'd be like if he liked it!'

Taylor butts in before she can say something else. 'Well, he don't like it.'

She's pretending to be fooled by his concerned look. They're enjoying my discomfort. She turns to face me. 'Why do you do it then, darling?'

I wasn't prepared for this. I could feel my cheeks going red before I could reply.

Taylor roars out, 'Because he's got tension!' Every head in the bar swivels round to stare at us.

'Tension!' she screeches, shaking her head, laughing . . . stopping just long enough to serve a customer. As she's putting the money in the till, I'm staring at her bottom. She turns – too suddenly to pretend I'm not looking. But her mind's not on her bum at the moment. 'Tension,' she says very slowly, as though I may not be able to understand, 'don't you know everybody's got it? You just . . .'

But Taylor's voice stops her. 'Of course they have,' he says. 'Even animals have it. But they don't go round getting drunk.' They both laughed. So everybody gets it, including animals. I laughed too. We all laughed.

After a few more drinks, Taylor suddenly asks, 'How would you like to earn a good few quid?'

'Easy, is it?' I asked.

'Yeah, simple.' He laughs.

'Why, what have I got to do then?'

'Only a bit of taking and driving.' He pulls out a big bunch of car keys. Now he's talking low. 'They fit any motor. All you got to do is go round the streets. When you see one not more than three years old, take it, drive it back to the mews.' He looks round to see if anyone is eavesdropping before continuing. 'I'll give you a tenner for every one I flog. But if I have to cut them up for scrap, it's a fiver – OK?'

'Yeah.'

'Oh,' he says, 'are you skippering?'

'Yeah.'

'Well, you can stay at the Spiv's place for a while, on the settee.'

'Will it be OK with the Spiv?'

'Yes. He ain't there and he won't be there for a long time.'

'Why? Where is he?'

'In nick, waiting to go up the steps at the Old Bailey ... passing dud fivers.'

Over the next few weeks I must have taken about a dozen fairly new motors. I couldn't keep it up – drink got in the way – or it got in the way of drink. Asleep on the floor one night, I was awakened by a painful blow in the ribs. Taylor was standing over me, aiming kicks at me. Staggering to my feet, I lurched towards the front door. His hands closed round my neck as I opened it. He was going berserk. I became unnerved. Turning suddenly, I kneed him in the balls. He bent down, holding his crutch, his body blocking the doorway. I tried to push past. He lunged at me in a frenzy. Picking up an old metal dustbin, I brought it down on his head. Dropping to his knees, blood pouring from the wound, he grabbed my legs tightly. I brought the bin down once more, opening his skull to the bone.

I was picked up the following night, charged with causing grievous bodily harm and remanded to Brixton Prison to await trial. I kept telling myself not every bloke's a psychopath ... just the ones I happen to meet.

'Hello, H.' The Spiv's voice interrupted my thoughts. 'What have they done you for?'

'Nothing much.' I tried to sound unconcerned. 'Had a fight with Taylor.' I could see out the corner of my eye that he was looking at me very deliberately.

He laughed right out loud. 'So you had a fight with Taylor, just a bit of fun really, and now you're up here on remand.' He shook his head. 'Come off it, H. It's either murder one, manslaughter, wounding with intent, GBH, ABH, attempted murder or assault. What is it?'

'GBH.'

'And he's grassed you?'

'Yeah.'

'Any other witness?'

'No.'

'That's it then,' he says, like he's just found the solution to some very mysterious problem. Then he asks me all about what's happening on the outside. Talking seemed to make the time fly. Suddenly the screws brought us in off the exercise yard. On the way to our cells, the Spiv whispers out the side of his mouth: 'I want you to do me a favour when you get out.'

I thought he was joking. I laughed: 'You'll be out so long before me you'll be giving me visits.' He didn't reply because just at that moment two landing screws told me to move back into my cell.

When I left for exercise the cell was empty. Now there was a young guy with wild-looking eyes and a crew cut lying on the bed opposite mine. Our eyes met. We nodded at each other. I walked over and threw myself on my bed. I rolled a smoke. We still had not spoken. Well, I thought, there's no hurry. We have a month to find out each other's names. The only book in the cell was a bible. Crew Cut was staring up at the ceiling without any sign of wanting to talk. I started reading 'and Sarah was begot by Iserria [or someone] and they went into the land of the Pharaohs and she was begot again.' It took me a long time to realize that Sarah was a bit of a girl and that begot meant having a bunk-up. After a bit more about Sarah and Ruth and Rebecca, I glanced over at Crew Cut, still staring at the ceiling. Well, although I haven't got any proper friends, I'm friendly. I coughed, then said, 'Fucking hot in here tonight.'

Still staring at the ceiling, he said, 'I never done it.' Then, looking at me, 'They fitted me up.'

'Yeah, I know, mate, they fitted me up too, the cunts. We've all been fitted up.' He started talking fast: 'I was all right in hospital until that other fucking doctor came.' The spittle was running down his chin. He kept talking in disconnected bursts, without expecting answers. As far as I could make out he'd been in a psychiatric hospital and had set fire to the place, nearly burned it down. I wasn't listening to him any more. Earlier on he'd put his hands behind his head. Deep scars on the insides of either wrist told all there was to tell.

About a week later on exercise, the Spiv called me over. As we circled the yard, he told me, 'Taylor won't be turning up in court to give evidence against you.' I didn't ask why. 'So the police will have to drop the case.' He continued, 'You know what I'm up on, don't you? It's a fucking dodgy charge, so listen carefully. What I want you to do is go over to this address. Tell the bird I sent you. She'll give you a suit and overcoat. Then go over to King's Cross. I don't know how you're going to get in. It's a lodging house. The landlord's scared to death: since I got nicked the law have been round there day and night looking for the bent dough.'

'That's it, then,' I said.

'What's it?' he asked.

'I'm the law.'

'Right,' he says. 'Now when you get in, go right up to the top floor. Go into a room on the left . . .' He stopped talking as we passed a screw. 'Open the window . . . hope you're not scared of heights.'

'Why?'

'Because you've got to climb on to the roof.'

'Fuck me gently.'

'No. It's OK really.' He laughed. 'You just got to put your hand up until you feel the loose slate. The dough is underneath in two carrier bags.' He nods to a couple of big cons. 'Now if everything goes all right you should be able to have a couple of hundred changed into straight money within a week easy.'

'Well, yeah,' I said half-heartedly. I don't like committing myself when something's got as many problems attached to it as this seems to have.

'Look, H, I know it sounds awkward what with one thing and another, but if you stay away from that fucking wine you should be able to do it, no trouble.' He shook his head. 'That's a madman's drink. Why do you drink that shit? It'll drive you round the twist.' But he didn't really expect an answer so I kept silent. He went on, 'Bring me a couple of hundred. There's a few grand there. Keep the rest. But bring me up £200 after you've changed them. OK?'

'Yeah.'

After getting a few books, I relaxed and read until I was brought back to court. No Taylor. No charge. I walked free. That's when I first learned about power. I called at an address in Finsbury Park. A woman of about thirty, with short dark hair, and the dry white look of a whore without her make-up on, answered my knock. I said, 'The Spiv sent me.'

She pursed her lips before speaking. 'Are you John?'
'Yes.'

She beckoned me in. 'There's a suit in the bedroom.' I changed. We drank coffee. She wished me luck. I left. I sipped a bottle of wine on the bus. At King's Cross I found the street and knocked at number nine. A fat bald bloke answered. 'Police,' I said, pushing past him and flashing a chewing-gum card that had a small picture of Popeye in the corner. He disappeared into a room. I slowly walked up the stairs. The door on the left was open, the lock broken. Must have been the law, I thought. After getting the carrier bags I left undisturbed. I hid the money in a skipper near Euston, took £500, bought a pint in a pub, and got change for the first one. They were quite well forged really. The only flaw I could see in them was a little pinkish discolouration on the right side which only showed up if you held them up to the light. I realized that I must try to keep sober. This kind of crime carries a heavy sentence.

I hit on the idea of changing them faster by getting into large company in pubs, sending different blokes out to buy various low-priced articles. After two days I was loaded with legal money. I meant to catch a taxi up to the prison to visit the Spiv, but was so drunk I ended up at Euston Station sitting on the bench surrounded by the lads and the women. What a party! I got bottles of whisky, vodka, gin – no wine or surgical spirits today! I carried on like this for a week, still changing the money, pissed all the time. I don't know how I was doing it. I sobered up quickly one night when I found myself on a chair in a police charge room. The law were slapping my face, asking where I got this funny fiver. 'Jesus.' I knew you had to be caught with two to be done (how many had they found?). I started to act silly, just a harmless wino. They looked at each other and then charged me with drunk and put me to bed for the night. I got off with a £2 fine next day. When I got back in the park no one seemed to want to know me. Then Frankie, a Jock from the Gorbals – thinks he's a hard man 'cause he's done a lot of nick – came over. Stood in front of me all flash-like and told me the big fellow's pals are going to cripple me when they get hold of me. The words came out so aggressively he frightened himself. You'd have thought I had leprosy. Everyone sort of shuffled away from me, except the whores who sat shivering with cold after being out all night, taking on all comers, with their backs against the wall, too knackered to care who's done what. But their ponces – all flash and bouncy, well-fed and rested – kept glancing over, weighing me up tactically – build, height, bottle scars – anything that might give them a clue to my toughness or lack of it. After a while I walked over to the station for a warm, and sat against a wall. I thought of getting a knife but, knowing my luck, I'd probably fall on it myself. I was feeling a bit sad when this bird came over and started talking to me and pulled out a bottle of wine. We sipped it between us. Then she left me to get some fags. Said she'd be back. I finished the bottle. What with the heat and everything it made me come over drowsy. When she came back she asked me if I would come down under the station and sit with her and she would get me another drink. I wanted a sleep really, so I went with her. I just got near the bins when two blokes jumped me. One of them hit me with a bottle, smashing open the side of my head and knocking me down. Then I felt the kicks – but I was gone. I woke in the hospital, had stitches in my head, bruised ribs and body. The next day I discharged myself.

The Spiv got five years for passing dud fivers.

So the days merge together more and more, each one like the other. You wake, rise, look for drink, fall asleep again, staring into darkness, seeing nothing, feeling nothing, hearing nothing. Time passes nonetheless. The toilet had been locked for three solid hours. This is a most serious state of affairs – interrupts the schedule of every dosser in town. Standing in groups, talking and spitting on the ground. A lone perv looks furtively across, eyes of unfulfilled desire, searching silently for the ultimate peep. Big-time gamblers talking in telephone numbers, slip on a 10p bet, their minds sick on the dream. One-time workers still got their boots on – age finally sacked them – look and wait for a genuine shit. Flop-house dossers, in between teas, scratch at lice. The Dipper hands me the bottle, pisses up against the bank, takes no notice of passers by.

'Hurry up, Dipper.'

'What we supposed to do?' Fuck getting nicked for pissing; charge you with indecent exposure. Sounds bad, looks bad, like you been flashing or something.

Flash-looking bird came out of the bank. Dipper says he'd like to give her one. She tells him, 'Go have a wank.'

'Have you got clean hands, darling?'

'Jesus, did you see her face?'

'Shall we rob the fucking bank?'

'What, with an empty cider bottle? Naw, there ain't no future in it.'

'Excuse me, sir, could you help us out? I'm a seaman.'

'Yes. What do you want?'

'I'm trying to get my fare to Tilbury.'

'Oh dear, how sad. What a pity. I seem to have left my cash indoors.'

'Excuse me, love, I'm trying to get him back to hospital. Could you help us with the bus fare?'

'What's the matter with him?'

'His mother died last night. He keeps taking fits and falling down.'

'I am sorry. Here we are. I hope he's soon all right.'

'Thank you, lady. You're very kind.'

Two coppers walked up. 'Come on, you two, you should know better than to be standing outside a bank. Fuck off, or we'll run you in for sus.'

The Sham was insensitive. One time we were drinking in the Early House. We followed a young businessman out. I started fighting with him – just mauling around. The Sham, separating us, put his hand into the guy's pocket . . . took his wallet. We walked on. Two pounds. I was happy enough – it would buy a bottle. Sham got nasty. The guy was on his way to the tube. Sham went after him, started to slap him round the face with the empty wallet. 'What kind of cunt are you? Why ain't you got more money?' The guy was too drunk to be scared and became angrily confused. Very stupid act this. I was trying to coax the Sham on to the tube. Suddenly the law pulled up in a van and grabbed the three of us. Luckily they saw nothing. Got to the nick, the guy too drunk to talk. Done us all for drunk.

Another time the Sham and I were smashed from a mixture of pills and drink. When we climbed over the wire down on to the platform of Finchley tube station, finding the station tool box open, we armed ourselves with a pick and hammer. Just as it started to dawn we smashed open the first fag machine. 'Leave the fags. We'll pick them out after we've opened all the machines.'

'OK. We'd better be fucking quick, though. These cunts open up early.' Both spaced out, we must have been on the third machine when the law came running down the platform. The Sham took a swipe at the nearest copper with the pick, missed. They were on us. They smashed the Sham's face into the broken glass, handcuffed his hands behind his back, dropped him with kidney punches. I was smashed over the head with a truncheon. Never felt it but took a dive anyway.

'You're both nicked,' said the sergeant, not telling us anything we didn't know. The Sham's face was a mess – that's what probably saved us from a good kicking. Next morning, up before the magistrate, we decided to act mad, perhaps avoid the Crown court, maybe get sent to a nut-house. Better chance of getting drink in there or even breaking out.

The police read out the charges. The gist was: 'They were smashing the glass in the cigarette machines when we apprehended them. They then assaulted Sergeant Watkins with exhibits one and two, sir.'

'These, officer? Oh dear, how disturbing.'

'Yes, sir, Carson had the pick, Healy the hammer. Sergeant Watkins is unable to be here today, sir. Unfortunately he's sick.'

'Oh, I am sorry. I hope he's better soon ... most distressing.'

'Thank you, sir. I'll convey your kind regards.'

With his black hair going grey at the sides and black moustache, the magistrate could have passed for anything – doctor, army officer, antique dealer, prison governor, Assistant Commissioner, or confidence trickster. Might even be Sergeant Watkins's uncle. Fuck this lark. Horrible comedown you get from them pills.

'OK, stand up, you two.'

'Ahem, now do you wish to say anything about these – ah – charges?'

'Yes, sir, it wasn't us,' I said.

'Oh, are you saying the police are lying?'

'No, sir, it was alcoholic hunger done it. We thought the machines contained chocolate. That's why we never took any cigarettes, but kept on smashing the new machines, searching for something to eat.'

'I see.'

'What have you to say, Carson?'

'Sweet holy mother of God, where am I? What am I doing here?' says Sham, dropping down at my feet in the dock.

'I want full medical reports on these two back here in three weeks.' They carried the Sham gently out of court, then pushed him down the stairs. He soon woke up.

'Alcoholic hunger, you pair of cunts! We'll have you,' said the CID.

We saw the head-shrinker at Brixton Prison. No need to act. He put us down as chronic alkies. Then we had a three-week laydown. In the meantime, I wrote to Clive Soley,[1] a probation officer, whom I met once at court – an intelligent-looking bloke, he seemed to be very straightforward. One Wednesday he came to visit me. Said if I wanted to try and give up drink he'd try to get me into a clinic away from London. Left it at that. Back at court, the Sham was given a conditional discharge. I got the same with a proviso that I stay in an alcoholic clinic in Oxford. Mr Soley drove me to Oxford. I was longing for a drink. We reached the clinic by late afternoon – a beautiful modern building surrounded by green fields, trees and bushes. The sun came out. I started to get very tense. It was a long time since I'd been close to any normal human beings. An attractive girl in a mini-skirt came up. Asked if we would like some tea. Seemed so relaxed.

'She's nice.'

'Yes, that's one of the nurses. They're all nice here. No uniforms. The staff wear their own clothes.'

After we drank the tea, Clive Soley left. I felt alone – I'd rather have been with a load of psychopaths. I liked looking at the nurses, but they seemed so calm compared with me. I felt sort of naked. I had only my aggression to relate with. If

[1] Former Chief Probation Officer, now Lord Soley of Hammersmith.

I couldn't use that, I couldn't communicate. A young nurse came over.

'Hello, John, how are you? Did you have a pleasant journey from London?'

'Yes, thanks.'

She was gorgeous. Her name was Kate. We were about the same age. I felt embarrassed in my dirty torn clothes, smelling of stale wine. I was shown to a dormitory upstairs. Men one side. Women the other. On the ground floor a dining room and group therapy rooms. A large lounge looked out on to a vast field of lush green grass.

Every morning group therapy; afternoons we'd go for walks in the surrounding countryside, accompanied by some of the nurses. Kate often came. I enjoyed walking beside her, but became exhausted with tension trying to relate to her with no drink. As the days went by I became worse. We were all living on will-power here. After a week I broke out. I drank all day in Oxford, returning to the clinic that evening. I gave Kate two mini-dresses I had nicked. She took them only to be polite. Walking me up to the dormitory, she told me she had a boyfriend, a doctor, at another hospital. The drink helped to soften the blow. After she left I went out to the village pub, got into a fight, and was slung out. Back to the clinic mad drunk. Two big male nurses tried to overpower me. I managed to drop one with a kick . . . ran upstairs. More came running, held me, got my trousers down, shoved a needle full of knock-out drops in me. I floated out. Came round two days later. Got slung out. Jumped the rattler for London. Back in the old routine.

It was hard to tell whether the full bottle in my hand caused the Dipper's face to light up or was he perhaps pleased to see me! 'Hello, Johnny,' he said as he sat down clutching at the bottle. 'We heard you were in Oxford. What happened?'

'I broke out on the drink.'

'Never mind,' he said, 'I know where we can get hold of the price of a good drink later on.'

Then I told him about Kate. I would have felt a fool telling anyone else but the Dipper kept making kind noises, so I added, 'And now I feel lonely every time I think of her.'

As I said this he began shaking his head, 'The best thing to do, Johnny, is climb to the top of the Post Office Tower and jump feet first – that gets rid of desires and passionate feelings. When you're madly in love you have to do that – makes your beloved feel guilty. If you survive, you'll have plenty of attentive females hovering over you caring for your every need.'

I managed to raise a laugh and that set the mood. By the time we reached Oxford Street I was a bit better and readily agreed to do a bit of shoplifting. The overcoats on show beside the exit were a giveaway, so we obliged, accepting one each. We soon got rid of them ... £5 for two £20 overcoats! It's daylight robbery!

In the greasy spoon we had two big bowls of soup. The Dipper looked a bit embarrassed when I asked him how he planned to spend the evening. 'Fancy coming to a meeting?' he said finally. Sod it – an alcoholics meeting! Sitting for hours crushed together on hard, wooden chairs with all that cigarette smoke burning your eyes and all them sad stories. Compelling listening they ain't, though sometimes you do get a funny if someone turns up drunk ...

Partners in crime seem to share a bond of intimacy like partners in bed, so I let myself be talked into it. On the way over, the bus was crowded and we had to stand. Dipper drew my attention to an attractive young woman who was certainly glancing at him from time to time. 'Have you got a comb on you?' he asked me. I hadn't. 'No matter,' he said. 'I think she fancies me.'

Suddenly she looked right into Dipper's eyes real friendly-like, then standing up said, 'Excuse me, would you care to sit down, Pop?' Sit down! He nearly fell down . . . and not on to the seat either.

The meeting was being held in an old mission hall over in South London. It was in progress when we entered the room. Two men sat behind a large, wooden table facing a crowd of odd-looking men and women. Their shabby clothes gave them a harmless, ragamuffin appearance, which was at odds with their battered and scarred faces, but we sat down amid friendly smiles. Having led impossible lives by the age of twenty-five they know how to laugh at themselves and at life. A newcomer looking around at the missing eyes, limbs, teeth and broken noses might be forgiven for thinking he was at a war veterans' convention rather than an AA meeting.

The younger of the two guys at the table told us he was an alcoholic. His name was Joe. At the beginning of his drinking career he'd been involved in a number of amusing incidents and we laughed as he related them in a happy-sounding tone of voice, but gradually a depressing sadness crept in as the incidents became more pathetic, frightening and horrific. Each one of us in that small group were thinking, 'That's true, that's true . . .' Then . . . 'Fuck it, I still want a drink!'

There was a break. Cups of tea and biscuits were handed round along with the collection box for Spitty Phil's funeral. Some have survived terrible beatings while too drunk to defend themselves; their scars heal up but their eyes never light up and their speech fails to make sense; like babies they sometimes feel uncomfortable but don't know why. Spitty Phil used to sit on the grass, a stream of silver snot trickling into his mouth – when enough had collected he would spit it out in a long, continuous jet. He would keep this up all day long without moving from his chosen spot. His speech was always slurred and his eyes were always dull.

Dipper tipped me the wink. Before it got any more depressing we slipped away . . . after that we needed a drink!

It was freezing cold, and I was sitting in the boneyard trying to think how I could get a drink, when it started to rain. It nearly made me cry; what a bastard! I wished it were summer; not that it's really any different from winter once you're drunk, but people are more tolerant, it seems, and will usually drop you a couple of bob for the simplest hard-luck story. It is always like this on wet days, sitting on a bench in the soggy park waiting for someone to walk in and coax life with a bottle. I don't need the sunshine anymore, nor the sky, nor the earth. Nor even the heavens, all I need is a bottle.

Shuffling out of the place, I bumped into Fenton coming in with a bird. 'Here, have a drink,' he said and produced a bottle, then passed it to the bird. I didn't mind waiting . . . waited all morning, a few more minutes wouldn't crease me up. She had a big swallow. (Leave some for me!) She wasn't bad looking – better than some of the scrubbers Fenton usually picks up. I took the bottle from her with forced casualness, put it to my lips and took a long swig, then passed it to Fenton. When he was busy drinking, the bird offered me a fag, at the same time weighing me up. You could tell by her unravaged face and relaxed way that she hadn't been on the wine for long. She was getting edgy to leave – she'd dismissed me as a wrong'un. They'd probably both got dough. She didn't want to hang around bottle-feeding a fucked-up wino. She was not desperate enough yet. Give her time though – in about a year she'll be glad to meet anyone, even if they've only got a bottle of meths! Fenton passed me the bottle again. We were standing in the rain. I took a big swallow and went to hand it back.

'No, Johnny, take a good drink. Cure yourself,' said Fenton. I didn't need telling twice. I nearly finished the bottle. The rain stopped and Fenton pointed at the bench. We all sat down on the wet seat, not really caring. I felt the heat from the wine rising up to my head – a good feeling, the best!

They started holding hands and making cooing noises to each other. It didn't look right so I just helped myself to the last dregs while they were courting. Suddenly he remembered the formalities. 'Johnny, this is Mary. Say hello to the wee hen.' 'Hi Mary, nice to meet you,' I said. 'Haven't seen you in here before.' 'She used to be an air hostess,' said Fenton proudly. An air hostess! She was the first high-flyer I'd ever seen drinking the old red biddy in here. I took a closer look at her – perhaps I'd missed something. She smiled at me worriedly, her eyelids flickering delicately for her descent into dosserdom. I gave her a little grin to show her I wasn't too evil, to let her know it wasn't that bad here really if you could find a warm corner and enough money to stay drunk. Certainly it was sadder in the rain – then everywhere looks a bit more smudged. 'We're getting married next week,' continued Fenton.

I didn't really know what to say. Fenton has been married three times already. They were all fairly near-the-mark birds, but neurotics, and drank like fishes; course, like all the others still hesitating to sell themselves, implied that they weren't in the habit of drinking in parks. Indeed! Probably needed a couple bottles before they even ventured into the park.

Helen and Tessa came in. Helen was small and thin with a face like a frightened child. She swallowed pills by the handful, washing them down with bottles of wine. Tessa was fat with blonde hair, black at the roots, falling down over her battered cheeks. The Sham said she'd always got a half-eaten chicken in her bag! They still carry handbags full of their women's stuff. I suppose whores could afford to eat and drink as well, sitting on a gold mine. I don't seem to get too hungry and when I do I'm too sick to keep the grub down. I get a few bowls of soup in the Major's Café each week and a slice of dry bread. Good job I don't eat much; I'd have to pull real dodgy stunts to keep both appetites fed! They sat down giving me a half-hearted nod. I didn't give them enough attention. I didn't mind really, but I didn't want to be too friendly: whores think all men fancy them, with or without the disease. There's enough trouble round here without incurring the wrath of some stupid whore's deranged pimp.

Fenton was at home talking with domesticated whores, some people like being drawn back; it saddened me though, talking about hair-dos and that sort of thing. It reminded me of my aunties and the girls that used to visit our house and all those far off things a long time ago. No matter how intense the nostalgia I couldn't see that it had any use here, so I didn't bother to join in the talk. Anyway, they'd probably be half-killing some poor straggler tonight before ripping him off. Not that I was any better. We're all the same here. They gave me a drink, though, and that's the name of the game. I was getting a bit thawed out and that put me in better shape – didn't want my joints stiffening up all the time, like some dried-up old dosser.

Jock Stone walked in with Dundee Eileen. She used to be Fenton's woman but something happened and now Stone's poncing off her. Stoney's small, with a sharp face, a couple of bottle scars on the cheek and the usual broken nose. He's got friendly eyes, though, like a woman's in a way; when he smiles, they go into a sort of almond shape. Dundee Eileen has lovely skin, nice features and slim legs – sort of country girl. I like her, she could be quite alluring, hard as nails one minute and calm and civilized the next. As she sat down I nodded at her. She smiled with grim tenderness, then Stoney pushed up beside me on the bench and the bottle went round, but Eileen became sullen because Fenton insisted on telling her how he felt. The air hostess began doing her eyebrows with a black pencil while considering herself scornfully from all angles in a little mirror which she had to adjust from time to time. Suddenly she started screaming, saying everybody was a cunt. She spat it out – nobody contradicted her. Stoney laughed then turned towards me, he made a big show of speaking to me. Everyone was feeling uncomfortable – except me. I was really calm and happy now. I hardly noticed the day passing. Between the blur of things I'd somehow got hold of a bottle, and even though a lot of fuckers I did not like came to help me drink it, I was still beautifully content and happy. Until the two whore masters, Stoney and Fenton, started arguing about Eileen. I don't know how it happened. I never heard the bottle smash above the gritty patter but Fenton shoved it right into Jock Stone's neck, and Jock just keeled over with a hoarse, broken sort of sigh, holding his neck on the grass. We all stared hypnotized as sounds burst through his clenched teeth in little agonizing cries. His shirt collar had turned crimson, the cloth could not absorb it, the grass could not soak it all up. His throat was bursting with it, it bubbled up into his mouth, nothing could muffle the sound of the blood gurgling out between his fingers. We all kept quiet. I couldn't make out if I was pissed or Jock was pissed – he'd clambered to his feet again then he'd sort of gone to walk away, gone round in a small circle and then in a stumble changed his mind and began coming back towards us, blowing awful bubbles. It brought immediate sobriety. Everybody got up and backed away. I was the only one left on the seat. He came towards me, his hands out in front of him, fear filling his eyes. I felt like helping him to sit down, maybe put him lying down, it would be easier on him. But I was scared of getting blood-smeared – evidence. So I jumped up and got the seat between us. The women had turned aside and had started to walk away to avoid those ugly dangers. Fenton was gone. Jock was wandering round in a circle again, making little blubbering noises. It seemed funny – he didn't seem to know where he was or what he was doing. I wondered how far he could go before he ran out of blood. There were a few bottles half full on the ground. I'd never seen that happen before – no one left drink behind. Jock had made it to the street. He was heading for Euston Station on the opposite side . . . suffering hell, he was walking straight out into the traffic . . . I started drinking one of the bottles. Now he was in the road. The cars were swerving and hooting, just missing him whenever he blundered in the wrong direction. It was comical really. Blood-splashed and exhausted, stumbling and jerking around, he was saved from toppling over by being bounced from car to car. What's going to happen first? I thought. If a car don't hit him properly, will his blood run out? I watched for a while but he seemed to be making no progress at all, so I just got stuck into another bottle. I wasn't really worried, there was so much drink left you couldn't really believe in death; in fact I did not think much more about it until later on, when I could not think where he had gone. So I shouted out to him.

That's the last thing I remembered. Woke up next morning in a cell. Stiff as a board – lying on one too – no blanket. My mouth was stuck, dry as a bone, couldn't swallow . . . rang the bell . . . it didn't work, they'd disconnected it. Flushed the toilet, lay along the bench, face down over the toilet bowl, and filled my cupped hands with water; most of it spilled because I had the shakes. Shithouse water! So now I wanted to be sick. Couldn't stop spewing my guts out, even after all the water came up; my stomach muscles were going into painful contractions. I'd have given my right arm for a bottle of wine and a fag. 'Fuck it!' I suddenly wanted to piss and shit – everything seemed to happen at once. There was no toilet paper – still got to shit though. Tore a bit off my shirt. Sod this – I went to stand up straight and came over all faint and giddy – hoped I wasn't getting the fits or something. Now it was coming back a bit; I began figuring it out. There is a copper here who was in the same class at school with me. He was a big bastard then, now he's the same only bigger; he's out to fit me up with a serious charge, reckons he's fed up seeing me in and out every month for drunk. Last night they were on about something in the park, I can't remember what or whether it's one of his fit-ups. Then he got funny and smashed his fist into my face from the side and knocked me off the chair. I can't remember if it was then or if I went down again, it's difficult to sit innocently in a police station without conveying some deception. So they gave me a few kicks. Still, they say they don't like doing it . . . 'But you were very awkward and refused to help us with our enquiries. Can't have that, can we? Got to get on with the job, upholding the laws of the land, son. No disrespect intended, but we can't have some fucking wino fighting a small little fit-up, can we? I mean, what you going to get? Twelve months? Two years? Three? It's nothing – you'll be out before you know it. Now we ain't worried about you, son . . . bit of shoplifting, and drunk – nothing. Why, we done some villain last year . . . Fitted him with life. Anyway, we know who's who, 'cause we drink in the pub with them every night.'

I know they do and I'll give you one guess who pays for the drinks.

The door flap opened, a copper's face looked in. 'You all right, son?'

'Yeah, governor. You got a light?'

'No, get you one later, son.'

Up went the flap and silence descended once more. I was surprised when the door opened a couple of minutes later. Two of the biggest CID blokes I had ever seen were standing there.

'On your feet, son. Hold your hand out.'

He handcuffs my wrist to his. I'd never known it to go like this before, on a plain drunk. Wait a minute, I thought, what if it's something else? 'Where are we going, guv?'

'We're taking you to Euston. They want to talk to you there.'

Bollocks to this. I didn't like the way he said that. Outside there was a squad car waiting and we got in the back. Nice motor. No poxy old sweat van for me this morning. On the drive over I could smell myself; that was bad. They were pretending not to notice. When we got to the law shop over Euston way, they pushed me into the CID room before removing the cuffs. I glanced round. The place was rotten with coppers, about half a dozen descended on me at once. This one gave me a fag, another rushed to light it, well he would have only he was in such a hurry the lighter failed to ignite so his mate shoved him aside and struck a match. He might even have smiled – I couldn't be sure, I was completely confused. They were treating me like royalty. They didn't appear to notice that I was stinking of my own piss, shit, drink; and I was probably verminous. I was also very worried. 'Right, Johnny,' said the senior detective. 'Where were you drinking yesterday?' (They usually begin by over-using your Christian name.) Didn't sound like a trick question. OK. Let's keep it simple, I'm too sick for mind games with this lot . . .

'In Euston Gardens.'

'Who was with you?' asked his mate, making a careful pattern on the floor with his foot.

'Ah, I can't remember.'

'You must remember something.'

(Yes I do. Though it's still a bit flickery and I'm too scared to think what I'm thinking.)

So on it goes. They ask me questions, hinting that they know the answers, and I can't remember or I say I fell asleep. 'Son, we're not going to fuck about any longer. You're wasting our time. We've got a witness seen you do something very, very serious before you fell asleep.'

Double-talk. A copper's trick. I did not want to look at his face. 'I done nothing. I was sleeping most of the day.'

'How do you know you were asleep?'

'Because I remember waking up.'

'What then?'

'I fell asleep again.'

'What for – to forget what exists and remember what does not exist?' One of them laughed, but softly.

No one has told me exactly what happened yesterday. Their patience was making me jumpy, hope I don't fall into a trap and betray myself. Keep calm, don't let them provoke you, you fell asleep. Woke up, fell asleep, and can't remember. Stick to that and keep it simple. The more I dried out, the sicker I got for drink. Because whatever way you looked at it, this was turning out to be a bad day, they were not going to just let me go.

But what can I tell them? 'Terrible things happen in the park at night.' 'But this happened in the afternoon.' 'Yes, but . . . you know what I mean, officer.' 'Indeed we do, son. Everyone's trying to protect their own. Why, others have suddenly fallen from that very chair you're sitting in so comfortably now. Passed away on us for no reason at all, and had to be carried out and dumped up a dark alley to protect the reputation of the force.'

What else could you tell coppers? I was there in the park yesterday because I've got a drink problem but I can't remember doing anything wrong. Alright, I wasn't asleep but I keep getting these memory blackouts when I've had a drink.

They would have laughed. Oh really – how terribly inconvenient for you – I mean, so unlucky, would you like to call a solicitor now or would you prefer to wait until after you've been charged?

'People talk,' he said. 'They tell you things, it is in their nature.' When I did not answer he bent over me. 'You know what I'm talking about.' I remained silent, because they could put almost any word they liked into your mouth if you opened it. 'OK,' he said. 'If that's the way you want it. He beckoned to the jailer to sling me back in my cell. When the door slammed shut I lay down on the bedboard. Looking up at the ceiling I noticed a little round gizmo that may or may not have been there before.

I was going to have to think this one out. Either Jock's badly done – it's GBH – or Jock's not too badly done and it's ABH. Fuck Fenton. Sod all the whores and their pimps. Where are they now?

'Johnny.' A voice called from the cell opposite.

'Yeah, who's that?'

'It's Eileen.'

'Yeah Eileen. What's going on?'

'Davy is dead.'

'Dead . . . !' I wanted to laugh but I couldn't bring it out because I was too busy looking over my shoulder to make sure that nobody had heard. 'Who says?'

'The police.'

Then Fenton's voice butted in and a few women. We keep the talk going for a while, but though fatally connected we were not a great comfort to each other. So I butted out and lay down. All afternoon I heard someone different being taken out for questioning – funny these big murder squad mob ain't beaten any of us up yet. Mind you, we ain't out of the woods yet. The flap made me jump – it was the duty copper with my tea and a cheese sandwich. I put the sandwich in the corner – can't eat it now, but I might need it if I'm in here too long. Someone had written on the wall 'Kilroy was here.' 'Dear Lisa, dear Angie, love forever, Jimmy.' Funny how people's minds think about someone they love when they're in a police cell. It didn't trouble me. I don't know any women to fall in love with anyway; and I don't like men. I could fancy some of them secretary birds that come through the park from the big offices in Euston. Most of the lads talk to them (especially Scarface Mick) and beg them for a couple of bob, which they usually get. Then they have a go at me for letting such easy begs go past without pulling them, but I could end up getting too fond of them if I was to start talking to them and they were giving me money. That's why I don't beg from women. I've seen those big gangster blokes crying and cracking up in nick over women, and they got everything outside. What chance would I have with nothing, only the wino monkey on my back?

I'm dry retching into the toilet bowl when it hit me, a terrible thought. What if someone out there decided to fit me with Jock's murder? I have this sense of letting go. It's not clear what I should do because eventually when they realize that the answers they are getting to their questions are no answers there are bound to be a few blows, after which someone is going to write down with a pen that has been put into their hand the words that have been put into their head. The gashed throat of a dying man is a thing of horror, why should I risk blame for another's crimes? Those coppers' fondness for facts was beginning to make them sound like reasonable people. It occurred to me that whatever I wished to say would be heard by them with sympathy – kindness even. I started pacing the cell, trying to clear my head. I was being carried dangerously far by my own thoughts ... Even so, I cannot play cat and mouse with six senior CID officers forever.

Bang. I jump. The cell door opens.

'OK, son, let's go.'

They took me upstairs again. The room was packed with inquisitive coppers. They sat me on a bench by the wall. First thing I saw opposite was this young woman. She's got a worried frown on her face, sitting on a chair in a short skirt with her legs crossed. It wasn't hard to imagine what she was in for. Then the head CID turns to her and started asking her something which caused her to look at me with a thoughtful squint. That's when I realized who she was, she was their witness! But what's she fucking thinking about? Three blokes go into a park, one of them gets himself killed, leaving two, Fenton and me. Obviously I never done it so that leaves Fenton. It doesn't take great eyesight to see that far. That puts me in the clear and I cannot help feeling a bit cocky. So I'm having a little breather, thinking I'm going to have a go at these coppers for interrupting my schedule, might even beg a couple of bob off them for compensation when it hit me. Fenton wasn't there – he'd nipped off quick, leaving me alone with Jock and what's worse Jock was still alive and kicking! Well, staggering around like me, but while I was staggering from drink he was staggering from dying. The woman who had been staring at me ever since I'd been brought into the room now began speaking to the big detective. But they were too far away to hear.

Suddenly I realized that he was the one who had told me yesterday or whenever that they had a witness seen me do something very serious before I fell asleep. The woman continued speaking to him, but he showed no sign he was listening – he seemed to be watching me. Even though I was forcing myself to sit bolt upright which always makes you look less guilty he still kept watching me. Then he called to the station sergeant, nodded at the woman and came over to where I was sitting rigid against the wall. I would have liked to have got up and stretched but I couldn't. I could only stare straight ahead. Then the detective bent down and put his jaw close to my cheek. He was huge. I could see the big nose on his face but not his eyes. Though you could sense they were poking around so that I began to fear that they might discover greater crimes than Davy Stone's murder. I couldn't swallow, the saliva was clotting in my throat. When suddenly he said, 'OK, mate, you can go.' Just like that.

I looked up at him speechless, then asked, 'So what's happened, then?' It was easy now that I was leaving, but he turned away without reply. I glanced over at the woman. My chief concern was to find somebody to whom I could complain. But she gave a thin smile and turned away too. My importance in their thoughts had dwindled. I was just another vagrant alky to them now.

'What's going on round here?' I said trying to intimidate the burly sergeant with indignation as he led me towards the exit.

'Fenton's done for murder,' he growled as he shoved me out the door. And though I had no money I was happy to have failed the audition. It was 8 p.m. I was back on the street. I've got to go some if I'm to make a bottle of wine before closing time. Here we go again.

'Excuse me, guv, I'm a seaman trying to make the fare to Tilbury – could you help us out, please?'

'If I knew the money that was in religion, I'd have been a priest. That's what Al Capone used to say,' Angel tells me, earnestly, at the same time handing me a bottle of Scotch. Yes, real whisky, cigars and two cooked chickens. Angel's just finished five years. He fell out with a bloke over a bird, broke into the guy's house, beat him unconscious with a lump of wood that was studded with nails. The poor guy snuffed it while Angel was in nick. Angel's a big young guy, moves very slowly, got an engaging smile, and when you bump into him you speak very slow and friendly so there can be absolutely no misunderstanding over aggressive intent. I've been told – I have no memory of it – that a few times, all through drink, I've got a bit lippy with him. Still, he's very generous and seems to have good time for me. I hope he doesn't recognize a kindred spirit or, worse still, see something I don't! I won't bother mentioning Angel's record of violence. Enough to say that women and drink have a lot to do with it. Liza's with him today. She's got such a sweet little face and a lovely schoolgirl voice. Big Mulvey was looking at that face and listening to that voice when she slid a knife into his stomach. Now he walks with a limp and his spleen's gone. I used to fancy Liza. Jesus, on my life, I'd rather sleep cuddled up tight to one of those tigresses at Regent's Park Zoo now.

Many more have come into the park and, after greeting Angel respectfully, they are all welcome to drink.

Everybody's talking as if they had something really important to say. All of us bursting with life. But in the mornings there is only sickness.

'I'm *persona non grata* in the King's Head,' said Michael the priest.

'What are you talking about?' asks Spikey Joe, giving him a sour look.

'Barred, old chap. Barred last night,' replies the priest, putting on a real posh con man's accent.

'Aw, fuck that, I'm barred everywhere. Can't even go in cafés,' says Spikey, fingering a scar across his forehead, giving me a treacherous look at the same time. The stupid bastard; it wasn't my fault what happened. A couple of weeks ago, these two young tearaways came into the park after the pubs closed, eating sausages and chips. Margo, Spikey and myself, we're the only ones there. Sending Spikey for some drink, they started kissing and cuddling with Margo. I never interfered – often snatched a cuddle myself. It's not like she were some innocent young bird; she's on the game. Perhaps she's letting them have a test run or something, I thought. Suddenly Spikey came back with the wine. They let go of Margo quickly. But Spikey had seen something.

'What's it all about, then?' he demanded, trying at the same time to look tougher.

'Here, have something to eat,' replied the tallest guy, offering a sausage to Spikey. Hunger got the better of him. He grabbed it and shoved it into his mouth. But he was not in the mood to let things go. He started on Margo. The tallest guy interrupted him. 'Mate,' he says. Spikey looked at him, mouth full. 'Are you enjoying that sausage?'

'No,' said Spikey, vexed.

Both tearaways started laughing at the annoyed look on his face. Then the tallest put a mean look on, saying, 'Well, you ought to.'

'Why?'

'Because it's been up your wife's cunt.'

I burst out laughing. But Spikey went berserk, lunging at the tallest, sinking punches into him. He was doing all right until the other guy caught him from behind. That's when I jumped in. We done our best – shouting and bawling, pawing and mauling – but they were well fed and rested. They also had a couple of knives. Spikey got slashed across the forehead. Trying to block a stab at my eye, I got my index finger cut to the bone. The blade severed the tendon. I can't straighten it any more.

Still, any time Margo refuses me a drink I can always point it at her honour.

A fine June day. The sun beat down. If you weren't loused up – squirming and scratching – you were almost comfortable.

Willie Lyons came out of nick after finishing a long one. Bought us all a good drink in the park. We call him Shakespeare because he likes doing the Post Office books. Only he wasn't away for that.

'What did you get done for, Shake?' I asked him before we got too drunk.

He gave me the nearest thing to an embarrassed look. 'Fuck it,' he says, 'I was prowling around just trying to drum up the price of a bottle, when I seen a crowd gathered round this bloke who was flat out in the middle of the road.'

'Don't tell us you got stuck up the poor bastard,' says Mad Gerry. We all started laughing. Anything can happen when you're on the wine.

'No,' continues Shakespeare. 'Nothing like that. I just stopped to have a look. It wasn't my intention to mug him, but seeing how he was laying there sprawled out, I thought I might as well try for a drink.' He asked the crowd what was wrong and hearing that the bloke had been knocked down by a car, he told them to move. 'Move back, give the man some air. I'm a doctor,' he says, at the same time going through the bloke's pockets and palming the guy's wallet. Then, springing up, he shouts, 'A phone! I must get to a phone! This man is a diabetic,' and off he went in the direction of a pub. Before he reached it, however, the law grabs him. 'My mistake,' said Willie sadly, 'was saying I was a doctor. They done me for deception as well as theft.'

He was tall – over six feet, could have been a businessman, well built ... maybe a bit too well built, I thought, when I saw him coming into the park with Pill-head and the Jockey. Perhaps they've slipped up. But after a while I decided he was too obvious to be a copper; putting him down as a poofter, I relaxed. That was until he caught Eddie's hand in his pocket and knocked him clean out with one punch. After that the horseplay stopped, the bottle went politely back and forth. I was very civil. Eddie's unconscious body stretched out on the ground was a grim reminder to keep both hands in my lap, although it didn't seem to have the same effect on the two lads, who kept nudging each other, not even bothering to conceal their contempt for the guy when his speech became slurred. 'I'm not looking for Miss Right, lads,' he mumbled! 'I'm looking for Miss Right now. Where can I have a piss?' he asked no one in particular. As he lurched to his feet I thought, this guy can't handle the old wine too well. All his movements had become disjointed. Then, as he tottered over for a piss, he banged right into a tree. That was when I realized they'd slipped him some sleepers. 'They're a great equalizer,' Pill-head was fond of saying. It was funny to watch the antics of someone when they'd been slipped some sleepers, but after you'd had a laugh you couldn't help feeling sorry for the poor bastard. Out cold, he'd be fleeced, but his troubles were only beginning: Mac or some other nutter would find him defenceless and give him a good kicking; someone else would take his clothes and, finally, the law would come in and seeing him unconscious, dressed only in his underclothes, they'd nick him for drunk!

But the best laugh was the day Pill-head got done himself. As he waited in the Kentish Town DHSS office, big Patsy Mulligan crushed up five or six Mogadon tablets into a bottle of cider and let Pill-head guzzle away. He was snoring loudly when the cashier called out, 'Anthony O'Grady, pay box B.' Up went Big Patsy, gave Pill-head's date of birth and signed for his Giro. Pill-head was still snoring when the staff started to close the office for the night.

Still, we've all been caught at one time or another, and it's usually for no other reason than someone wants a laugh. But it's a fucker realizing you've been doped and having to crawl into some lousy skipper in the middle of the day to sleep them off.

Nobody tries to die on purpose from an overdose round here. What happens really is that you're sitting in the park hung over, sober, when somebody pulls out the Jack and Jills – you take a few, of course, then later on, just to be sociable, you take another few and so on until someone shows up with a bottle which you may or may not drink from because by this time you're so spaced out that you just up and wander out and into the first off-licence you see and grab your own bottle. You don't remember much about it, so later maybe you grab another bottle.

When you do finally get round to where you're remembering things again you find that you're lying on a damp rubber mattress on the floor. You're a bit fuzzy and your mouth's all scummed up. There's a funny sort of machine by the side. It's got a needle hovering over its face. Then you notice that you're wired up to the machine. It's helping two nurses nearby to tell at a glance whether your heart is pumping sufficient blood through your clogged-up veins to get your brain functioning properly again – well, at least enough to where you can get up off the mattress they poured you on to when the police brought you in a night or so before.

It was very cold. Macglaccan had just got released from nick the day before, fit and looking for a fight, mean like a head butcher in a slaughter-house, eyes like a pair of black slits – a cobra would envy them. Not a guy to trust or cross. Everyone was feeling edgy. Mac was buying the drink and didn't we know it! Slapping backs and patting everyone. He knew the tell-tale rattle of money. He knew who was holding out! We all kept quiet, sensible. No one getting provoked into rash acts this day. Doyle tried it once. Mac sliced half his cheek off with a broken cider bottle. They stitched it back, but it never looked right – as though his neck was joined to his cheek.

Dipper and Long John one side of the tube platform, Mac and me on the other. 'Sit down, Johnny. We'll finish this last drop.'

'Right, Mac.' He handed me the bottle. As I put it to my mouth, he caught me by the throat. I dropped the bottle with pain and shock. He was slowly squeezing the breath out of me. No talk. I was looking into two mad eyes. Felt like I was drowning. Got my thumb under his fingers, trying to prise them loose when a girl passenger suddenly let out a loud scream. Mac looked. I smashed my left fist into his eye, his head dropped forward, hand still round my throat. I stuck my thumb into his eye. He grunted with pain, but still kept gripping my throat, while regaining his strength. Desperately I tried to grab his bollocks.

'What the fuck are you two doing?' Four law swooped on

us and, separating us, hauled Mac along in front, me between the other two behind.

Then Mac did it. 'You shower of fucking bastards,' he said. 'What?' They left me and pounced on him just as a tube was about to close its doors. I jumped through them, falling on my head inside the carriage as it pulled away.

Waiting, waiting, waiting. Nurse called out a patient's name every half-hour. After two hours she called my name. 'Mr Healy, please wait in the cubicle.' After another half-hour the doctor came by. Stopped and talked to the pretty nurse. Took my card. 'What's happened to you? Your hand will have to be X-rayed.' Two hours later I got out of there, my hand in plaster. Broke two fingers. Fuck Mac. Useful for begging though.

Mac got three months, sending out death threats to me. (Must remember to avoid Mac's parties in future.)

The Dipper gave me the bottle. 'Come on, Johnny, don't nurse it.'

'What, is it a rush job?'

Outside the station he gave me a pile of *Old Moore's Almanacs*. 'We're going to work the oracle!' I shove an *Old Moore's* in the businessman's face to cover the Dip's hand on his wallet – which he then slips to me.

'Don't forget your *Old Moore's*, madam.'

'Oh, thank you. Very much.'

'That will be 50p, lady.'

'Dear me, I thought these things were free.'

'Goes to a good cause, love. Disabled servicemen.'

'Oh gosh. How thoughtless of me. Of course, here's a pound.'

'Blessings of God on you, madam.'

'I'm going for a bottle.'

'Don't come back pissed – fuck the game up.'

'I wouldn't get pissed, Dip.'

'Not fucking much, you cunt.'

'See you.' Got to get the magic fluid. Sham and Long John were sitting without a drop. Lots of good hoisters and panhandlers here today. I'm the paymaster, and paymaster is God until he falls down pissed. When the jackals have fleeced him, he wakes up a plain old wino again.

Time passes, stands still, moves on again. Sleep is oblivion, annihilation. And even when I wake there are spaces of time that are blank to me.

So Pill-head and me are sitting in Dr Shiva's surgery. Windowless room. Dirty stale smell, graffiti and spit-stained walls – place is worse than a skipper – full of dejected-looking people, scruffy kids playing in the middle of the floor. Shiva's a fat little Indian junkie. The lads call on him from time to time, like once or twice a week. If he's in the mood, you can score for a prescription. Other times, you have to knock the phone out of his hand when he's calling the law. Everyone's coughing and sniffing like they're far worse than the next person. Nobody's getting any sympathetic looks for their act. Pill-head seems the worst. Saliva dripping from his mouth, he spits on the floor. Mothers call their kids away. No one looks at us except the kids! Pill-head slips me a couple of blues. 'Can't hang about here all night waiting for that fucked-up abortionist.' I follow him into the surgery. Patient looks up surprised. 'Get out of here this instant.'

'Sorry, Doctor. Must see you now. My wife died last night. I'm totally distraught.'

'Yes, yes, please wait your turn in the waiting room.'

Pill-head breaks down sobbing. Big croc tears.

'I can't wait. Can't you see, I'm torn apart with grief? He's with me, he's my only support.'

'No, no, both of you out. I'll call the police.' He lifts the phone. Pill-head grabs him round the neck.

'Get the pills out the cabinet!' I put four cartons in my bin. Shiva's screaming like a stuck pig. The place is like a madhouse – nerves going a bit. Pill-head's trying to rob him. Now Shiva's clawing his face like a cat, screaming all the while. We make a run for it.

A new guy arrived in the park – young and tough as nails. He didn't give a fuck about anything. I liked him. His name was Jarvis. He had threatened to kill Mac – which was another reason I liked him. I would've liked him even more if he did. We hit it off from the start. Used to nick anything we could lay our hands on. A good partnership. Were never without drink. Big Reardon enjoyed drinking with us, though he had a wife and young son of four years. He also had a house in Kentish Town; took me and Jarvis there for the night. We were all skint. In the morning, Reardon did his own gas meter before his wife got up. Then we got out quick.

One night, going back to Reardon's, we saw all these milk bottles smashed outside a phone box. Went into the box, started to prise the money container open. A copper came along, asked what we were doing in the box. Said we were sheltering from somebody in the flats who was throwing down bottles. Copper kept looking up to try to catch someone opening the window. We bade him good night. Got home quick!

Another morning Jarvis and I came out of a skipper. Shoes were leaking. Snow about three feet deep. Nicked the road sweeper's shovel and brush while he was in a café. Got over to Parliament Hill, started getting a few bob clearing the rich people's pathways. Started nicking the paraffin money left under the letter box for the oil man. Got a few quid quickly. Went into a pub.

* * *

Awoke one morning in a skipper, about six of us on the floor. Empty bottles everywhere. Looked to see who the others were. Noticed one of them was the Sham. Beside him on the deck was Dublin Tommy, a nice quiet harmless person, always doing part-time washing up in cafés and restaurants – known as Pearl Diving. Tommy had a thing about giving up drink – would go to AA meetings and had been in a number of dry houses. A great man for self-analysis, given to fits of loneliness and depression. Now we were all awake, all trying to roll a smoke out of dog-ends and old tobacco dust in our pockets. I had no money left and was eyeing the Sham, hoping against hope that he or one of the others had the price of a bottle. Tommy broke the silence, saying he was fed up with this life. If he could get the fare he was going to a probation officer who could get him into hospital; no one took any notice. Tommy continued, 'My problem is . . .' He got no further. The Sham fired an empty wine bottle catching Tommy straight in the face, shouting, 'Fuck you and your problems – you're only a cunt.' Poor Tommy flew out of the skipper, holding his nose. No one spoke.

Skippering is illegal; also rough. Some skippers are fair; most are bad. One feature common to both – they are all lousy. It is hard to describe to a clean and healthy person just how uncomfortable and degrading it is to share your clothes day and night with a load of parasites: apart from the terrible irritation there is the nasty feeling of self-contempt. Fights break out in the night; the police come in, nick you or throw you out, depending on their mood; any nutcase can walk in, burn the place down while you're in a drunken stupor. You try to sleep in the attic with the birds but end up in the basement with the rats. One day Long John told me about a rough skipper he used now and then when he had some pills – a coal cellar under the road, no house above. There was a bomb site. You got to it over a wall and then through a hole in the wall. It was approximately seven foot long, six foot wide and four foot high. There was an old mattress, wet and soggy. It was continually damp – water running down the sides. The butchers used to throw chicken heads and remains over the wall, landing in a pile at the entrance. This attracted some wild life – not the sort you see in pet shops. There were long, hungry-looking rats, mean, crazy cats, sly-eyed mongrel dogs and loads and loads of pigeons and gulls. They worked shifts too: rats and cats at night; birds and dogs in the day. I started to sleep there. No one would ever come near it, I thought, not even the police. It allowed me to switch off.

One night I was sick. Awoke about 4 a.m. Big fat Tessa – Ginger Payne's woman – was lying beside me, her face and nose bashed in. She had two very deep razor scars – one down each cheek – which she got from Ginger. I was fumbling in my pockets for a dog-end. She awoke . . . looked in her bag to see if she'd been robbed during the night. She gets a few quid on the game. Things seemed to be in order. So she gave me a fag and a light. Pulled out a bottle of wine. What a delightful awakening! Drank the bottle between us. It didn't seem to cure me yet my companion became completely rejuvenated. Rummaging in her handbag she swiftly pulled out a little mirror and began powdering the badly stitched gashes on her battered cheeks. Then, breathless from her efforts in the narrow light she turned towards me (though she herself would have warded tenderness off with a broken bottle). She put her arms round me, snuggling up, started kissing. I had not thought about such a thing happening. All her snot and saliva going in my mouth and face. She started getting more sexy. Fuck this lark. I know God said you should love your neighbour, but you couldn't when they were all full of snot and slobber. It might have gummed us together for ever. Struggling to get out from under her, I saw

Hogan right up against the back wall, grinning, enjoying my discomfort. Got out at last . . . Tessa shouting and screaming after me, Hogan roaring and laughing.

Sitting in the park, thinking I'd like to be in bed with Sophia Loren. Maybe Hogan will put it about, say I'm a powder puff. The lads would fuck Tessa. They'd fuck anything. I like attractive women, but attractive women don't fuck with park bench winos. No lust in the dust.

Ginger came out today; caught me pissed. Caught me with a bottle too – said it was for trying to shag his misses. Needed stitches in my head. A few days later I caught him in the park, drunk. Broke his nose and kicked a couple of his ribs in – now we're even.

Heard the Sham was in hospital; got run over by a lorry. He's lost the will to live; he's also lost an arm, poor cunt. He should do well begging, though.

I'd just opened the bottle when they came over. Four young tearaways. They said nothing. One picked up the bottle and stood it on his head. I was scared. He passed it to his mate. I could not let it go – word would get round I was easy. The weakest dosser would do it to me every day. Lashing out, I dropped the one drinking the bottle and ran for the gate, but not fast enough. They jumped me, their kicks accurate and painful in my ribs, head, face and spine. I woke up on a mattress on the floor . . . nice pair of legs one side, the same on the other . . . nurses! I wanted the toilet. Lifting me up between them, they half carried me over. I sat there, straining; the pain was bad; I couldn't let go. I didn't care that they watched me. 'Come on, big strong lad like you, try to go.'

'Can't, let me lay down flat again, please.'

They put me back on the mattress. I fell asleep. When I opened my eyes again the quack was standing over me. 'Well, how are we feeling today?'

'OK, Doc. What happened?'

'The police found you two days ago, unconscious in Euston Gardens; you have severe concussion, bruised ribs and a badly bruised coccyx.'

'What?'

'Coccyx – it's the bone at the base of your spine.'

'Yeah, it's murder when I move.'

'Well, um, yes, of course, it will take about three weeks to heal. We've taken X-rays. Your nose is broken but your face will heal up in time. Who did this to you?'

'Some young lady, Doctor; I refused to go out with her.'

'Really! Ha, ha, ha. Oh well, hope I don't run into her.'

I discharged myself a week later. I needed to get a drink. That hiding slowed me down for six months. Murderous tension in my head, difficulty in walking. Reminded me of when I was healthy and feeling good; frightened me too. Maybe I will never feel that way again. Had to drink surgical spirits with old Ernie and George – easy to get, hard to drink, deadly on the eyes and body. No choice, too weak to steal or defend myself. Shit, piss, talk, laugh; the only thing I wanted to do was sleep. The jake was easy to get all week in any chemist, but Sundays we had to travel to Marble Arch for it. We'd jump the tube, George leading the way with his one eye (lost the other in a fight over a bottle of wine. Maybe that's why he only drank jake now); Ernie next with only one hand (lost the other with gangrene). Me hobbling along behind with my fucked-up head and body. We'd cut the jake with pisshole water.

Once Steal the Horse was sitting there, a disgusted look on his face like he ain't never been subjected to such indignity as this before. He was hoping a live wire would come in with wine. His only claim to fame was when the mounted copper came in the park and got down all flash in a jangle of spurs to have a go at old Mary. Steal the Horse jumped up in the saddle and galloped away up Oxford Street. They caught him near Tottenham Court Road. The judge gave him eighteen months for theft. Steal the Horse told him he'd been a cavalry officer in the war, so the judge gave him another six months on top for cruelty to animals – said good cavalry officers should know better.

Then Alex the Grinder came in, looked round, blew his nose in his fingers, wiped them on his sleeve, produced two bottles of wine and sat down. We stuck some in the jake. Old Mary came out of the bushes, trembling for a drink, stockings falling down. Just given the Paper Man a blow job. She took a swig and handed it to me. Very disgusting practice. Always happened when there was no health inspector in the area! Think I'm a bit pissed or pilled?

Mary got funny habits like putting uppers and downers in the boys' drinks. Good park this. Plenty of tourists. Many good begs. 'Hello, Vicar.' 'God's everywhere. God's love will help you all.' 'God help you, you cunt, if you come over here.'

Beautiful classy women in this park. It don't seem possible Old Mary and them are the same species. Fucking noisy bastards at Speaker's Corner. Transvestite Jan just begged a toothless old perv. 'Oh no, dearie, I don't do that sort of thing.' 'Don't look at me Jan, neither do I.' George and Ernie came back with a bag full of chicken bones. They've been down the dustbins again, back of the restaurants. Everybody welcome to lunch. Yeah, we're all going to catch some horrible unspeakable disease. Not today perhaps. But time is on the dustbins' side.

The bottles are smashing. The fighting is starting. Really must dash. Got a tube to catch. Nice feeling rolling about on the tube. Can't seem to get my tube legs. George got his quick – the sympathy he got for his missing eye! He's a good old beggar. Now Ernie doing his bit. I got to do mine. 'Excuse me, lady, could you help us out? I'm a seaman trying to make the fare up to Tilbury.' 'Thank you, love, you're a fine woman.' 'Governor, hey guv, here help us out, guv.' 'What do you want?' 'Help us with the price of a bottle.' 'You've had more than enough already. Here's something for a meal; no drink though.'

I woke up in a skipper with Ernie and George, a box full of surgical spirits and bottles of lemonade. When the mind halts, all memories go. Mouth feels like a sewer.

'How did we get back?'

'Don't know, Johnny.'

'At least we got a drink.'

'I think that fucker, Steal the Horse, nicked Ernie's matches.'

'You can't trust anyone lately.'

It took us a week between drinking and sleeping to get through that jake. No need to leave the skipper for water – we had the lemonade. Pot black and beat, we hit the street. Spit on my hand. Try to plaster my hair down. Beg two guys. 'It ain't how you look kid, it's how you smell.' Yeah, he should know, he's drunk enough of the shit. I can't take any more of this. Fuck off up the High Street. Try to clean up down the toilet.

Been prowling around for three days now. Not a bite to eat – just a drop of wine here and there. Enough to keep the horrors at bay but not enough to get drunk on. Haven't met one friendly face and I don't know where the lads are – most likely they're nicked. Thinking about death – it's bad. (The thoughts, I mean.) Still, millions have died, including many who had everything to live for.

As I passed the alley where the whores usually take their punters for a knee trembler the dry retch got me. Nothing come up, only phlegm. Hard green lumps, then yellow, then white, off white, clear white, whiter shades of pale. Finally nothing except groans from the pit of the guts. It don't half leave you weak when it grips you for a couple of hours. Still, at least I was doing something. Sitting here, unable to do anything, is the worst. Desperation sets in – beyond loneliness, sadness and fear. Then it's bloody-mindedness time. I feel I am just one inch away from killing someone – one of the psychos, a fellow vagrant, anyone – man or woman, young or old, big or small, strong or weak, fit or crippled. Why stop at one? Yes, keep on going, throwing, strangling, mangling, gouging, kicking, ripping, slashing, stabbing. Bodies crashing, dead and dying, everywhere. What a frenzy! Could do with a drink after that.

If you don't stay drunk, then you get the horrors. It's as simple as that really. They're always waiting: hanging around the edge of the mind. It was more a dream that I got. Not like some of the horrible weirdo stuff I've had before. It reminded me of that song – 'Don't sleep in the subway, darling.' You've got no chance of that. I must have been pissed out of my mind. Thought I was in a coffin or something. Black as pitch. Hemmed in on all sides. I could not move, and someone was locking me in. Lying on my back on top of shovels, picks and other tools, I pushed upwards with my hands, but the lid would not budge. Sick as a dog, there was nothing for it but to go back to sleep and await events. A scraping sound made me jump out of my skin. Only trouble, there was no room to jump. Up went the lid. The light flooding in blinded me for a second, but not before I'd had time to make out two big coppers staring down at me.

'Fucking hell, now we've seen it all,' says one of them. 'Come on out of it.' That's when I found I couldn't move. The drink had worn off, leaving me stiffened. But the big ones soon hauled me upright and out of that tube station tool box. To cut a long story short, I got a month for vagrancy and trespass.

II

I was knocking around with Long John at the posh houses, on the drain-cleaning game. At the last house in a tree-lined avenue the door was opened by a slim, smartly dressed middle-aged woman.

'Good morning, madam. We're cleaning the drains. Do you have any blocked?'

'Yes, I'm having quite a bit of trouble. Please come in.' I turned every tap on in the house for effect. John coupled the rods outside, lifted the manhole cover, shoved them up the drain. Messed about for half an hour. John pulled out the dead rat he kept in the rod bag. Told me to fetch the lady. As we came out John was shaking his head, looking at the ground. The woman followed his gaze.

'Ugh, what's that?'

'That's vermin, madam. You don't want them in your drains. Good job we came by today before the Sanitary Inspector seen it.' She was annoyed. The implied threat was obvious. She looked straight at me. I felt a bit sorry for her, but our need was worse. Returning her gaze I said, 'We better get rid of this before someone does see. It might get round the area.'

She walked into the house followed by Long John. I put the rat and rods back in the bag, replaced the manhole cover. John came out. In the pub he gave me £10. We got legless. Our prospects looked bright.

One cold February morning we called at a house in Highgate. A tall, grey-haired serious-looking woman answered. 'Yes, I'm having a problem. They seem to be blocked.' We set to work. Up in the bathroom, John produced a bottle of wine he'd nicked from the kitchen. It was very bitter. We finished it . . . became a bit over-confident. I took a half-full bottle of Scotch. We finished that. Gave her the rat treatment. Got paid. Ended up in a pub at the end of the road. We were a bit drunk when the woman came into the bar with the police.

'That's them, officer.'

We were charged with deception and theft. John tried to wriggle out, asking for the rat to be produced as evidence! They had enough without it. We got six months each. The magistrate called John an 'arch rogue and a charlatan'. John started spluttering and coughing like he was going to bring up a lung.

Back in the nick, into reception, four nights of the horrors. Finally allocated to B Wing. Worst fucking place in the nick. Full of nutters. A fit and a fight a day merchants.

In the rag shop I saw a guy that appeared to be very popular with the villains. He sat in the best position at the end of the table, just under the observation screw: Harry Collins, known as the Brighton Fox, never came in for less than six months, always for villainy. One day I passed his table. He looked up. 'All right, son?'

'Yeah.'

'Here a minute,' he said. 'So you're the one that's been drinking all the soup.' He was hinting at my nickname – Oliver Twist. They all laughed. So did I. They were playing chess on the table. The screws never seemed to bother them. All the rest of the cons in the shop were stone raving madmen. The Fox and his henchmen were all dead shrewd. The Fox had once been done for murder but had managed to beat the charge. He was an alcoholic and was married to a woman in Brighton. The day before he was discharged he gave me some tobacco and his tin. I liked him. He was always laughing and fucking about. I gave him some split matches. A box lasts a week if you split each one in four with a needle. Everybody was pulling strokes, doing deals, and panhandling all day long. Just passing the time.

Macglaccan came in for fourteen days. He told everyone I cut his eye with a knife. Tried to start a fight with me in the recess and made me lose my remission. He wasn't doing long enough to worry. Bastard got discharged in a couple of days; but he'd be back. Some were ending a sentence; some just starting. Big Rob Penman came in doing nine months. He'd just come on the wing and got a terrific job. Red band, sweeping the yards. He could walk into any wing he liked without an escort. He nicked me a Spanish onion out of the kitchens. Nice with a bit of cheese.

Fast Eddie came on the wing doing six months. Had some news from outside. Macglaccan was dead! Got nicked for drunk. Found dead in his cell next morning. Saved me a lot of trouble!

We were kept banged up again all day. A black bloke stuck a needle in a screw's eye as he peeped through the Judas Hole. The Heavy Mob nearly killed him. There was blood on the floor all the way down the landing.

One of the hospital orderlies got a gate arrest this morning. Charged him with pushing drugs on the wards. Fuck his luck.

Moved over to reception ready for discharge. Hardly anyone can sleep here. We've all got gate fever!

I've not seen or heard from my family for years. Last week Mulvey told me my father was dead. Funny, haven't bitten my nails since!

* * *

A few of us were sitting on the metal crates in the picture-house doorway drinking a bottle. Big Dawson and Williams came into the company – no money; no drink; plenty of flash talk. I don't like Dawson – lowest type of ponce. He and his wife adopted children, then spent all the kids' allowance on drink, tobacco and food for themselves. In the end the council took the kids. Then he put his wife out on the game.

'Can I have a drink, Johnny?'

'There's only a drop left.'

'Only want a drop, son.'

'So do I.' I put it to my mouth and finished it.

'You flash cunt, Healy.' He swung at me and missed.

I lashed out with a right and missed. He grabbed me; tried to knee me in the bollocks. He held me by the lapels, Williams picked up a milk crate and smashed it over my head. Fucking pain, but couldn't get away from Dawson's grip. Felt a bottle bounce off my head. Went out like a light. Woke up in the stinking doorway, covered in blood. I felt so weak . . . grabbed the wall for support . . . just as the law pulled up.

'Drunk again, Healy? Come on, you cunt.'

Threw me in the van. I never had a leg to stand on. Ended up getting a month.

Talking about legs, I shared a cell with Tin Legs Alex, an old wino. He fell on a railway line in Scotland dead drunk one night and only woke when a train had gone over his feet. He had to have them both off. He's still a good laugh though.

I was drunk. I wanted to piss. Went into an old office block – facing me a wide curved staircase; to my right a long corridor with large photos of stern-faced old men with smug expressions like they knew something others didn't. Perhaps they did. Hearing an office door opening somewhere back along the corridor, I ducked through the nearest door – a broom cupboard under the stairs. The voices got closer – a man's and a woman's. They stopped right outside the cupboard. Holding my breath, I imagined at any moment they would open the door of my hiding place. Eventually, they walked away. Picking up a mop bucket, I pissed into it. I felt shattered. Lying down among the cleaning kit, I fell asleep. I awoke. It was pitch black. Opening the door slightly, I saw it was night. I crept out. The main door was shut. It was very quiet. I went into each office, searched every drawer. Nothing. Not even a spastic's collection box. It was hard to believe. There must be something some-where. I tried again. No luck. I found an unlocked door on to the street. I needed a bottle. The shops and offices all along the wide street were closed.

'Have you got the time please, guv?'

'Nine o'clock.'

A cold wind had come up, giving me the shakes. A bit too fucked up to beg! Decided to nick a bottle. I sneaked a glance through the first off-licence window. The assistant looked too big and fit. My nerves were raw. I had to have a bottle or face the night with the shakes. The sight of an old man at the third shop made my heart soar. Waiting until the last customer left, I walked in and picked up a bottle of wine. The smile vanished quickly from his face as I turned and fled. For an old man he had a very young shout!

As the few little flowers skirting the edges of the park started to bloom, Liverpool Lil passed away.

I remember when she first set foot in the park, cheeky and smart, not bad-looking for a whore. The lads fancied her like mad. She teamed up with Kelly the Tinker. They made the boneyard their home, pulling strokes, panhandling and hustling from there. Looks fade quickly. Hair turns grey, teeth fall out, wrinkles appear on top of wrinkles, sight fails, bodily func-

tions fail, the mind deteriorates, memory goes, pity goes, to
be replaced by aggression. Violent acts quickly punished by
further violence deteriorate mind and body more and more
until eventually the Chief Psycho puts the final boot in.

After that Kelly lost weight, spent days without speaking,
nursing the bottle. Suddenly he'd fly into a rage at someone,
over a long-forgotten incident. Sometimes he'd win, but mostly
he'd lose. Never a fighting man, his body couldn't take it. He
was found close to death in the park. Someone had given him
a savage kicking. Taken into hospital, he lasted a few months.
As the flowers slowly withered and died, so did Kelly. Drink
is a hard master. Someone got a collection up. Someone else
drank it. Someone managed to get a week's money from the
Social, using his name and date of birth. No one really cared.
The only sad part was when Scarface Mick dropped a full bottle
of wine. The red liquid spread out slowly, like blood from a
knife wound.

It was getting dark as I made my way over to the park with
a bottle. Sat down on the bench opposite the bushes where
what seemed like a bundle of rags had been dumped. As I
pulled the bottle from inside my coat, it clinked, touching
a button. The bundle of rags moved; unfolding slowly, they
took the shape of a man. I recognized Taffy Tommy's withered face as it popped out from layers of filthy cloth. He could
have passed for sixty; really he was thirty-five. He peered
over. He could hear wine bottles tinkle where others heard
only the wind.

'That you, Johnny?' he said as he struggled to his feet.

'Yeah.' He looked like the Hunchback of Notre Dame with
a hangover, lurching across for a drink.

'I thought it was you, son,' he said. I gave him the bottle.

'Thanks, nothing like a good bottle of wine.'

'Yes, and this is nothing like a good bottle of wine. Ha, ha, ha.'

'Know what a workaholic is?'

'What?'

'A bloke who's gotta have a drink before he goes to work.'

As he handed back the bottle he told me, 'Rabbiting Jock was in here this morning. Couldn't get a drink. Said "Fuck it, I'm off to Glasgow" as if it was just round the corner. Then walked off up the road north.'

'Fuck him, he'll be back.'

'Yeah.'

I looked at Taffy. He had three overcoats on, one on top of the other. It was a pantomime. Every time he got nicked, the desk sergeant would nearly have a fit as the contents of his pockets started to pile up on the charge-room table. An old mouth organ, half-eaten toffees with bits of tobacco stuck to them, elastic bands, broken combs (not that he ever combed his hair), fag ends, bottle tops, bottle opener, matchboxes . . . endless crap. The copper having to write it all down in his property book starts fuming when he realizes there are another two coats to go! finally he's had enough, shouts, 'Fuck it, lock him up, lock him up!'

Taffy screams back, 'No, no, wait! It's my property! I want it all put in the book.'

The day was pleasantly warm as I sat with a few of the lads on the grass verge, near where the old seat used to stand. It had been removed at the beginning of the week to discourage drinking – a park-keeper's nod to prohibition?

The Sham came walking down the broken tarmac path. He held a carrier bag in his right hand, the empty sleeve of his left pinned roughly across his chest like some Mexican soldier. As he drew near, I shouted, 'Good morning, General.'

He looked a bit embarrassed when he put down the bag. 'Hello, lad, anyone want a drink?' Mad Freddie opened a bottle, handed it to him first. Then the party got under way.

The Sham's eyes met mine as I opened one of the bottles. It was the first time we'd met since his accident. 'You have very small hands, Johnny.'

What could I say? I coughed and spat on the ground. 'Must have got a bad bottle in the Greek's last night. Here, Sham, get into it.'

'Good man, thanks.'

'Are the hospital looking after you?'

'Are they, fuck. Put me in a poxy doss-house, got loused up in it, had to go over to the health centre to get deloused. Can I skipper with you?'

'You can. But I'm in the Hole. Will you be able to make it over the wall?'

'How do you manage it?'

'Ha, ha, ha . . . yeah, fall over it pissed every time.'

'I'll do the same.'

Came out of the skipper this morning, the March wind cutting through my clothes. Had to use all my strength to walk against it into the park. A heavy frost in the night had left long silver smears down the bark of the trees. I sat on the first bench – first, last or middle doesn't matter. None of them got any shelter. No one about today. Most of the lads are doing time for drunken fines, others on more serious charges, but all in warmer climates. Found a few dog ends in my pockets; finally managed to roll a smoke. The first drag brings the blood rushing to my head. I'm shaking like a leaf, feeling the horrors coming on, getting paranoid. Who can I go and see? No one. Where can I go? Nowhere. That's sorted out my social life. Nowhere I can get a drink, either.

Talking about paranoia and drink reminds me of O'Rourke. He's just out of nick after doing two years for nothing. He went off to the convent for the cup of tea and the dry slice the nuns give out at five o'clock. The convent is situated at the top of a steep hill in a posh part of St John's Wood. When, after much effort, he finally reached the top, the CID grabbed him and fitted him up with attempted housebreaking. They also got the Sham once. He called them all the names under the sun, wanted to know why they couldn't have nicked him at the bottom of the hill, especially as it was high summer at the time! Two evil bastards from Kentish Town nick have done poor O'Rourke a few times. He's done about six years – all fit-ups. A bit potty now, he's petrified of the law – thinks everyone's a plain-clothes man. The Cat Woman's just come in. She's always in plain clothes. Never smiles. Got a face like the Mother Superior of an orphanage.

She comes over. 'Hello, luv,' I said.

'All right, son? Where's all your other friends today, then?'

'Gone. Left me.'

'Ah. Why, dear?'

'Said I drink too much.'

'Te, he, he . . . Not that lot. Probably gone 'cause you ain't drinking enough.'

'Yeah. Could you help us out with the price of a bottle, Ma?'

She gave me a sly look. 'Haven't got anything left, luv. Spent it all on food for my cats.'

'You like cats?'

'Oh yes. They're my babies. I better go. They get terribly lonely on their own.'

'See you, luv.'

'Ta ta, dear.' Wish I was a fucking cat today!

* * *

I knew it was night-time because it was dark. Had a bottle of brandy in my hand. Don't know how I got hold of it. I'm sitting in a pub somewhere, with a pint. Every time I take a swig of the pint, I wash it down with a swig of brandy.

Loud voices shouting jerked me awake.

'Fuck me, Bill, he's still pissed.'

Seeing the blue uniform, I shut my eyes again; tried to turn towards the wall, hoping that somehow they would leave me to die in peace.

'No, you don't. Come on, son.' Grabbing my lapels, the copper pulled me to a sitting position on the wooden bench against the cell wall. 'Come on, mate. You're going to court in a minute.' For a second I didn't know what he was talking about. The blood rushed to my head as the coppers lifted me to my feet, half dragging me out to the street where the sweat box was waiting to take us to court. As I was put in the van, I noticed my face reflected in the shiny metal. Someone had done a demolition job on it: eyes swollen to slits like a blind puppy. Nose two sizes too big. Dried blood covering my lips. Cheeks just two purple bruises. Fell fast asleep in the van. Woken at the court.

My turn came. I thought it was just a drunk and disorderly until the clerk read out the charge: 'Smashing up the bar in a pub, assaulting the governor and his barman with a broken chair . . .' The clerk's voice droned on and on. Now and again the copper would reply to a question. Jesus, were they talking about me? I sat down without being told. Couldn't care less. Too sick today. Remanded in custody to appear at the Crown court for sentence, where I duly appeared after a further few weeks. I got eighteen months and was sent to Wandsworth Prison.

We new receptions were allocated to different cells. My cell had two beds, but I was the only occupant. That's the way I liked it. After making my bed, I was just standing in the open doorway, looking along the landing, happy that I'd managed to get a single cell, when a tall, massively built con came mincing along the landing to shouts and wolf whistles from the two screws.

'You've got a right wiggle on tonight, Trixie,' said the nearest screw.

The big queer turned his head, smiling, saying, 'You should see me in bed, darling.' Reaching my cell, he stopped and looked at the number. The smile vanished from my face as he said, 'Out of my way, son, I'm in here too.' I was speechless as I watched him making his bed: big strong arms and shoulder muscles rippling as he shook out the heavy prison blankets as if they were handkerchiefs. I was afraid to speak: if I spoke soft, would he think I was bent too? If I spoke hard, that wouldn't do either. I got undressed quickly, sprang into bed fast and closed my eyes, feigning sudden sleep. Then he spoke. 'Do you always sleep like that?'

I opened my eyes. 'Like what?'

'Without sheets. You've not put your sheets on your bed.'

'Oh, fuck me.'

He smiled over at me. Jesus, I shouldn't have said that. I was becoming confused. Getting up, I put the sheets on, remaking the bed, asking him at the same time how long he was doing. 'Four years,' he replied.

'What for? Thieving?'

'No, throwing the landlord out of the window.'

'You can't get four years for that!'

'You can if it's five floors up!'

Fuck that! Thought I was tough, but I was nervous as a kitten lying there trying to sleep.

A few evenings later Trixie asked me if I was married.

'No, but I've got a bird,' I lied. I don't like these kind of conversations.

'You married?' I asked.

'Yes.'

'Ah,' I say. 'That's good.'

He lowered his eyes. 'No, it's not good, it's no fucking good at all.'

'Why? What's your missus like, then?'

His eyes took on a hopeless stare; he was looking at me like some martyr: 'She told the law where to find me, the slovenly cow.'

'Fuck that,' I said.

Then a ghost of a smile appeared on his face: 'I would rather have a nice, clean, young guy than a dirty old woman any time.'

I went back to my book. Sometimes I got a bit worried about Trixie; you never knew whether he was joking or serious.

During the following week, Trixie's queer friends kept coming to the cell, talking, acting and smiling like women. They squealed with delight over red-bound books, which they made great efforts to obtain. They would wet a finger, smear it over the cover, then apply the dye to their lips. They were OK, but I felt uncomfortable round them. Also the other cons were winding me up all the time. So I was glad when, after two weeks, Trixie got moved over to a job in the hospital wing.

My next cell mate was called Max. He was about my size. Not a bad-looking bloke when he smiled, but he hardly ever did. He was doing four years for manslaughter. He didn't look hard, but he'd battered a bloke to death with his fists in a fight over a woman. He used to attend the Alcoholics Anonymous meetings in the nick every week. Talked about nothing else. One night he got on to me about it: 'Why don't you come next week?'

'I'd rather read a book, Max.'

'Look, you can read any time, and the screw gives you two fags if you tell him you're sorry that you drink.' Looking at my face he added, 'Better still if you really are sorry, Johnny.'

I wanted to laugh, but felt sorry for him – thinking them cunts cared about him.

'No, I don't fancy it, Max.'

'Listen. Two tasty-looking posh birds come in from outside and give us a cup of tea.'

'Who are they, then?'

'What the fuck does it matter who they are?'

'It matters to me,' I joked. 'I don't want to get mixed up with any old slags in here.'

He smiled. 'You cunt. They ain't no slags; they're two right little darlings.'

'OK. Next week then,' I told him.

Two very attractive young women sitting up straight and relaxed on the hard wooden prison benches watched as we filed in. I took a seat opposite them, looking right at them. They looked right back, their eyes calm and direct. One of them had thick black hair, the other was blonde. They were terrific – apparently unaware of how desirable they were.

Everyone in the room seemed intent on what was being said, perhaps hoping that talk would replace will-power in the fight against drink. I kept stealing glances at the women. Why were those gorgeous, posh, educated females interested in what happens to us thieving, violent, uneducated, penniless cons? I was playing a game, trying to decide which one I liked best. It helped to pass the time. What if they came over and said I could take one of them back to my cell for the night? Jesus! What a choice! And what about the one you didn't pick? Better if the screw was to allocate me one. Then I wouldn't have to make such a big decision. The blonde started talking. I noticed she had a wedding ring on her finger.

'Alcohol is very devious. No matter how you try to manage it, it will sneak up on you. It destroys the brain cells. The only way is to cut it out altogether.'

A young con whispered out of the side of his mouth to me, 'Is that so? And what do we put in its place? I bet her old man's falling all over the cocktail bar right now, unless he's at home giving it to the au pair girl.'

The screw cleared his throat before speaking. 'Yes, yes. How very true, Ann. Most of these men are doing long sentences for crimes committed while drunk, and of which they have no recollection when they are sober.' The old bastard, he loved it, and the cunt hadn't given me the two fags yet either.

Her eyes came over all sad as she said, 'Oh dear me. How tragic. What a waste!' Yes, she really was the best. I'd have her and I'd never even glance at the au pair girl.

The screw's eyes started roving until they came to rest on me. Putting on a serious, concerned look, he spoke to no one in particular. 'I see we have a new face here this evening.' Max and the rest of them looked over at me as if they were seeing me for the first time. The screw continued, 'Would you like to tell us a bit about yourself, lad, just so as we can all get to know each other?' He gave what he thought was a smile; looked more like an old timber wolf deciding which part of his victim to bite first. Well, the spotlight was on me, but I wasn't about to make myself look silly in front of the women, just to give everybody a show. Say just enough to put me in for the fags. Leave it at that.

'My name's John and I'm an alcoholic, doing eighteen months for violence.'

Everybody waited silently for more. After what seemed a long time the screw broke the silence, asking a young Jock, who had a face like an Italian mobster, if he would like to say something. The screw prompted him. 'I know you've had a couple of sentences in the past for smash and grab, Jock. What is it this time?'

Jock, pushing his hair back, started speaking. 'I came out of a pub well drunk. Stopped in front of a shop window. Pulled the hammer out my pocket. Smashed the glass, put in my hand, grabbed a gold watch, tried to run. I was nay fast enough. The squad car caught me at the bottom of the road. In the police station I turned out my pockets. They put the watch on the table. It was made out of chocolate; it had broken into bits in the gold-coloured paper. They gave me two years for intent.'

The screw gave his wolf smile again. 'I bet that's put you off drink, Jock.'

Jock looked right at him. 'No, but it's put me off sweeties!'

I came out of nick fit, fed and rested. Got a bottle of wine. Drank it slowly, nursed it all the way; not drunk, not sober; felt a bit mad, fearless, vengeful . . . About ten of the lads, some on the milk crates, greeted me as I walked in at the back of the picture house.

'Hello, Johnny. Have you just come out?'

'Yeah. Here, Eddie, get a few bottles.'

Gave Fast Eddie the money. Chatting away, Big Pat Dawson came up with Williams. Thought they'd got me where they wanted me now. Both a little cocky, looking for easy prey. Eddie came back with the drink. Feigning friendliness, I offered them drink. 'Go on, Pat, get stuck into it.'

'Good man yourself, Johnny.'

Every time the bottle came to me I put it to my lips without drinking. Passed it to Dawson or Williams. At last the pair of bastards sat down on the ground, backs against the picture house exit. Relaxed, I waited. Dawson put the bottle to his lips.

I put the sole of my shoe up against it; shoved it hard into his mouth. Unable to scream, he keeled over with pain. Three hard kicks to the head put him to sleep. Blood trickled out of his smashed mouth. Williams never made it to his feet. Half-way up I kicked him down. Kept kicking his head and face till the other lads stopped me. Funny, the bastard was still conscious, trying to drag himself away. I wanted to move in and finish them. Too many witnesses!

'Jesus, Johnny, fuck off. Quick. Before the law comes.'

'OK. No one seen anything?'

'You know us.'

'OK.'

Fear plays a large part and he who can produce the most fear gets the most drink for nothing. Everyone and everything is full of tension. There are no tomorrows; tomorrow can't be relied on to come in this vagrant society. Nothing can be taken for granted. Each day you have to prove yourself anew in toughness or lack of it, in stealing, fighting, begging and drinking.

The Sham made two mistakes that a man of his calling should not make; first he stopped instilling fear and then adopted a yield-and-ye-need-not-break attitude. Though for a while he did enjoy the benefits of being disabled, especially when he brought in a big bottle. Then they would extend many little courtesies, like removing the cork for him, brushing the bench before he sat down and of course offering him the first mouthful. But they soon forgot or did not bother. One day when there wasn't much drink or anything else about somebody pushed him so hard he fell off the bench and cracked his skull open on the tarmac. Though he himself had been responsible for much more deplorable incidents in the past, he could not accept that his own turn had come. Fear had made him human. Weakened enough already by hunger and the loss of a limb it was apparent that he would not be able to endure much more. Struggling to his knees, one hand dangling uselessly, he began to choke and sob. But in the sober grave-yard they longed to be one less and screwed up their faces for the certainty, the shape that their memories had taken. From where I sat darkness and trees screened most of it, though not altogether. Then the night closed in more grimly, its thickening darkness muffled sound . . .

Soon after that his lifeless body was fished out of the canal.

12

Small and thin and ravaged by drink and pills, Charlie looked like you could blow him away. That is, until you noticed his eyes. They burned with an intense life. He had a flat by the sea in Southend. He was married to an attractive middle-class woman, half his age, called Wendy, who had lived a so-called sheltered life – that is until she met Charlie! I met Charlie in the nick, both doing three months. We were discharged on the same day. Bought a bottle of wine. Chas asked me, 'Where are you living?'

I stood up. 'In the parks.'

'Well, I suppose it ain't too bad this weather. Must be fucking murder in the winter.'

'Yeah. It's fucking freezing. So you gotta keep well pissed.'

'Why don't you come down and stay with us for a while?'

We caught the train to Southend. Drinking and begging, shoplifting and thieving. We were off our heads after a week. Then some big, hard-looking guy in an expensive but crumpled suit got into our company. He took a liking to Chas. Seemed sorry for him. You could tell at a glance this guy would not normally be seen dead with us. However, circumstances alter cases. We just knew he was on the run from the law. He was a proper-looking villain. He had no money. We gave him a drink. He said, 'I'll get something later when I go to work.'

'What do you do?' says Chas.

'I'm a cat.'

'A what?'

'A cat burglar.' A second-storey man! The three of us were sitting in Chas's front room, Chas and myself lounging drunkenly in the armchairs, the Cat sprawled on the settee, just finishing the last bottle of wine, when Wendy came into the room. She sat on a chair over by the window, her legs crossed, unknowingly showing plenty of thigh. The Cat seemed surprised by this unexpected view, casually looking from the legs back to Chas's face. The legs were built to last, but Chas didn't look like he would last the week. Suddenly noticing the interested gazes she was getting, Wendy tugged her dress and shyly stood up, leaving the room, followed by the Cat's eyes. Turning to Chas, who was unaware of all except the story he was telling, the Cat said, 'I'll do you a favour before I go.'

Chas stopped in mid-sentence, looked at the empty bottles, then back at the Cat, 'What, mate?'

'I said, I'll do you a favour, Pop. I'll give her one for you!' nodding his head towards the kitchen where Wendy was washing up. Chas went pale. He was speechless. Silence.

I said, 'We'll have to get another bottle. Who's got any dough?'

'Come on. Let's go out,' said Chas. 'We might be able to nick a couple of bottles down the town.'

We settled down on a park bench with a couple of bottles. After a while the Cat noticed an open window in a posh-looking house three floors up. A bit pissed, I lay back on the seat. I must have dozed off for a couple of minutes. On opening my eyes, the Cat was half-way up the drainpipe that led up the wall of the house. A few more feet brought him level with the window. Grabbing the sill, he disappeared inside the house. I looked over at Chas. He was fast asleep. I lay back to await events, but fell asleep too. When we both awoke it was dark. We nicked two bottles of wine and headed back for Chas's place. An old wino called Seagull was there. We all talked and drank for a while and he told Chas he'd been working, washing up in a restaurant. Before he left, Chas tapped him for a couple of quid, sending Wendy down to the pub for more wine. It was high summer. All the windows were open. We continued drinking. About two o'clock in the morning we were all well pissed. Chas started shouting at Wendy to keep her dress pulled down. They were shouting loudly and furiously at each other. Neighbours started banging on the walls. They took no notice. Wendy went down into the front garden with a glass and a bottle of wine. Sat in the deckchair screaming insults at Chas, who was shouting out the window at her. It went on and on until Chas asked me to help get her back into the house. Down in the garden, as we tried to coax Wendy to keep quiet and come in, a big gypsy-looking guy dressed only in his trousers came up saying, 'Keep the fucking noise down or I'll swing for you, you bitch.'

I was very drunk; just wanted to go to sleep. 'Did you hear what he called me, John?' said Wendy, putting me right up front with the guy. He drew back, intending to crush me with a punch.

Waving my hands in the air, I said, 'No, no, guv. I've just had a heart attack.' He stopped still. I added quickly, 'I've been sent down here for convalescence.'

He shook his head, turned round and kicked the air with frustration. 'Fucking good, isn't it? The cunts fuck you about all night long, then you can't even have a go at them.'

We all got back in the house fast. Chas and Wendy continued arguing. I went to sleep.

There's a policewoman here. She's got a terrific figure, blonde hair, handsome face. But when you look at her eyes, desire dies. They're cold. They shine with hate. Loves to kick the drunks when she finds them asleep. The lads call her Pussy Galore.

Pussy came along last night with two male coppers. Threw Brooksie and me into the van. She sat opposite Brooksie who was lying on the floor. I could see up her skirt. Smashing legs. She noticed Brooksie looking and kicked him hard in the guts. He doubled over, puking. She kept kicking him up the arse . . . anywhere she could. I pretended to be knocked out. The van kept going. We seemed to be travelling a long way. The ride got bumpy. We stopped. The doors were opened. They carried us, one at a time, into the rat tip. We fell asleep, woke up shivering on Hampstead Heath among the rubbish. Started walking. 'Take your time, Johnny. I'm fucked today. How come she never touched you?'

'I don't look up ladies' dresses.'

'You lying cunt. Even the law was looking.'

'She don't mind them. And she never caught me.'

We hobbled on. Found a tyre lever and an iron bar. Brooksie kept watch while I done a phone box. We got a couple of bottles. As we were drinking, Brooksie showed me his legs. The skin was black. I think he's dying from cirrhosis of the liver. Pity. He's only twenty-eight. Same age as me.

'You'll be OK,' I said, 'you've got better legs than Pussy Galore.'

'Ha, ha, ha, you cunt. Give us that bottle.'

Funny how things work out sometimes. I thought of every way I might get to wash my feet and change my socks. I've been unable to take my shoes off for a week or so and the socks have rotted. They're not so bad when damp and sweaty. Somehow you can handle that, squelching along. It's when they're icy they become a bit lethal – sharp slivers cutting the toes painfully. And this army marches on its feet! It's not so much a problem to get clean socks – Woolworths is a benevolent society for those with quick hands. But where to wash a pair of rotting plates of meat? I know the toilet washroom, if you can find one open, seems the place, but the days have long gone since I was nimble enough to lift one leg up for that balancing trick.

Nothing worse than getting nicked sober; and soberer than the soberest judge was I when they came in and done me for a fine. As soon as the cell door clanged, I eased my shoes off; took my socks off slowly, peeling the tattered bits gently away from my toes like some second skin. A rest to get the breath back and then the final part of the operation, and the happiest. Sitting on the bed board, I rolled my trousers up, swung my feet over, placed them in the toilet bowl, and after a few pulls of the chain, they were as clean as this makeshift foot shower could make them. It don't half make you footloose. Pity about the lock.

As I lay down, through the door comes the soft coaxing voice of the gaoler. 'Son.'

'Yeah, guv.'

'We got another little charge for you.'

'What?'

'It's an enclosed premises to steal.'

'When?'

'Last Monday night.'

'I was in here last Monday night.'

'Don't be awkward, lad. You weren't in here.'

'Yes, I was. You booked me in yourself for drunk.'

'The book's been lost, son.'

Here we go again, waiting in the corridors ready to go into court at a moment's notice, straining at the leash, copper and prisoner alike, waiting to make our grand entrance, go into our act, tell the truth . . . the what?

'The truth.'

'Don't fuck about. Let's be sensible today, eh, son?'

'Well, are you going to tell the magistrate I've been out of trouble for a while, guv?'

'No, he's a busy man, so don't start whining about all that nonsense.'

'OK, guv, but you know I never done it, so I'm pleading not guilty.'

'You're what? You ungrateful little bastard. So that's how you repay me after I gave you my last fag and all.'

'Oh, I'm sorry, guv. Please don't take it so hard. I know it was your last fag and all, but I might get six months for nothing.'

'Don't be a cunt all your life, son. Take a day off. Six months won't harm you, and think of the good you'll be doing. My record for arrest is well below par. You wouldn't believe the troubles I've got, son.'

'But I never done anything.'

'Don't keep saying that, lad. You're like a broken record. And talking about records . . .'

'I don't want to talk about records, guv, especially my own.'

'That's just it.'

'What?'

'Your own . . . that's what does you every time.'

'Jesus! What evidence you got?'

'You were out after midnight.'

'That's nothing. So is high society.'

'You comparing yourself to high society?'

'No, guv, I just meant . . . Oh, it don't matter.'

'Well, then, shut up and listen. Sergeant Willis will be along any minute with evidence against you.'

'There ain't no evidence.' He leans over like he's going to tell me a real secret now.

'Oh, yes, there is,' he whispers slowly. 'He's been up all night working on it. Marvellous chap. So imaginative. Wasted in the police force really. Should have been an inventor. Look at the state of you. I mean, you look guilty. So pull yourself together.

Sign this little statement and I'll see if I can't get you another smoke.' He smiled, trying to convince me that he only fitted up people he liked.

'Can I go for a piss, guv?'

'No, there's no time. We're on in a minute.'

'You said that half an hour ago!'

'I know. And I'll say it in another half-hour's time too. Now, are you going to sign this statement?'

'Can I have a piss then?'

'Yes.'

'And a fag?'

'Yes.'

'And a shit?'

'Yes.'

'Cup of tea?'

'Now don't get greedy, son. Anyway you're in no fit state. You're beginning to shake.'

'I know. I need a bottle. And I'm pleading not fucking guilty!'

We were just talking about the Dipper, wondering where he was. None of us had seen sight nor sound of him for the last three weeks. Is he dead or alive? In heaven? Or hell? . . . Is he in nick? It doesn't take long for the rumours to start. Someone said he was begging . . . stopped this posh, rich woman and she took him away in a big car. Another, that he's out in the country staying in a monastery.

Talk of the Devil and he'll surely appear. To our surprise, he turns up in the park today. (The Dipper, I mean.) He looked really well: all his jaws filled out, eyes clear as a baby's. Stood in front of us easy and relaxed in a faded but clean double-breasted suit – not the type of fashionable clothes that straight people would wear, but he was going to get himself rigged out proper after he got a job, he informed us, and he wasn't going to be seen dead round the parks again.

'Nothing so bad as a reformed whore,' whispers Gerry to me as the Dip was busy explaining to Big Conners how he'd conquered drink.

'Jesus, you've got terrific will-power,' says Big Con, knowing that's all he wants to hear. Maybe he'll leave us the price of a bottle when he tires of letting us know what cunts we are and how great he is. Perhaps he is great. I was beginning to think so, looking at him standing so relaxed without a drink, until Mary asked had he any Jack and Jills? Did he? Only enough to sink a battleship – every size, shape and colour, too, it seemed. He dropped us a few each. So much for giving up drink. More like exchanging one bottle for another.

On a cold January night that would freeze the snot in your nose, as it started to snow me and Big Conners went into the Hole in the Wall, thinking to beat the cold by sleeping. We weren't drunk enough. Spent the night turning this way and that, begging morning to come. No telling what time it was. When we did hit the street, little halos of yellow light round the street lamps in the early morning fog said all there was to say about the weather. Arms and legs moving like puppets, stiff with the cold, we headed off towards the toilets for a warm. Shops and stores closed at this early hour. Streets deserted except for the odd early morning cleaners hurrying past on their way to work. As we came up to the corner, about to cross the road, a sudden fierce gust of icy wind and sleet made us jump back, taking shelter in the doorway of an old office block.

'What a bastard wind, Con!'

He turned. His face blue with the cold. 'That's fucked it. We won't be able to pick up any smokes either.'

I felt the outer door of the office give as I leant further back against it to avoid the wind. It must have been opened by the cleaners. Were they still around? No matter. I pushed it open without a word; Con followed me inside. Standing by an old wooden staircase that had a new bike chained to it, we listened. Voices coming from upstairs told all we needed to know. We looked silently at each other and at the chain attaching the bike to the banisters. I held the bike while Con, with two swift blows, smashed the wood, pulling out the broken banister as I lowered the bike to the floor. Put it up on my shoulder. After hiding the broken wood, Con followed me out.

More people up and about now. We crossed the road. 'We'll knock it out to the barrow boys, Con,' I said, breathless with the effort of lugging it on my shoulder. 'They're the only ones up.' I had to rest, putting the bike down just as a copper came into view. We both saw him.

'Jesus, Johnny, shall we make a run for it?'

'No. I'd never outrun him. He's a fit-looking bastard.' I leaned across the saddle with my legs hiding the lock and chain. Con got the message. Moving in to cover the other side, he started shouting at me, just as the young copper came close. 'I've just finished unloading all the fruit without you! If you can't get up in the morning for work, Mr Gusman says you'd better find another job!' Luckily the copper didn't know us by sight. Hardly giving a glance or an ear to the petty squabbling of two market workers, he passed by, turned the corner, and was gone. Only then did I realize that my fingers were burning with cold, locked round the metal of the bike. As I was prising them loose, Con burst out laughing. 'Poor old Mr Gusman! Why ain't he got any decent staff?'

After flogging the bike in the market, we got into the early morning pub.

I woke up on top of a pile of earth and rubble that the workmen had dug out of a trench on the side of the road. My nerves were a bit shattered and a biting wind was cutting me to the bone. No one with an ounce of sense would stop long enough to be begged on a day like this. I went into Scraggie Aggie's café for a cup of tea and a warm. When I first came on the streets I used to detest this place – full of dirt-flies and always stinking of some foul odour. Not any more: now it could be the Ritz; in fact, Scraggie's is more useful than the Ritz.

Most of the women were there that morning, including Margo. She tipped me the wink and, as soon as I sat down, slipped me a bottle – covering me off while I took a good drink. The whores have started bunching together again, talking friendly, acting mannerly and more than willing to give a man a drink. You wouldn't think it was one of the same crowd of girls at all. Is it because Mad Joey's around? He comes out of the nut-house now and then. He killed his own mother with an iron bar – at least, that's what he imagines when he's pilled up and drunk. The truth is it was a woman who surprised him after he'd broken into her house, and he strangled her. He was a teenager then. There are a lot of stories about Joey – all bad. He never seems to sleep, prowls around all night with a jemmy bar under his coat. Seeing the bulge in his coat for the first time gives you a moment's hope: you think perhaps it's a bottle!

The wine and the heat have thawed me out a bit. Delia's at a corner table, beckoning to me with mad, outlandish gestures. I don't want to upset Margo by going over; besides, I might lose a drink. Margo nudges me; leaning over, she whispers in my ear that she's going to buy me a bottle, only she's a bit tipsy, so she leans her lips and face up against my ear. One or two of the workmen mistake the action and Scraggie Aggie shouts out, 'Come on, cool it, you two.' Delia follows us out and in the off-licence they're vying with each other as to who's going to pay for the drink. On the way over to the park they can't stop talking about Joey while throwing sidelong glances at me

– which I ignore. They end each sentence with '. . . he's a nice bloke really, though.' But the fear in their eyes tells a different story. They seem like two shy little girls at the moment. You have to make the most of these uncertain calms . . . perhaps, when I've had a good drink out of them, I'll let them know Joey's back in the nut-house: he got picked up by the law yesterday.

And time goes round and round. I was pleasantly oiled. Couldn't remember where I got the drink. Couldn't care either. It was a long way to the skipper up a posh part of Hampstead. Bit stupid to use a rich area but there's a couple of warrants out for me for non-payment of fines, so you have to keep moving if you want to avoid getting slung inside.

I know this skipper. Poor Danny had been skippering there with me. One night last winter, both stupid drunk, we lit a fire on the ground floor. I was warming myself, Danny was trying to split some more wood, when he let out a fierce scream and fell down holding his hands over his eyes. I tried to make him shut up – his screams were tearing through my head – but he got worse, shouting that something was in his eye and he couldn't see. I coaxed him into the street but he continued to scream and couldn't be comforted so I took him up the hospital, where they put him on a stretcher and stuck a needle into him, just under the eye. Then I left him.

When I got back near the skipper, the fire brigade were there and smoke and flames were leaping from the windows. I shot off quick. I met Danny over the East End six months later. He had only one eye. It was a splinter of wood that he caught that night.

I was on my own this night. The inside was gutted. The wooden slats showed through the shattered ceiling and dust from the fallen plaster was everywhere. But there was one room at the very top that was OK . . . In amongst the junk and filth, broken tables and chairs, there was an old mattress on the floor. Some of the stairs were missing and there was no banister, to climb the stairs required daring, so no one was likely to come in on me unawares. Anyway, for a peaceful night's sleep I'd risk most things. You're lost at this game without sleep.

Funny thing, the day before, coming out late in the day, a big bloke grabbed me: 'What're you doing coming out of there?' (middle-class accent).

'The cat,' I said.

'What?'

'The cat, governor. It got stuck in the railings. I saw it struggling as I was walking past.'

'Oh, I see. Well, I'm the doctor from next door and I don't want to catch anyone on these premises or it'll be a police matter.'

'Let me go.'

The well-fed bastard, I would have loved to make a hospital matter out of him. But I hadn't been eating properly; my bones showed through my skin and I felt weak as a cat so I moved off.

I made it up the stairs and threw myself on the bed. I was just lying there, luxuriating in the dark on the thought of a nice sound kip, when all hell broke loose as police cars, their sirens screaming, skidded to a halt outside. I can't believe it. When I peep out of the window the road is packed with coppers and there's about six squad cars and a van. They even had a searchlight, which they're beaming all over the windows. Before it slashed my face I got down on the floor. This is bad. I think they're looking for Harry Roberts, who's on the run after shooting three coppers dead in south London last week. If they catch me after they have gone to all this trouble, they're going to fit me up something rotten. It's hard to think what to do. I could hear them on the ground floor. They had a dog with them . . . let one of those bastards get at you and it'll chew your throat out while they pretend to call it off, laughing. (Happened to Mad Gerry two years ago; now he's going round with half a face.) What a turn up. I was busting for a pee and they were already on the second floor. Nothing worse than unfamiliar footsteps in a derelict house at night. You could hear the stairs protest against their boots. I quickly pee into the mattress to muffle the sound, throw my old overcoat on the deck and squeeze behind the wardrobe, right up tight against the wall. I'd already opened the wardrobe door, so they could take a little dekko without looking too close. I can feel the cold eating into my bones. It's gone very quiet, not a whisper, then the loose board on the landing gave a dangerous creak and my nerve went because I could end up having a nasty little accident here. If they are looking for Harry Roberts they will be fully armed. But who else could they be looking for? Certainly not vagrants like me. But that's just what Roberts is like now. Fuck it, I remember that the headlines had said so – since no one could afford to harbour a cop killer he had to be living like me. The silence was serious and I knew from the stillness I was caught. I wanted to give myself up, but I couldn't think how to do it. Should I just shout out 'I surrender', but to whom and for what? After all I was only a rough sleeper, but how could they be sure? They might be in such a mood over their dead colleagues. In blind rage, the stupid cunts might start shooting at me, or they could throw me down the stairwell and say I fucking fell.

Bang, crash, wallop. In went the door. The beams from their torches are scanning the room. I can hear the dog fretting as it sniffs out my fear, then one of them shoved a table aside so hard he overturned it. I have never been up against a situation like this one before. I held my breath until I heard a voice say, 'It fucking stinks in here, MIND! don't tread in that shit!'

Thank God for small mercies. They were preventing the dog from picking up my scent! For a while, except for the dog's panting, there wasn't a sound. The coppers seemed too intent on keeping their boots clean to move around. But I sensed by the absence of torch beams, coupled with the rattle of the rickety wardrobe's flimsy door that their eyes would have been trained directly on me if the back panelling had not been so dense. The next thing I hear is footsteps out on the landing, they stamped around for a bit before going back down the stairs.

Good job they never let the dog off the lead. Out in the street I can hear car doors slamming and the sound of their engines as they roar away. Jesus, that was close. I was out of breath from it all and wanted to lay down but I was so shocked I was too frightened to move. I stayed where I was, rigid up against the wall and that's when I realized why they hadn't let the dog loose. Because they were worried that in such a confined space it might have got shot if they had to use their guns. Suddenly, someone silently pushed the door in. I could see his crouching shadow on the wall. He began clambering over the debris towards the window, he was about five inches away from me, now his shadow was huge upon the wall. I shrank into my clothes as he began fiddling with the window, he seemed to be having some trouble with the sash. Finally he got it open, thrust his shoulders through and shouted down to the police officer waiting below.

'Nothing, Sarge.'

'No, OK . . .'

Then out he went and down the stairs. What sneaky bastards! I was lucky to escape. Finally I came out of my hiding place, put my coat back on to thaw the mattress and lay down. But my skin started to crawl and I began to scratch – from the lice there is no escape.

* * *

Next day I was sitting on a bench near Frognal in Hampstead. Can't go back to that skipper any more, but don't want to go round Euston for a while. Where the fuck can I go? Some old girl sat down beside me. I thought, she ain't no dosser, can tell by her face, handsome with a sort of brave, bold stare. I started to beg her but she cut me short, advised me to pack up drink, etc. I agreed. She gave me £2 to book a bed for the night in the Sally. Soon as she left I got a bottle in the off-licence. Ended up that afternoon meeting Charlie. He was a drug addict. Stayed in a large room with a load of other addicts and pill-poppers in Hampstead. As he was leaving he told me to call round for a kip that night. On the way round I got the urge to smash this chemist's shop window, so I got an old metal milk crate and heaved it through. Filling my hands with transistors and anything else I could hold I went round to Charlie's. I put the gear down beside the dustbin in his garden, went back for another armful of stuff, planted it and went back again; but by this time there was a crowd of people and two coppers. I begged a smoke off one of the crowd, then left and took the gear into Charlie's. He could get rid of anything, any time, any place, so I told him to get me two bottles of wine and sell the gear for me.

There were about twenty young men and women in the room. Funny, all these guys looked wasted in mind and body, yet they had some terrific birds with them. One bird called Dominique was very good-looking – bit slim, tasty though. Only one thing wrong: her hair had fallen out. It didn't even bother her, she still had that middle-class way about her, sort of politely fearless.

She got up slowly, saw me clocking her legs and said, 'I'm going for a pee.'

They were all doing that now – the posh birds, I mean. Said it as if it meant, 'I piss out of it too; I got no secrets.' When she came back, I wanted a pee too, but I didn't tell her about it. She came over and sat next to me on the deck; rolled herself a joint. She was hinting that I was a bit of a lad coming in with that gear. I hadn't meant to say anything . . . but the way she kept looking at me, I couldn't help boasting about what I'd done. (Many a person gone away for boasting.)

After a while Charlie came back and gave me some dough (you could see he had already helped himself rather generously to his own cut by the way he was buzzing around, eyes glowing with a kind of psychedelic glimmer). They all started to fix up on White Sally.[1] Then we were all on different wavelengths. When I woke up some hours later everybody was knocked out. They all pair off here to pull a stroke together later in the day. But everybody would have a different idea in mind and they all end up double-crossing each other at some point on their transcendental wanderings. I slipped out and went to the Early House in Covent Garden for a good drink. You don't need to worry about a friend double-crossing you down here.

Because in the Early House you never met a friend.

[1] pure unadulterated heroin.

13

Woke up lying in a puddle of water at the bottom of some iron stairs in the basement of a house. Got up as quickly as the stiffness in my body would allow. Climbed the stairs. No one around. Slid out onto the street – a street lined with tall trees, rich houses, well-kept gardens and expensive cars. Looking the way I did – dressed in rags – I was a sus man's delight. Caught round here, they'd throw the book at me. Knee and back playing up, I shuffled along to Hampstead tube. Got in the lift. Waiting for the train, the warm air put me to sleep. Woke about an hour later, thawed out, jumped the next rattler to Euston. Pushed passed the ticket collector.

'Hey!'

'Bollocks.'

Couldn't care less today. Could do with a month's lay down.

Out into the station ... made my way over to the waiting room. The Monkey was being very spiteful, bending my neck and head down. Shot into the toilet, threw a splash of water on my face: white as a sheet, sunken jaws, eyes staring out madly like an over-stressed cat, overcoat three sizes too large. Looked like an extra in a Dickens film. The few people in the waiting room were genuine travellers, smartly dressed men, women, children, luggage, pets. A few heads looked up as I passed near them. It's not how you look; it's how you smell!

Sat on a seat at the far end where I could keep my eye on the door . . . kept trying to find a comfortable sitting position. I tried in vain. In the old waiting rooms the seats were designed for maximum comfort. They must have got this design off the Spanish Inquisition. Every public place, eating house, even toilet seats seem designed to discourage the punter from relaxing.

Finding it hard to keep my eyes open with the smoke and heat, I was just dozing off when Mad Rafferty came in with a bottle. He was growling like a dog.

'Hey, boyo, you're looking well.'

'Yeah, I know . . . I'm dying, you cunt.'

'Get a drop of this down you. That'll soon cure ya.'

I took a slow sip. It tasted vile. Spewed my guts up. Horrified glances. Leaving Rafferty, I got out on to the station. I lay with my back up against the heater. The continual stream of passengers helped take my mind off the sick feeling in my guts.

Women's legs . . . knees . . . skirts . . . high heels . . . ankles . . . shapely calves . . . tall girls in flat shoes . . . earth mothers in sandals . . . secretaries in boots. Just looking was too much. I dozed off. A sudden sharp pain in my legs made me jump. Two big law had a foot each pressing all their weight down on my shins.

'Come on out of it.' Grabbing an arm each, they pulled me up and ran me head first at the glass door.

I just managed to swing my shoulder forward in time, bouncing myself off the glass, sideways out into the forecourt. 'Don't let us catch you here again.'

Limped over to the park. Lay across the seat. Start to doze off. Horrors again . . . I've got them bad . . . hundreds of rats, each threatening to bite before racing past. Kept spewing up. Didn't even fancy a smoke. Fuck the drink. What could I do? I felt sad, lonely, and depressed. Jumped a bus to the Morgue, a massive old workhouse run by the DHSS for homeless men.

Joined a queue of shabbily dressed, battered-featured vagrants, some with limbs missing, others on crutches. Even the young looked old here. Time dragged as each one slowly shuffled up to the check-in window to be processed into hell. My turn came.

'Name.'

'John Murphy.'

Insurance number, date of birth, height, etc., etc. Gave him a load of bollocks. Only truth in it was the colour of my eyes. And I'm not too sure of them lately.

In a large old room with a very high ceiling and bars on the windows, we waited a couple of hours before being called into the bath-house. An odd sound made me look round. A wizened old man, sitting on a little wooden cart with four small wheels, used his hands – each covered by a thick pad – to push his legless body along. The staff were big and well fed, dressed all in black; with their big boots and shiny peaked caps, they looked and acted like a death's-head division in a German concentration camp. On taking off their clothes, old men – some senile, others just plain mad – were hustled into a bath by two of the staff while their mates searched clothes for money and valuables to steal, all the while shouting at the old guys to keep them confused. After a bowl of soup, I was given a bed. Slept fitfully, shivering and shaking through the days, going into the horror dreams each night. In spite of – or because of – the people around me, I felt alone and a little afraid. After a week, I felt better: got up, washed, shaved, dressed and left before they had time to check up on me. Not even Oliver Twist would have wanted seconds there.

Heading for a skipper, drunk. A young blonde whore came towards me with a bottle of wine. 'Wanna drink, baby?'

'Yeah,' putting it to my lips. Heard the scuff of a trainer

behind me, go to turn round, blondie smashes a hammer over my head. Black whore grabs me from behind. I lash out with my foot. Catching Blondie in a private place, she bent over holding her cunt. The black lets go, moves just out of reach, screaming all the while for their ponces.

Blood spilling out my head, I ran.

The bitches followed, screaming with hate. 'We're gonna kill you!' Screams will tell their ponces where we're at. Made one fast run. Sped round the corner. Dropped down, rolled under a parked car. (No sense mugging a wino. Must be a very bad case of mistaken identity here.) Heart pounding, breath cutting my throat. The whores and two blokes came loping by. 'Down this way, Leroy, he must be down here.' I was beat. Laid where I was. My breath calmed down. Rolled out from under the car, doubled back to the skipper.

Aches-and-Pains was lying on the cardboard boxes that made up my bed. He's got a huge purple face between two small red ears. He was told he only had six months to live twenty years ago! He's always complaining about his health. Sticks his tongue out. Asks everyone what colour it is. He's slipped up tonight. Usually manages to beg enough money for a bed in a doss-house. In ten years I've never seen him come into the company with a drink.

'Move over, Aches.'

'Oh, Johnny, is it you?'

'No, it's Chief Superintendent Monkhouse, you cunt.'

'Ha, ha, ha, have you got a light, Johnny?'

'No, don't start striking matches or making noise. There's a couple of spades prowling round looking for someone.'

'Did you see them?'

'Yeah.'

'How'd you get past?'

'They're fucking colour blind.'

'I'm going to see Shiva tomorrow,' says Aches.

'To get some pills?'

'Ah no, it's me old chest playing me up.'

'If you got some pills, you wouldn't know you had a chest.'

'I never touch them after seeing Mad Gerry up the convent pilled out of his head.'

'What happened, Aches?'

'He caught hold of the Mother Superior, told her he'd love to ride her.'

'What she say?'

'Said she'd pray for him.'

'When, after he'd fucked her or before?'

'Ah, it's no joke, Johnny boy. He'll ruin it. They'll stop giving out the soup.'

'Don't worry me. Until they start giving out the wine, I won't go up there.'

'There's rats in here.'

'Oh, bollocks, let's get some sleep.'

'The law came in the park today.'

'Who were they looking for, Aches? New faces in hell?'

'No, old ones.'

'Why?'

'Couple of whores ripped some businessman off. They were loaded.'

'Plenty of drink?'

'Yes, but they wouldn't give me a drop.'

'Tight cunts.'

'No, there's not a tight cunt between them! Have you ever had a pain in your chest that makes you feel groggy?'

'Yeah, I've got one now. Good night, Aches.'

* * *

Never had a hangover to touch this one. Wedged up against the doors of the old picture house, eyes piss red, mouth tasting like a shithouse, trying not to move an eyelid for fear of bringing on another spasm of head and gut pains. Michael is paymaster. He must have done a post office book. The ground is covered with bottles of wine and cider. The Priest had been training for the cloth in Ireland. Got caught stuck up a nun or choirboy. Can't remember which, but it all came down the same way in the end. Had to leave for England. Still, he never let the education go to waste. He's a great con man. The women in the Cider House love him with his middle-class accent and posh manners.

There's a right mixed crew. A few Jocks from the Cross have joined in but mostly it's the lads from Ireland. Myself and Cockney Fred are the only two locals. Frankie Peel's talking in Glasgow gutter slang to Williams. Both giving me hard looks. I'm pretending not to notice – mad pair of cunts. Glad I'm in the doorway. Wind's howling mad. Bitterly cold. Peel never feels the cold, or so he says, even in this arctic weather. He's only got an open-necked shirt on. Trying to hold on to a bit of sanity can make you vulnerable in lots of ways.

A sip every now and again is bringing me round. The conversation's got a bit more variety too. Usually everyone's trying to outdo each other with tall stories about their begging techniques. Not today. Peel and Williams are shouting at each other.

'The worst screw in the nick is a fucking Jock!' Williams shouted, meaning Jock Lynch, a screw who beat a young con to death with his truncheon.

'Fuck you and the screws and the nick.'

'You fucking ponce.'

Williams grabbed Peel's shirt collar . . . tried to nut him. Peel wrenched his body sideways, leaving Williams holding two handfuls of ripped shirt, in the same instant grabbing Williams by his thick curly hair and pulling his head up against his teeth. Williams screamed with pain. The shock caused Peel to let go. Williams fell back on to some of the lads who had been too slow or drunk to get clear. I had enough drink in me not to be worried, but it still surprised me, when Williams took his hand away from his head, to see the lobe of his ear hanging off, held only by a bit of skin, brilliant red blood flowing down his neck. Took a good long swallow before passing the bottle to the Priest. Taking a quick shot, he passed it back.

'I'd better dash, John, before the law come. Only those untouched by sin, venial or otherwise, can afford to hang around here today.'

'Yes, Your Holiness.'

'Ha, ha, ha.' He'd have the devil of a job explaining away so many different-named Post Office books hidden in his shoulder pads! Come to think of it, I'd better make myself scarce too.

I turned into the High Street. Williams was lying in the middle of the pavement still bleeding, pissed out of his mind, shouting and cursing at the passers-by. Spinning round, scattering the midday shoppers, I pushed through the door of a clothing shop, slowed down, got my wits together enough to nick a couple of shirts, walked out down the High Street just as Williams was being put in an ambulance. Knocked the shirts out in the market, got myself a bottle, drank it down the tube, passed out.

The narrow street was lined with cheap boarding houses, each displaying a bold sign: 'Bed & Breakfast'. Those with exotic names, a recent lick of paint and curtains on the windows, looked as if they might attract the odd tourist. But mostly they were flop-houses. Stopped outside 'The Corina'. Pushed the door. It wasn't locked. Found my way along a dark narrow corridor to number seven; knocked.

'Hey, Willie.'

'Yeah, it's open. Push it.'

Swung the door back. Willie was sitting on top of a packing case in a corner of the room with his back against the wall. There was neither carpet nor lino covering the bare floor. A mattress alongside the window – burnt, covered in piss stains, dried blood and vomit – was the only other thing beside the packing case.

'Hello, Johnny. Pull up a floorboard and sit down.'

'This dump's worse than a skipper, Willie. Anyone can walk in.'

'I know. Asked the landlord for a key. Said I didn't need one, 'cause there's no locks on the doors.'

'Fuck that. Any young bird could walk in at night and rape you.'

'Ha, ha, ha. I'll leave the window open too.'

Willie didn't look too healthy. Ragged clothes covered a skeleton-thin body; a woollen hat, keeping his head warm and his hair down, looked out of place. He'd not shaved for a week. One side of his face was all gravel rash and dirty. He kept screwing his left eye shut, then peering around with the other. Seeing me staring, he gave an embarrassed little laugh.

'Been taking wobblers. Banged me eye on the deck a few times. Can't see out of it now. Keep testing the other one out when I'm sober, in case it fucking goes too.'

'Ah, it'll be OK when the weather gets a bit warmer and you get a few buckets of soup down you.'

'Yeah, I hope so.' He laughed.

I noticed a small sink in the other corner. (Well, at least he's got an indoor toilet.) As I pulled the bottle out of my pocket, his one good eye lit up. Passing it back and forth, we talked about boxing. Willie had once fought for the Scottish lightweight title. Suddenly, tiger-like, he throws a few phantom punches and for a second you could see the class he'd once been. He's been in a lot of hard nicks, including Biederfeld military prison in Germany. Brought up in a Glasgow tenement in the Gorbals, he learned his boxing and drinking there. Every now and then he kept testing his eye out, with that funny giggle.

'You on Jack and Jills, Willie?'

The giggle got a little crazier. 'Only got a few. Here's a couple.'

He handed me two blues. Swallowed them with a mouthful of wine. After a while, we were both talking at once, talking to ourselves, each other, the walls, happy as sandboys.

'You seen that woman been hanging around the station the last few weeks?' asked Willie.

'Who? The German one?'

'Yeah.'

'She ain't bad-looking.'

'She helps me home at nights.'

'Do you give her one, Willie?'

'Give her one? I give her six!'

'Ha, ha, ha. You cunt.'

Willie's two eyes were coming out of his head. As he fell forward off the box, crashing on to the floor in a crumpled heap, I took another drink. 'Willie, you OK?' Crawling over, I shook him. He was out for the count. Dragged myself on to the mattress before finishing the bottle and falling asleep.

Opened my eyes. Felt stiff as a board. Willie was lying on the floor. Then I remembered. Still in the same position. I shook him. Nothing. Needed a bottle. Got out.

Dipper, myself and Fred were all in the same cell, waiting to go into court, charged with nicking a box of wine from an off-licence. We'd given the law phoney addresses. (No fixed abodes can't be considered for bail.) Eventually we were brought out into No. 1 Court. After hearing the charges, the magistrate remanded our case until the following week and allowed us bail. A few days later, the three of us decided to skip bail. We jumped a train for Oxford and bought a few bottles of wine for the journey, but no tickets. At the ticket barrier our way was blocked by a ticket collector and some porters. We fought our way through them with punches and kicks. In the confusion the ticket collector had his ticket clipper pushed into his face. Outside the station, a long narrow road led us towards a pub, in the distance. Just before we reached the door, two black squad cars purred silently up behind us. Three or four big coppers jumped out, swiftly outrunning and overpowering us. Taken to the local nick, finger-printed, charged with causing actual bodily harm. Slung into separate cells. Slept soundly until the following morning when we were taken into court. After hearing the charges – travelling without tickets and fighting, occasioning actual bodily harm on a member of the railway staff – we were again remanded, this time without bail, to Oxford Prison for three weeks.

As we waited in the cell to be brought into court, Freddie got into one of his mad moods. 'We can beat this charge.'

Dipper smiled at me. 'How we gonna do that?'

'Listen, you cunts, we'll say the fucking ticket bloke attacked us with the clippers and he accidentally got them in his own face.'

'Yeah, Fred, and along with being accident prone we'll tell the court he's got a terrible persecution complex too! That should do it nicely; we'll walk out of this one easy,' I said.

Fred jumped me. We grabbed each other by the throat. Dipper got in between us, just as the copper came to the door to open us up. As we stood in the dock facing the magistrate, the sun shone in through an old-fashioned window, lighting up a coat of arms emblazoned on the wall above the magistrate's head. Fred shouting recklessly at the copper's evidence brought my mind back to the trial. It all sounded good until they brought in the ticket collector with a plaster on his cheek. Then they showed the court exhibit A. Funny how vicious-looking ticket clippers appear to be when the law hold them up in a certain way. We got six months each.

Just settling down in the Oxford nick, when the Governor told us they had found out we were wanted in London on theft charges. Sent back under escort the following day. We received five months each on top of our other sentence and were sent to Pentonville Prison to do our time. Eleven months. Not a bad result. On reception we were split up – Dipper and myself allocated to B Wing, Fred to A Wing. I never saw Fred again. Years later I heard how he was thrown from a doss-house window three floors up and landed on the spikes below. He was robbed as he lay impaled. Some things I know about. Some I only hear.

The screw escorted us over to the alky vat – the rag shop. The Dipper didn't look too sharp, shuffling along, face drained, eyes blank. Quiet as a church mouse. On reception, he'd over-acted, trying to work his ticket to the cushy hospital wing. They weren't fooled. The hospital screws gave him the liquid cosh – filled him so full of Largactil he doesn't know his arse from his elbow this morning. All the heads at the top end of the shop looked up as the screw's keys jangled in the lock.

'Two on from B Wing, sir.'

'Thank you, Mr Rose.'

The observation screw altered the board count from thirty-nine to forty-one. The walking screw, a big iron-featured old bastard, points us to our place without a word. There must have been over a hundred cons in the shop, most of them sitting at long heavy benches unravelling copper wire from Post Office cables; some walking towards the toilet or else coming back from it; others bending over the shoulders of their mates, whispering out of the corners of their mouths. We were all dressed in grey trousers, heavy black shoes and blue striped shirts – so full of starch they feel like straightjackets at first, but after a couple of days' wear they become limp as a wet lettuce. I was in between two cons who looked and acted like Dipper did earlier on; only difference is these two ain't been subdued with Largactil. Taking a piece of wire from one of the bundles in front of the old con beside me, I start to unravel it half-heartedly. 'Bump!'

Big Hunter, the screw, throws down a pile of wire on my hands, then leans over me all flash-like. 'Let's see you do some work for a change.' The bastard's on the biggest fiddle: three-quarters of the men are retards through the drink, working like zombies for Hunter who gets paid by the Post Office. I'll have to be careful. He knows he's got me for a while this trip. Most of the cons suck up to him. I hate the bastard and in the past have been stupid enough not to hide my feelings. Before he walks away, Hunter smiles to a young con opposite me. 'Going out tomorrow, Jenkins?'

'Yes, sir.' Hunter walked off, purring like a ginger tom.

Everybody loves a discharge; but a reception . . . that's another thing. As he nears his office, a fit merchant throws a wobbler, falling backwards off his chair. Jerking and shaking on the floor, the chair caught up in his legs, making an awful racket like it's attacking him. The cons at the table jump out the way. Hunter stops. Walks over. Grabs the epileptic by his shoulders and pulls him clear out into the middle of the shop. One of the trusties rushes up with a pillow kept in the office for just such emergencies. Hunter grabs it, puts it under the e.p.'s head, stands up straight, runs his eyes over the shop, nods to the watcher in the box, walks on down to his glass-fronted office. I ain't looking forward to sitting in between a bunch of nutcases, day in day out for the next seven months. Besides everything else, it might start to rub off! Got to think things out a bit. I'm in a single cell. That's great. Only trouble is it's got three beds in it. I already gave the No. 1 half an ounce of tobacco to put me there, but if they were to have a sudden crime wave on the outside . . . So I've got to get rid of them other two beds. Then any busy screw is gonna think it's a natural single cell.

The hard-digested food constipates the whole prison. With one recess shared by fifty cons the smell is foul and the queue is long. The door is waist high – others waiting, perhaps leaning over every now and then, glancing down with agitated faces. It's no longer a natural function. It's hard to go, harder still not to.

It was raining, so outside exercise was cancelled. We were allowed to walk round the landings for half an hour instead; gets rid of pent-up emotions, as the Deputy Governor puts it. As I'm passing the recess Stanton grabs my arm, falling into step with me. He's interesting enough if he's talking about what he's nicked for – knocking off antiques, oil paintings, stuff like that – but anything else, which means his girlfriend, how hard prison is, etc., creases me up with tension. Today it's the girlfriend – he hasn't had a letter for three weeks. He shows me her photo for the hundredth time and asks me what I think is wrong. He just takes it for granted that I'm supposed to know about girlfriends and that I'm a bit of a gangster on the outside, even though I've told him I'm a wino and, to keep it simpler still, that I have no family. Passing back the photo, I told him what a darling his girl looks but his eyes went watery and I wished I'd put it another way. Anyhow, you could see by the photo she wasn't the sort of girl to be sitting in every night knitting, so I said, 'It's them fucking screws, they're lazy bastards and if they know you've got a tasty bird waiting for you they get jealous and sling your letters to the back of the pile.' With that he cheered up and started on about some old-master painting he nicked one time.

I was glad when exercise was over, pleased to be back in my cell away from Stanton who couldn't tell the difference between a lust-pot and the girl next door . . . Thought he was in a hard prison! Well, the hardest thing about it as far as I was concerned was trying to have a shit in the recess. It was grim-looking (the prison, I mean), but then so were some of them holiday camps, and people paid to stay there. I remembered another prison all them years ago and that other good-looking bastard, Borthwed, with a new girl every night looking into his eyes while he took an hour to drink one pint; and the fight in the cell with that tough bastard and the big provost sergeant with the scar down his chops, the staffs with their sticks, every last one of them stone raving mad – and us risking life and limb for a smoke. Some good blokes, some cunning psychopaths, a lot of them gone now. Some dying in police custody, others in prison cells, but most because of the impossible life on the streets.

I see Jock's eyes again, full of silent agony, writhing, struggling, sinking back trapped, his life slowly flowing out from the wound in his neck.

And I'm still here drinking and smoking, doing my little bits of nick. It seems such an idle boast. I'm neither proud nor ashamed of it. It just is. As I'm rolling a smoke the spyhole clicks – the night watch checking the count. For some reason I burst out laughing. He gets confused perhaps thinking that I'm cracking up – and starts cooing through the door, 'Take it easy, son, you'll be all right.' I couldn't stop. 'What's the matter, why are you laughing?'

'I don't know really.'

Then he made me roll up: he said, 'Do you believe in God? You should read the Bible, I shall say a prayer for you.' I laughed and laughed. Turning out my light he shuffled off mumbling to himself, convinced that I had finally cracked.

I don't hear the dinner bell go until the screw's voice hits me. 'Stop work, stop talking.'

The first batch of cons gets in line as the escort screw drags over the low box platform. He throws it down on the floor with a bang, an annoyed look on his face, kicks it into position like he could do without such heavy labour. 'OK. Let's have you.'

The first con takes out his tobacco tin and other stuff he's got in his pockets, steps up on the platform, spreads his arms out shoulder high. The screw runs his hands over him, checks inside his tin, taps him on the shoulder, gives him the all-clear nod. He steps off to form a line by the gate. The screw, a bored expression on his face, beckons the next one on to be frisked. When everyone's been checked into line, they take us over to the main wing for dinner on a tray, then bang us up for two hours.

A couple of days later, the guardsman, Blake, comes on the wing. 'Hello, James. What you doing?'

'Nine months for demanding with menaces.'

'How'd you get caught?'

'Aw, you know how it is – one bottle led to another. What landing you on, Johnny?'

'I got a single on the Ones. Where you at?'

'In a three. It's fucking murder.'

So I take him along, show him my place. 'Help me get rid of that extra bed and you can move into the other one. Square it with the number one.'

'Great. I'll see that number one now.' He's back after five minutes. Tells me it's OK, so we take the extra bed down and stick it in the number one cell.

Time went on.

Sometimes after we got banged up for the evening, Blake

would be telling me stories about the ladies he got in with. Plenty of lies in between the truth. Then the night would fly. By day, in the rag shop, it seemed as if Hunter had fixed the clock on the wall not to move. The air would become heavy. I'd look round at the other cons' faces: lips moving, trying to shout their secrets above the blasting roar of the wireless, or just talking to themselves. At these times, talking becomes hard labour. Hunter should be done for GBH on our ear drums over that radio. Still, it makes you keep your eyes open 'cause you can't hear the walking screw until he's right behind you.

They brought a con into the shop one day just before dinner time – young-looking, crew-cut hair, solidly built, about six foot tall. His eyes were the thing you noticed most. A sort of diluted blue colour that bore straight into you or anything else they settled on. Big Blakey reckoned he's a Jock awaiting transfer to the local nut-house and that he's also a psychopath. I had to laugh. I seemed to remember Blake had done some time over killing a guy for a bottle of wine. Perhaps it takes one to know one.

Mad Gerry was brought before the Governor accused of attempting to nick pills on the hospital wing. Told the Governor the screws were lying. The Governor nearly had a fit: 'If my officers told me you were caught riding round the landings on a motor cycle, I'd want to know where you got the petrol from!' He lost two weeks' remission and got a week in the punishment block.

Most of the cons reckon the food's horrible. I agree – especially if you stand in the dinner queue behind a fit merchant when he throws a wobbler and fires his trayful of mush backwards all over you as he goes down. It's all hurry up and wait. Wait in lines of twos for the screws to open the gates into the bath-house once a week; wait outside the canteen for half-an-ounce of tobacco; for food; everything and everybody's waiting; for the screw to let them out the front gate.

Time moves slowly on. Now and then an old wino is found dead in his cell from the easy living. Another morning, a guy got a 'Dear John'. Fired himself off the fives, landed in the safety net. No real damage done – mashed his face up a bit though.

Dipper's back to his old self again. Jumped out of his cell in his underpants this morning, then asked the screw, 'What time's supper, have I missed it, sir?'

Screw got nervous as a cat. 'No, no, lad, plenty of time yet, let's get you back in your cell and put some clothes on in case you catch your death.'

With Dipper still winding him up, he walked off, a faraway look in his eyes, wondering why he didn't get a job in some nice, quiet nut-house.

I was looking round the shop trying to give my eyes a break. Hunter was talking to the young crew-cut Jock, both standing out on the middle of the floor. Suddenly, without any shouting or fussing, Crew Cut shot out a right, catching Hunter on the chin, knocking him back against a bench. He rushed in trying to hit him again. Hunter slid over to the side, grabbing Jock round the body, pinning his hands to his sides. As they wrestled round the floor, the box screw hit the alarm bell. They were still rolling round when the heavy mob rushed in. All four of them dived on Jock – smashed him unconscious. Didn't care who seen them advertising either. Then, picking him up between them like a sack of spuds, they carted him off to the punishment block.

Before he went into his office, Hunter turned his head, scanning the shop with his eyes.

Soon as Blakey wolfed his dinner down today, he was up straightening his tie in the shaving mirror and combing his hair. After about the twentieth combing, he gave up trying to improve on his already immaculate appearance and took to pacing up and down the cell like a caged tiger. 'How do I look?' he asked me for the sixth time.

'You look fine. What time's your visit?'

'One thirty. Hope she comes.'

He was really chuffed when he'd received a letter from one of the posh ladies he'd been telling me about, saying how she had heard about where he was and was coming to visit him. A few minutes later, the screw's key rattled the lock.

'Blake.'

'Yes, guv.'

'Visit outside.'

Blake came off his visit into the shop, beaming all over his face. Gave me a big wink as he made his way over to the Jocks on the Waterloo table. Back in the cell that evening, just finishing my tea, when he slings a tenner on the table.

'Fucking hell, Jim. How you get it through?'

He roared out laughing at my surprised look. 'Laura's got a magic kiss. Passed it into my mouth! Ha, ha, ha. We're going to have plenty of smokes and plenty of grub from now on. I'm going into the tobacco business.'

'God bless Laura!'

'Yeah. Tenners out her mouth.'

'Here, Jim, how much you think might come out if you kissed her somewhere else?'

'You cunt!'

'Ha, ha, ha. That's what I mean.'

14

Big Pat Conners came on the wing one day – doing four months.
With his hair cut to the bone, he always reminded me of a
soldier in the French Foreign Legion. Fit and tough-looking.
We've pulled a few strokes together in the past. He was looking
very serious when he greeted me. 'Hello, Johnny. Did you hear
about Long John Flynn?'

'No. What?'

'He's dead. Fell under the train at the Angel tube.'

'Jesus. But how?'

'Drunk. Lost his balance. Fell right out in front of it.'

I felt sad as hell. Long John was a great guy.

Then the Fox came in – doing nine months – and things bright-
ened up in the rag shop. First thing he done was to fix with the
screw for me to sit opposite him at his table. Next we straightened
the doctor's orderly with tobacco, so I got a jar of malt every
week and a pint of milk every day. I was getting as strong as a
lion. We were fucking about on the table all day, having a laugh
and telling jokes. The time started to fly. I had about a month
to do when the Fox said to me one morning, just after we'd got
in the shop, 'Listen, if I told you about a game that if you were
waiting for seven o'clock on a Sunday night for the pubs to open,
and you was playing this game, you'd forget the pubs wasn't open
and not worry about the time, what would you say?'

'I'd say there ain't no such game.'

'There is, Johnny. It's not really a game though – more like olden day warfare. It's called chess. And I'll teach you the moves if you want to learn.'

'OK,' I said, not really interested one way or the other.

Harry drew a board in between us on the prison bench, made some chess pieces from little bits of paper, and showed me the moves. After a week, I managed to play a game without forgetting how the pieces moved. Harry let our first games go on until he got tired of messing around. Then he'd make a few quick moves and I'd find the knife at my king's throat, forcing me to resign. I was falling slowly in love with chess and was delighted when Blakey told me he could play. What a joy. Now my games didn't have to stop when I was locked in the cell. Blakey wrote out to Laura, asking for a chess set. Our games became even more enjoyable after it arrived.

I met many players in my brief chess career. Most of them were clever, many of them were brilliant. Some of them were even geniuses, but none of those games gave me the same thrill as those first games I used to play with Harry and Blakey. I forgot to eat, such was the power chess held over me in those days. Even the time needed for a visit to the loo was begrudged if I was in the middle of a game. Even Hunter turned a blind eye when some con would leave his place to come over to me for a game. I usually won all the games against other players except Harry. He told me great chess players are called masters; the absolute greatest are called grand masters. It gave me the feeling you have when you get a crush on a classy woman, but can't get near her. I decided I was going to get very near them grand masters though. Harry thought I was going too far and tried to stop me getting disappointed.

'Listen. The experts, champions, masters and grand masters are all middle- and upper-class people. They start about ten or twelve years of age and lead normal lives, going to good schools and universities. They drink tea instead of methylated spirits, and they don't, etc., etc. . . . Of course, if you packed up drinking, you would be able to play much better than you can now. But at your age it would still be impossible to win a tournament and play so well that they'd put your games in the paper.'

I took no notice. Flushed with excitement, I said, 'Well, if that's what it takes, I'll pack up drinking.'

Yes, it happened just like that – no dribs or drabs. Chess is a jealous lover. Will tolerate no other, especially in the form of too much drink. I gave myself to her completely, body and soul, and for the first time in my life I began to live without a constant nagging desire for drink. I was like a person who finds God, only this God was a warrior made out of wood who derives his power from man. A nudge of the finger alerts the bishop contesting control of a diagonal. Another touch and the knight springs into action – with his peculiar way of moving causing many a heedless opponent's sudden downfall.

I was thirty years old and had become besotted with chess; ate it, drank it, dreamed about it. It had replaced everything in my mind. What would I need to do? I wrote two letters, one to Clive Soley at the probation office; the other to the Ley Clinic, Oxford, asking to be considered for another spell there. Clive Soley came to see me. I told him about the chess. He said he'd help me any way he could, if I wanted to beat the bottle. Left it at that. The clinic wrote back to say that they would have me, but one smell of drink and I would be out for good.

Christmas came and went. Then in January I was released. Eight o'clock in the morning. It was still dark as I stepped out the front gate on to the driveway.

'Hello, Johnny.' I was surprised to see three of the lads waiting for me in the frosty morning air.

'Hello, you fucking scallywags, what you doing out this early of a morning?'

'Come to meet you.'

I had a £4 discharge grant; gave them £2. 'I'm going to try and get off the drink, lads, so I'll be seeing you. OK?' They wished me all the very best of luck as they headed off to the Early House for a drink.

Had some breakfast in a café. Hung around till nine o'clock when the probation offices opened. I got in. Waited for Clive Soley. Then he drove me over to Paddington Station. On the way over we picked up a chess set for a pound. We had a cup of tea. Then he wished me luck, we shook hands, and I was off on the Oxford train. The first person I met when I walked into the clinic was Kate. As we shook hands I realized I still had a crush on her. Felt sad as hell that she was going with a doctor. Sober now, I became self-conscious about my ragged clothes. I was going to tell her I could play chess but it seemed such a silly boast. I wished I was a grand master. I was running out of things to say and I was glad when another nurse called me over to sign in. I was starting to get really tense. I wasn't used to being sober after coming out of nick. She was bent over a book writing as I came towards her. Looking up, her sudden friendly smile startled me. Funny how being locked up for only a few months makes normal things appear so interesting. What a pity it doesn't last.

'Hello, John, how are you? Have a seat. Did you have a nice journey up here?'

'Yes, thanks.'

I played chess with everyone that would give me a game and was soon able to beat everybody at the clinic. The only one to better me was a Polish cleaner. Later on I joined Oxford chess club. Never won many games there, though. The days consisted of group meetings and lectures on the effects and dangers of alcohol. One day they showed us a film about how one gets a wet brain. If half of it was true, mine was already going down for the third time.

The weeks had flown by. Now it was February and I had been one whole month without touching a drink. They allowed me to stay on at the clinic for a further week in order to be able to fix myself up with a room in Oxford. However, I considered London would be better for improving my chess. Leaving one morning towards the end of the week, I arrived back in London, going round to the probation office to see Clive Soley. He was surprised to see me back but very glad I was sober. He took me over to an alcoholic dry house in South London. There were six guys staying in the place and they had house rules about everything. They had been staying there some time and were suspicious of anything and everything in their efforts to keep off drink. They were not very friendly and talked only among themselves. After dinner each evening, when the table was cleared away and everyone settled down to watch the TV, I took out the chess board, set up the pieces, and studied tactics and strategy. The lads didn't seem to like chess. After about a week they got a house rule up about playing in the lounge. So I had to play upstairs after that. Only trouble was, there was no heating up there. Stuck it for a few days, but I couldn't concentrate with the cold. I brought the chess set back downstairs again. Everyone started mumbling and growling. It came to a head when the big guy who was acting as the house warden started shouting and pushing me out of the room. I dropped him with a left in the guts and right to the jaw. The probation bloke was quickly contacted. He was there within the hour. He said it was bad but was pleased no drink was involved. Then he lent me some money to book into a bed and breakfast.

It was a cold March evening when I called round to my mother's council flat. I rang the bell . . . waited . . . my mother opened the door. Of course I was expected, but my sudden appearance was still a surprise, though her face gave nothing away. It was the look in her eyes. We'd not seen each other for over ten years.

'Hello, John. How are you? Come in.'

'OK, Mum.'

My youngest brother, Dermott, was sitting with his girlfriend on the settee. I felt a bit awkward . . . a barbarian trying to adapt to a more refined way of life. I chatted with Dermott and his girl while my mother went into the kitchen to make tea.

'Oh, this is Janis,' said Dermott. I shook hands with Janis. She was a bit of a darling.

'Got any sisters, Janis?' I asked. She laughed.

'Yes, I have.'

'Put in a word for me?'

'Yes. But you'll have to wait, my sister's only seven.' We all laughed. I was pleased when they told me they could both play chess. My mother came back with the tea. After Dermott and Janis drank theirs, they went out. We sat quietly without saying a word for what seemed like a long time. Finally my mum looked at me. There were tears in her eyes.

'I never thought I'd see you alive again.' What could I say? 'I read in the paper where you came out of prison one morning and were arrested in the afternoon and sent back the next day.' I nearly laughed, but my mum looked too sad.

'I heard terrible things about winos fighting and killing each other in the parks at night. I couldn't sleep wondering where you were . . . maybe beaten so badly you couldn't move, lying in some dark cold street. Then I used to pray to the Virgin Mary for you.' I was embarrassed by her tenderness for me and stupid enough to try out a joke.

'There was a woman called Mary down there all right, but I don't think she was a virgin.' My mother ignored me. I poured us some more tea.

'There was a terrible story in the papers where an alcoholic was killed with a broken bottle, fighting in Euston Park! Why did you never contact us?'

'Look, Mum, it was the drink. You live their way or die.' Changing the subject, I told her about the chess. Then her face and eyes gradually grew calmer. She told me about her new job as a secretary in the Post Office, about Terry who was married now with kids, as were my two sisters, Bernadette and Philomena, who had emigrated to Australia some years back.

'Where did you get them clothes?'

'Off the welfare,' I said.

'They're two sizes too big for you and they're all crumpled and creased. Do you sleep in them or what?'

'Yes, I do.'

'Haven't you any heating in your room, then?'

'Oh, there's an electric fire, but I spend any money I get playing chess in coffee houses. I want to become good at the game.'

'Do you want to live here with us? There's plenty of room upstairs.'

Did I? 'That will be great, Mum. I'll go back tonight for my chess set and come back in the morning.'

She gave me a key and a warm smile.

15

A lot of straight people were unemployed. So no one was going to employ a thirty-year-old wino and ex con. I joined a chess club in a college. It was open every night except Saturdays and Sundays. I played every week night with Mr Kaufman. On the chess board he was a conniving old wolf, a mauler, cunning as twenty devils. No one enjoyed playing against him. He was a very tall, massively built old man with a large head and watery blue eyes that would become increasingly mocking, the deeper his opponent's chess troubles became. The old grey suit he wore was covered down the front with soup, gravy and tea stains. His trousers were held up with an old tie. I played him endlessly; and endlessly he smashed me. After we'd been playing for about two weeks, something clicked in my chess mind and I started to think before making a move, instead of making a move and then thinking. What a thrill – I had him on the run. I pressed my advantage cautiously. But he dug up moves from nowhere. He managed to survive every sudden lunge; but slowly, bit by bit, my advantage began to tell and I was just on the point of checkmating him. He mumbled something about the heat, got up and stood on a chair to open one of the large bay windows. As he stretched further up, his tie came loose and his trousers fell down round his ankles, leaving him fumbling with the window in a pair of long johns. The room became quiet as both men and women students stopped playing to look at Mr Kaufman. He never batted an eyelid: he turned round, pulled up his trousers, and got down off the chair, at the same time hitting the table with his free hand, scattering the chess pieces all over the floor. A new move? But after that he never won a game against me. The club secretary put me in the first team where I won all my match games for the club.

One night there was a big league match. I found myself placed on the lowest board in the lowest team. I asked the secretary why, given that I'd won every match so far. A little embarrassed, he told me that the players had complained. They had official grades and demanded that I be relegated as I did not have a grade. In a fit of anger I challenged the whole team, adding that I would play them simultaneously. They jumped at the chance to make me eat my words. I got a little worried in the week leading up to the display; perhaps I shouldn't have spoken so hastily. Anyway come the big night, half the team showed up: four of the strongest players, and I was playing them together! After an hour I had secured a winning position on each board. They reluctantly resigned but not before searching each position desperately for a microscopic flaw, a misplaced piece, a loose pawn, a bad bishop, a useless rook . . . witchcraft, my sudden death, anything that would redeem a crushed ego. Chess seems to turn the most sensitive of souls into mindless maniacs or 'tournament soldiers' as ex-World Champ Mikhail Botvinnik used to say. When you enter competitive chess the game enters your blood.

I gave up playing for clubs. Entering tournaments instead, I played in the open or highest section where, after winning a game, one is paired against increasingly stronger opponents – strong club players, candidate experts, experts, nationally graded players and so on.

All tournament games are played with a chess clock – that is, two clocks joined together. When one player makes his move, he presses a button which stops his clock and starts his opponent's clock. A red flag drops on the player's clock. Whoever fails to keep the time limit, regardless of the position on the board, loses the game. Weekend congresses with a fast time limit and long sessions of play up to twelve hours a day are very strenuous and result in fatigue and time troubles. The play is quite sharp. Active attacking chess is the order of the day and it's difficult to hold up a sustained, precise defence against such play. A score of the game must be made as you play. The moves are written down on a score sheet which must be handed to the tournament marshals at the end of each round. The only thought in everyone's head is to win.

Into this gruelling, competitive world we threw ourselves each weekend, seething with aggression, hunched over our boards like hawks mantling their prey. As in all sports, the opponents come in different shapes and sizes, temperaments and habits.

Talent and youth – that's what's needed for success at chess; with the emphasis on youth. Some approach the board with a slow purposeful manner without giving you a second glance – you simply don't count. No matter if you were God Almighty, it would not make the slightest difference to the result. They seem to imply that the outcome is a *fait accompli* for them; you only have to accept it with good grace.

One morning I was paired against a well-known player, who later became an international master. He sat down without a word and, with a flourish, unfurled a copy of *The Times*, raising it between us in a gesture of contempt for the fools he is sometimes forced to play. Then he made his move. I took advantage of his heedless approach to mount a sacrificial attack which gained me a winning position but, in the process, tangled up my pieces. It would take time for me to regroup but, after that, it would be all over for my opponent. He knew this. He also knew that time is of the essence and that to keep me at the board would result in no dinner break for me, no little rest before the next game; so I'd probably lose in the end, through weariness and fatigue. What's in it for my opponent? Nothing except revenge. I may be playing his mate in the next round!

A certain champion threw in a cunning sacrifice. It's an offer you can't refuse. He hated to lose and would sacrifice his grandmother to keep the title. 'Still, all good clean fun – lots better than drinking with a gang of maniacs,' he informed me with a cute little wink as he accidentally knocked a cup of tea into my lap. It didn't help him: he lost in the end.

Then there's the opponent who must leave at once – their mother's sick, their wife's bedridden, their father's dying of mysterious ailments – otherwise they would play on. But *under the circumstances* could they have a draw? Never mind that they're only a few moves away from losing altogether!

At other times I could have cut iron with my teeth; I felt so mad I'd have loved to throttle some of the buggers. After analysing the game with them, they'd pooh-pooh all my suggestions and negate all my strategies with a dismissive flick of the wrist – it simply wasn't done that way! It was against the code, the old school tie and all that! Never mind that I didn't belong to their school, wasn't I a chess player now – just like them? Nothing less than the best behaviour would be tolerated, old boy. Part of the code is to shake hands, win or lose, with friend and foe alike. This ritual is repeated before and after each game, regardless of results. Over come the hands: small, large, medium, enormous, clean, not so clean, dainty, delicate, strong, weak, hard, soft, limp, damp, dry. After this sporting gesture one is free to cheat, lie, hustle, harangue, pace up and down, fart loudly, laugh, sneeze, bang the pieces down, intimidate, glare and stare until the game ends, once more with a gentlemanly handshake.

Then there was Little Yabs, a talented schoolboy with a flair for mathematics, who had the habit, when making a move, of screwing the piece down into its new square with such force as if no other move were possible.

At the end of a tournament everybody is jaded and disorientated. Some leave for Cornwall and end up in Scotland or else they land up in hospital, suffering from brain seizures. Some forget who they are; others disappear completely; some go straight to a psychiatrist; a few crack up right on the spot, holding their head between their hands and letting out loud pitiful moans – hard to know whether they're venerating the grand masters or in genuine pain.

Gradually my game became stronger.

I played and drew against three county champions. I decided I was strong enough to play for the county title, a match of six games. I won my first two. Then I was paired against Vearsman, a very strong player, who only a week previously had defeated a famous master. A clean-cut smart young executive type, he shook hands at the board, polite enough, saying, 'Good evening, Mr Healy. I'm surprised to meet you. They say you are a tramp off the streets.' I saw red and fell for it. Grabbing him by his tie, I dragged him over the table; with my free hand I caught a fistful of his hair, pushing his face on to the chess pieces. It was an act of sudden aggression, instantly regretted. Suddenly a hand wrenched my neck back. Others grabbed my arms, my legs; then lifted me up, face down, carrying me out. One of them squeezed my balls so hard, I got a pain in my guts making me dizzy.

Outside the four bastards were just about to lay into me when a match captain called Mike Crenus intervened. 'All right lads, he's OK. Leave him with me.'

What could they do with an unexpected witness around? Crenus was a very good guy. Two days later I received a letter from the Middlesex County Chess Association banning me from that and any future championships. Mike Crenus told me I'd better write and apologize to the Chess Association or they might take it into their heads to ban me altogether. I wrote and apologized. I was very surprised a week later when I received a letter back saying that after hearing evidence about the incident from my opponent (no less!) they had decided to let me continue to play if I so wished. I was very pleased. Vearsman was a real sportsman too. We met in March a year later, both turning the board into a bloodbath in our efforts to prove something, but the game eventually ended with a quiet draw.

My game kept improving. After playing an unusual sacrifice in a match against the Civil Service, the former British champion and theoretician Leonard Barden spoke to me. He was influential at the time in helping Britain's juniors to become world standard players. Although I was too old to be considered for this, he none the less recommended me for a Slater Award. A few weeks later I drew against a grand master. The sacrifice of a pawn in the opening gave me a raging attack, but eventually the grand master neutralized the position. My attack burnt out. But I was delighted with a draw against my illustrious opponent. A businessman called Frank Foster saw the game and sponsored me too. What a bit of luck! I was released from money worries, allowing me to travel around the country, playing in the strongest tournaments.

Sometimes I played against so-called celebrities. Usually they lacked strategical understanding. I was surprised, however, when playing against the Shah of Iran's nephew, Prince Bauman, to find myself forced on to the defensive. After the opening moves, I just managed by a hair's breadth to survive his powerful attack until he got careless. Then I beat him. Found out after the game that he had an international reputation.

Another night my opponent was a nineteen-year-old kid. He

refused to shake hands, giving me a world-weary look instead. He was a chess genius and later became a grand master. I never knew all this and sacrificed my queen against him. After staring at the position for fifteen minutes he mumbled his resignation and left.

For fun I used to give simultaneous displays of chess where I would play around fifteen players at one time, moving quickly from board to board, usually winning all the games. About this time I started to play blindfold chess – not really blind-folded – just sitting with my back to the board while my opponent had the board facing him. I also won or drew most of these games. Eventually I could play six games at once while blindfolded.

The Russian grand master Raphael Vaganian, who was rated second in the world at the time, came to England. I managed to draw a very difficult game against him. Got a bit carried away: challenged a young British grand master in front of his mates at a chess coffee house. He took no chances. He played cautiously, eventually grinding out a win after a two-hour fight. Refused to play a return match. There was a tournament being held in the club where I'd been barred over the county incident some years back. There were fifty-four seasoned London League players competing in it. I entered too. I wanted to win it. So I gave up smoking and started to practise yoga, breath control and meditation. Working alone, using books as my teacher, I made a little progress. We played one match game each week. I kept winning, until I had ten straight wins. No one could match that score. I asked for the winner's shield. The old chess master said I now had to play last year's champion.

'Did last year's champion have the same score as me?'

'No. It doesn't matter, you still have to play him.' Seemed like a bit of a middle-class fix. What could I do? The meaning was becoming crystal clear. He was a young guy studying at university. It's easy to be a chess champion if you learn the game young – takes some going if you're over thirty. We shook hands.

In the first game I played cautiously to force a draw. We met again. We drew once more. In the third game I opened quietly; the simple development of my pieces encouraged my opponent to play boldly with an ambitious plan. For a while it looked like last year's winner was going to become this year's winner as well until I found a sacrifice which crippled his daring attack; after a further few moves he resigned.

Now I was a chess champion. Strong players invited me to their homes. Hadn't been to many homes before. They were nice. They had everything. We'd play on a large wooden table, violin music in the background, oil paintings on the walls, tea served in patterned cups by wives in lovely dresses and sensible, low-heeled shoes. They spoke of trying unsuccessfully for babies, the state of the Government, high income tax, the cost of children's school fees, daughters that came home far too late at night. Was I married? Did I have a good job? Where did I live? And we talked about people who'd perhaps be better off if they played less chess.

Although these homes seemed peaceful, within that calm there was strain. I began to wonder about chess: the players living on their nerves, full of stress, myself included. No matter how good one became, there would always be someone to beat you. And anyway, the greats all had names like Alekine, Capablanca, Nimzowitch, Bogolubov, Bobotson, Stallberg, Tschigorin. What chance would I have with a name like mine?

In that world I had no real friends. The game of chess is about competition, not friendship. The only friends I'd had were back in the parks. Perhaps I knew I wasn't going to be a grand master.

More than anything else I needed friends; I'd throw away winning games just for the company. I wanted to be a part of those homes, but each time the chess game was over I was back on the street. The tension was back. Chess was like the drink. It was going to be a big wrench to get out of it and I had nothing to take its place.

I was still getting money from the chess grants. I started to go to the seaside – spent hours walking along the beach. Pure air seems to stop one's mind racing – at least, it does mine. I tried oil painting, copying a Gainsborough I'd seen on a wall. I bought prints of some other famous paintings. I liked the rural scenes best; they reminded me of the farm in Ireland.

Since I considered that my small efforts at meditation had helped me win the chess tournaments, what, I wondered, would be the results of bigger efforts? I read many books about it and practised for half an hour twice each day.

Apart from feeling more relaxed, nothing magic happened. But I kept at it. After about a year I saw an advertisement in a magazine. An address was given where deep and spontaneous meditation could be induced. It made me laugh at first, considering my own feeble results over the last eighteen months. The young lady who answered the phone assured me that the advert was true – the severest austerities required of a student were to navigate the rush-hour traffic to reach them. At the centre it was explained that there is an energy, known as Kundalini, lying dormant at the base of the spine. A form of Shakti could be awakened, after which it would slowly move along the spine to the brain, purifying nerve centres, until finally, after many years of intense meditation, the mind itself would become purified. Wasteful or mundane thoughts would no longer be manufactured, leaving one with a tranquil mind, thus enabling one to receive a clearer understanding of the consciousness that gives motive power to every single thing. That's roughly the theory; practice is another matter. I started to meditate with the people at the centre every week. I certainly felt an increasing calmness in my everyday life. I was really enjoying it.

One night a lady came to give a talk about the meditation master, a Siddha yogi, who was the lineal head of this form of yoga. The talk was very interesting, but the lady more so. They say meditation calms and slows the breath. This woman took mine away completely. With her thick shoulder-length black hair, beautiful high-cheekboned face, sparkling grey eyes full of Shakti that would light up, dancing with ecstasy, as she talked of the yoga path, her otherwise austere countess looks would change to those of a young girl when she laughed. Her long slender form sat easily in the lotus posture. What a gorgeous figure of a woman! After the talk we had tea and cakes. Everybody wanted to ask her questions. The only question in my head was would she come out with me? I found out that she attended the centre every evening. Her name was Marianne. She was descended from the Hungarian aristocracy and had fled the Russian invasion with her mother. Her father had been killed in the uprising.

I also became more interested in meditation and I too attended the centre every evening. She seemed very friendly and whenever we met she gave me a nice smile. I nicknamed her the Countess and approached her after meditation one evening – asked if she fancied coming to the pictures one night. She looked straight at me with those beautiful grey eyes. My heart skipped a beat. 'Yes, I'd love to.' What a thrill. She smiled. I didn't know if meditation could transform my mind, but the Countess's smile certainly could.

The following week she phoned me and invited me over.

The road was in darkness owing to a power cut but the frost was twinkling on the trees as I made my way to her house. All along the pavement little dabs of snow reflected the moon's rays and, in the absence of street lamps, acted as natural cats' eyes to guide the way. I pressed the bell and waited. The cold air gave me a light-headed buzz and I was floating in contentment as she opened the door. It was a large old mansion-type house. Her mother, who owned it, was a nice regal-featured old girl who was fond of playing bridge. She occupied the top half and the Countess occupied the ground floor.

She gave me some tea and cakes and made conversation easy: all that was required of me were a few well-placed yesses and noes and ohs and ahs. But I knew that I couldn't go on like this. I'd told her I was a professional chess player all my life (slightly true). I was desperately trying to guard against making a sudden blunder. As we became more used to each other she would naturally expect to know more details – fine if she was Liverpool Lil's sister . . . She was pouring more tea when the gloomy thought struck me that the Countess and her world were totally beyond my reach. It wasn't just the money and education, more the personality and feelings. Mine were hyped up and geared to attacking and warding off threats, so even the most innocent question worried or startled me.

I said, 'That's a pretty dress you're wearing.'

She thanked me but when she asked, looking sideways at me, 'Do you really think so or are you just saying that?' I was taken aback. Not many people, and especially classy women, had ever been concerned about my opinion of them or their stuff.

'No, no, you look terrific,' I managed to stutter and was rewarded with a lovely smile.

She had charisma, this Countess of mine. Everything about her fascinated me: from the way strands of her hair would fall loose on to her face to the way her dress would swirl if she stopped suddenly, half turning to greet someone. At the time

I thought it might even be madness, but a madness that I fully enjoyed. Sometimes when I called she would be playing the piano. I got to like Schubert, Mozart, Bach and Co. I felt sorry for Liszt though – a lifetime spent chasing birds and the one he really fancies enters a convent and he ends up in a monastery! We would go to the cinema, or sometimes she would take me to visit her friends. When the Countess introduced us they would look straight at me with clear and guileless eyes, not a mark or blemish on those healthy faces. No sudden movements either; all their actions seemed to me slow and deliberate like they had all the time in the world to say 'hello' and repeat your name. No mumbling out of the side of the mouth here! It had the effect of lifting me out of myself. I'd get a feeling that somehow I had developed a knack to charm their fullest attention.

They all seemed tall and shapely, especially the women. Their boyfriends were big and fit-looking. I was surprised at first that they didn't use their size to threaten with. Perhaps they didn't know how; but they knew other things like how to make £2 into £5 and tell each other how to do it. Then a girlfriend would glide up and talk about a little restaurant she'd found where a certain wine tasted delicious with the duck and orange sauce; or how Cynthia was just finishing her job to go abroad for a time, while Gloria and her boyfriend had just returned and were already talking about going off again.

What did I talk about? I didn't talk about anything. There didn't seem to be any kind of hook to hang our stuff together with.

Over the next few weeks I started to talk less freely. Thinking before speaking replaced what little spontaneity I previously had. One evening as we were walking towards the tube, laughing and talking about the funny habits that some people who practise yoga possess, I said that perhaps they, too, considered us to have odd ways – although I didn't think we had. A serious expression crossed her face and she said, 'Well, I think we have. I'm a bit bitchy myself, and I don't know, John, but I find you a bit secretive.' Glancing at me, she added tactfully, 'Oh, I don't know, I suppose we're all a bit secretive in our own way really.' I wanted to put my arms around her, tell her I loved her, loved her more than anything; tell her about my past, everything.

I was besotted by her. But, painfully, I began to think of myself as her inferior. Class, her accent, her education . . . money. Then we seemed not to be so close. After a while she told me she was going to India to stay with the Master for some months. The evening before she was due to leave they held a farewell party at one of her friends' houses. There was a lot of wine about – everybody was laughing and giggling. I was sad as hell. Marianne came over – asked me why I didn't consider visiting India too. I wanted to put my arms round her, kiss her, hold her, stop her from going away. Instead I said, 'I might go to India sometime.'

As the weeks went by the sadness would not go. She was always in my mind. The quick solution would have been alcohol. I was fighting a very bitter battle with myself, avoiding taking that way out again. I didn't know what to do until a couple of other devotees, Liz and Alan, asked if I'd like to travel to India with them. I thought I might be better off being hopeless near the Countess. If the grief could kill me I might see her once more before it did. I still had some money from the chess grants. I gave it to Liz and she booked the flight.

We landed in India. That day should have been most auspicious – the one on which a disciple meets a master. The only master I wanted to meet had black hair, grey eyes and honey-coloured skin. The Master Swami, Muktananda, lived in a large temple at Ganeshpouri, surrounded, I was told, by beautiful gardens. We walked to the station through a market town full of stalls, animals, smells, heat, flies and people hustling us to buy. Only one thought in my mind, the Countess. No conquering hero coming to the welcoming arms of a lover here; more like a peasant begging an audience with a lady.

But what other way could she see me? What could I offer her? Penniless, jobless, no formal education – the more I thought about it the more hopeless I felt. The dream was collapsing, I couldn't face her. Many people were boarding the train for Ganeshpouri – I caught a train going in the opposite direction to Bombay.

Standing packed like a sardine, I became aware that all eyes were on me. Then I felt a tug at my back pocket and realized that the hunt had begun. I put my bags between my knees and my hands on my pockets. Then I felt the heat. It hit me like an electric fan, the sweat rolled into my eyes and the old tension started to build up around the neck and shoulders.

When the train got to Bombay all I saw was brown faces and staring eyes. After walking for an hour I felt really weird. I realized that I was thirsty, but I didn't know where to get a drink. I was surrounded by people, but I might as well have been on the moon. At last I spotted this shed which was really a shop. I got a tea, and in the process learned that to purchase something in India can be a severe hassle.

As I was drinking the tea I noticed them. They seemed to materialize from under rocks and stones, their little hands outstretched, mutely begging.

They did not seem like children but reminded me of tiny clockwork toys that just glided silently around. I started off again. I walked for hours. Was I weary! Must find somewhere to stay . . . Every now and then I stopped outside flop-houses calling themselves hotels – all smiles until I asked the price, then they priced themselves out of business. I sat down opposite a picture of a famous Indian saint who seemed to be an authority on who made the best puja tables around there at the most divine and heavenly prices. All the billboards, pictures of film stars, adverts and awnings were dreamy, soft and watery, as though the artist was too frightened of running out of paint to lay it on any bolder.

Two guys were standing with their backs to me talking. They had been behind me since I left the station. Hoisting my bag up on my shoulder I crossed the street and tried one more hotel. No luck. The bigger the dump the higher the price! The two guys stopped every time I did. Hard to be brave when you're weary, so into the Sheraton I went – one of the most expensive hotels in the world, never mind India. I sat down in the reception area. How the rich live! Must have cost at least £200 a night. And you can only sleep in one bed. Gave it about half an hour, then hit the street again. The two bastards were still outside, leaning against the wall smoking, calm as you please. Fear and frustration got the better of me, I walked right up to them. They never batted an eyelid at my approach. 'Don't keep following me,' I said viciously. I was in a right temper and also afraid.

'What are you talking about?' said the heavier one, coolly and in very good English.

'You know what I'm talking about, so fuck off, you pair of cunts.' I saw their eyes go, my guts tightened, but they didn't react to that. Instead, the same one stripped his teeth, trying to work his face up into a smile that wasn't going to make it all the way up to his eyes.

'Have you any traveller's cheques to sell?' he asked me.

'No, I ain't got anything to sell.'

He acted like he hadn't heard me. 'How many have you got?'

'You pair of cunts, why don't you listen? Better still, fuck off!'

That did it. They started waving their hands about like two demented monkeys, shouting, 'Why are you using that filthy language in this most sacred country?'

By now, a small crowd had gathered. They weren't saying anything, but all eyes were fixed on me. There wasn't a lot I could say either, except repeat, 'I told you not to keep following me.'

'He is a most disgusting person,' said the second one, trying for the sympathy of the crowd. He didn't have much trouble getting it. Most of them were growling by now anyway, unless it was their stomachs rumbling. I'd already sussed I wouldn't be able to make a run for it, and where would I run to? My first attempts at international relations were off to a terrible start, and to top it all the crowd joined in . . . looking ferocious . . . shouting, spitting.

How the hell did it get to this? It was like a scene right out of the Bible. And what happens there? Not a lot; they just stone you to death!

Pack it up, I told myself. Don't panic. It's only a bit of fear got at you because you're in a foreign country. They can't kill you. Even so, there would have been lots of pain if they'd all attacked me! I couldn't kid myself out of that one. How many blokes have I known who could have given a good account of themselves there without a drink? Not many, but there have been one or two. How I wished I was one of them. Not that I was much good with a drink either, but at least it would help to keep that old fear down and deaden pain.

Two big blond blokes, each about seven foot tall and six foot between the shoulders, elbowed their way through the crowd right up beside me. Everyone went quiet.

'Vot is zee trouble for you?' asked one of them.

Before I could reply the two hustlers started shouting frantically at them, 'He has insulted us, using the most foul language.' It was hard to see what they hoped to gain out of this unless they were in league with the church.

'Ah, zat is most distressing,' said the other blond guy.

'What?' I roared. 'The bastards have been following me all afternoon at the hustle and . . .'

'Yes, yes, I see vot zee trouble is,' said the first one, at the same time catching my face between his hands and giving me what I take is a wink to keep quiet. Then, lifting my eyelids up, he started making clucking noises. Everyone went silent watching this performance – looking on with the same awe an audience has for a magician.

'Yes, one of zee most severe cases of sunstroke I have seen for a long time. Come along, we must get you into hospital right away,' he continued. Then, putting his arm round my shoulder, he walked me straight through the crowd and slowly on up the street, all the while repeating, 'He'll be all right now, we shall take care of him.'

I sagged with relief when we finally got clear of that mob. They asked me what it was all about. I told them, making a big point about the two guys following me. After I finished they said I should go straight to the ashram, 'And be careful what you say to people here because there are some things up with which they will not put!' They stopped a taxi and bundled me into it, telling the driver to take me to the station. We soon got there . . . Seemed I'd just gone round in a circle!

I still hadn't found a place for the night. Maybe I could sleep out in the country in a haystack? With this idea I caught the Ganeshpouri train. I kept looking out of the window for a haystack but I didn't even see any hay. Then I remembered that they'd got snakes in this part of the world and wild tigers. This was getting complicated. I left the train at the end of the line. Now I wasn't thinking straight. I sat down in the street.

The Indians were looking at me, but I didn't care. Everything seemed to have gone quiet. All the people's lips were moving but no sound was coming out. This struck me as really funny. Maybe it was the funniest thing I'd ever seen, but somehow I didn't feel like laughing, so I sat there very quiet. I became aware that an old man was talking to me. For how long I don't know. But at last I heard his voice. 'Bus for temple. You for temple?' Yes, of course I want the temple bus. I fell asleep on the bus and awoke at the temple, a beautiful white building like a fairy-tale palace. The devotees were chanting the evening lays, so I was allocated a bed and, after a shower, I fell asleep.

A slow whining drone suddenly awoke me. The sound seemed a bit eerie. I didn't like it. While I was lying there, puzzling out what kind of fly sounds like that, it stopped, and I liked that even less. 'Bloody hell!' I must have jumped about ten feet in the air as I realized what it was. It was the dreaded old mosquito. In all the films I have ever seen about hot countries, whoever got bitten by a mosquito died, after first shivering, shaking and sweating all over the screen. Not even Sophia Loren was safe from those bastards. I shot out to the showers. When I got back I dressed quickly and sat on the edge of the bed. It was about 4 a.m., but even at this hour most of the people in the room were up. Suddenly there came the throb and boom of conches and the blare of trumpets. The sounds echoed and re-echoed around the dormitories and neighbouring country-side. Everyone dropped what they were doing and made their way to the temple. I followed them. Everyone filed in and took their place, each adding to the colourful scene. The white robes of the temple priests; the light orange of the Sannyasins or renunciants; the saffron and red saris of the women, and the white garments of the men. All sat cross-legged in lines of about ten deep.

Suddenly all became still, so quiet that I could hear my own heartbeat. The priests and male devotees started to chant; then the women would answer this call and the response seemed to produce an intoxicating effect. They went on and on in this way, from one to the other, back and forward, repeating the age-old chants, *om namah shivaya*, their voices rising and falling. Dinner hour came round. I forced myself to think of something funny as I joined the line of men and women winding their way down to the dining hall. I took my place among the lines of men sitting on the floor cross-legged in long rows – women at the far end and the men nearest the entrance. The servers came and ladled out vegetables and rice, passing along the rows, giving each of us the amount we asked for, as no one was allowed to waste the food he took. Great care was taken to ask for the amount which was wanted. I finished my dinner.

As a newcomer I was allowed three days to get acquainted with the ashram routine before being assigned a job, so I started back to the dormitory. On entering the forecourt, a well-loved voice greeted me – it was the Countess. She looked terrific. She was dressed in a simple short-sleeved dress and no shoes. 'Hi,' I said. But I didn't look directly at her. I knew that if I looked at her eyes and her face I was lost.

'It's John,' she said to the young blonde woman beside her, as I gave her a kiss on the cheek. Then she asked me how I liked being in India. They waited for my answer without any sign of impatience.

'I think it's smashing,' I lied. She introduced me to her friend – Daphne. There was an awkward silence; they expected me to talk some more. But the elegant way they were standing there unnerved me. I felt like some thick, country bumpkin who suddenly finds himself in the company of the king's beautiful daughters.

Daphne prompted me. 'We're short of two things here, John, English sweets and gossip!'

I gave an uncomfortable laugh, I felt foolish. Only children or the pampered rich could say such things and mean them . . . 'No sweets! What a shame! Still it's smashing here,' I laughed.

'You've already said that,' Daphne told me irritably.

The Countess smiled tenderly. 'John doesn't like gossip.' I don't dislike it, I thought to myself; I've not really had much practice. But if that's what they like, I'll see what I can do.

The next day, as the Countess was taking me over to visit one of the surrounding villages, I suddenly got tired, partly because of the fierce heat, but mainly on account of the mad rushing thoughts in my mind. Trying for the most favourable way to put things, in the end I blurted out, 'I want to tell you something.' She looked at me suspiciously. We were alone, surrounded by fields. I told her that I had not been a chess player all my life as I had claimed . . . then, briefly, I told her the truth about my earlier existence, trying where possible to make it sound normal. She listened quietly. When I finished, she looked sad. But I didn't know if she was sad at what she'd just heard, or sad because somehow she felt she'd been conned. 'And there's something else . . .' But she looked worried, so I just said, 'It doesn't matter, I can't explain it to you very well anyway.'

After all, how do you talk about love after a life spent relating to others through violence, aggression and fear? I know I'm a bit too common for you and my social skills are a bit lacking, but I love you, so could you keep with me while I tune them up a bit? We walked on in silence for a good length of time before she spoke. When she did it was in a relaxed, kindly sort of tone – about the guru and the ashram, about how everything

was as it should be because it was all consciousness, etc., etc.
. . . Fuck consciousness, I thought. What about us? Her peace
of mind had taken enough knocks for one day and I wasn't
brave enough to face any either, especially a hard one in the
form of a clearly stated rejection.

It was getting plainer every day that I wasn't part of her
thoughts. She was becoming more and more absorbed in
following the guru and her spiritual contemplations.

Funny how heavy work followed me. I was given the job
of breaking up boulders with a sledge-hammer for the flower
gardens – hard labour under a very hot sun. Take your shirt
off to cool, the mosquitoes bite you to death; put it back on,
sweat to death. Hard to hold anything together.

Against ashram rules, I took to wandering off, down dusty
paths and narrow tracks that led to little shanty villages scattered around the area. One humid afternoon I found myself
walking along a path I had not been along before. Two wide
draining ditches, damp and slushy, on either side allowed
thick, green shrubbery to grow effortlessly under the wilting
sun. That simple bit of irrigation gave the place a cool thirst-
quenching effect. The path stopped at a clearing. Half a dozen
wooden huts made up a village where swarms of flies buzzed
over animal droppings, and squawking hens in wicker baskets
strained scrawny necks to catch the flies.

The place seemed empty but smoke was coming from one
of the huts and there was a strong smell of spices in the air.
A rough, wooden sign, faded by the sun, nailed to the door,
made my heart jump: 'WINE'. The cure for everything! A radio
blared out an old rock 'n' roll song in a foreign language. It
had been a hit in England when I was a teenager.

> Listen to the patter of the pouring rain,
> Telling me just what a fool I've been.

The only girl I ever loved has gone away
Looking for a brand new star.

But little does she know that when she left that day,
Along with her she took my heart . . .

An old Indian looked out, surprised to see me standing there;
he gave me a welcoming smile. Wherever you find them, pubs
seem friendly places. If I just had a little drop of wine, it would
soon get rid of the sadness. My nerves were tight as I walked
away.

One day looking through a book dealing with 'the nature
of consciousness' to get away from thinking of the Countess,
I came across a passage that went something like this: 'What
matter if my beloved have kind and gentle ways, beautiful and
loving, if she be not kind to me?' Well . . . others had been in
the same boat! A woman could bring a sage to his knees, and
not just for prayer.

My mind was bogged down in constant sadness. Trying
to walk it off was useless. Whichever direction I went in, I'd
bump into groups of young, middle-class men and women,
clean and fresh, whom it didn't seem possible that life had
touched, discussing in posh, educated voices the hardships
that had been handed them until, on the point of suicide,
they had found yoga! It became maddening. Every time I tried
to start a conversation they immediately brought it round to
yoga. Some seemed very sincere and were really nice with it.
But most wandered slowly about and when they met you their
faces took on a tender look which quickly turned to irritation
if the conversation veered away from the ashram or the guru.
They seemed devoid of memory or concentration, or any of
the fine attributes that meditation is supposed to enhance.
Others sat around the café drinking tea, ecstatic expressions

on their faces – appealing for attention. Scoundrels? Perhaps. Who's not?

Now, sitting before Muktananda like this, I no longer knew what to do. A spiritual master, he is said to have transcended the mind. His teaching is: 'Nothing exists except pure consciousness.' Sitting cross-legged surrounded by other devotees, I tried to weigh up Muktananda, but as one who had only known the lowest forms of consciousness, it was nigh impossible for me to judge the highest. I watched his face; he's got terrific eyes. Sparkling with childlike innocence, they suddenly give you a knowing look. I would experience a feeling of contentment. Perhaps it was the air or the place. But whatever it was, it never seemed very long before I was back thinking about the Countess. I was old enough to know better, but I couldn't help hoping some magic might happen there – it seemed to be that sort of place.

I persevered with the meditation for a couple of weeks, but realized that I was not doing myself or anyone else any good by staying there, so early the following morning I packed my bag and left. As I stood waiting for the bus to Bombay, I looked back at the temple dome. It made me feel sad as hell.

On the way I met a guy who was fond of playing chess. He helped me to get lodgings in Bombay. Apparently his uncle was ambassador for Austria and he would go around conning money out of the other embassies. He wanted me to join up at it with him. But I had already been down that road . . .

I had to wait a week for a flight to England, so one night I went to a place where there is a massive temple hewn out of the solid rocks of a mountainside. In the temple I got into a relaxed, peaceful state and the night seemed to pass very quickly. As I came out it was dawn, just turning to light. Everywhere was wet with dew, so I placed the only thing I had – *The Book of the Guru Gita* – on the ground and sat on it while I waited for the bus. A group of well-to-do Indians came up, also waiting for the bus. I was surprised when one of them spoke to me in English: 'In India we do not sit on holy books.' I didn't reply. They started talking seriously among themselves. Then the self-appointed guardian of the holy scriptures spoke once more – dawn light softened his voice dangerously – : 'That is a most sacred book . . . What kind of a devil are you . . . ?'

But I was too empty to answer. Back in England I never met the Countess again, nor did I play in any more chess tournaments. Time clouding memory cured my longings for both.

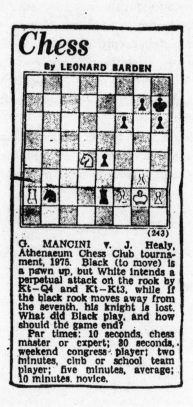

Chess

By LEONARD BARDEN

(243)

G. MANCINI v. J. Healy, Athenæum Chess Club tournament, 1975. Black (to move) is a pawn up, but White intends a perpetual attack on the rook by Kt—Q4 and Kt—Kt3, while if the black rook moves away from the seventh, his knight is lost. What did Black play, and how should the game end?

Par times: 10 seconds, chess master or expert; 30 seconds, weekend congress player; two minutes, club or school team player; five minutes, average; 10 minutes, novice.

Evening Standard, 5 April 1975

Afterword
by Colin MacCabe

The Grass Arena, a substantial typescript, sat on my desk for several weeks before I got around to reading it. It had been recommended to me by Jo Spence, the photographer, and I should have known to trust her judgement. However, my current job consists principally of reading potential film scripts and one result of ploughing through large quantities of banal and predictable writing is that one comes to dread reading instead of turning to it with anticipation, pleasure and excitement. But from the first page of *The Grass Arena*, and its traumatic introduction to father and son, a routine chore was transformed into a rare privilege. This was writing of the very highest quality. The pages turned themselves and the clock went unconsulted as I concluded John Healy's account of his life at a sitting. It was obvious that this was a work of great importance which deserved as large a readership as possible. I was delighted when Faber responded as positively to the text as I had, and was only too pleased to be asked to introduce it.

The simplest way of recommending this text is to say that, perhaps like all great books, it leaves you permanently altered. 'Read it and you'll never be the same again' is the adman's version of the truth that writing can offer experience of the existence of others which enlarges and transforms one's own. To read this book is to descend into the 'grass arena', to roam the parks and streets of inner London as a vagrant alcoholic.

By the time I had finished reading this extraordinary document I saw the streets of my native city – which until then I had thought so familiar – from a new angle and with a different light that revealed a whole society of which I had only ever seen isolated individuals.

It would be wrong, however, to stress the importance of this work as a sociological document. Certainly it reveals a subculture that no ordinary researcher could ever penetrate but the interest of the book lies in the precision and the accuracy of the description. Figures like the Sham or the Dip are brought into sharp focus in a few clear sentences; given meaning and identity in a world that, before this book, would have viewed them merely as pedestrian hazards. Equally it would be misleading to classify it in the 'confessions-of-an-alcoholic' mode. If the corrosive energy of drink has rarely been more graphically and disturbingly described, this is not a manifesto for Alcoholics Anonymous but the record of a life which, even in this too much recorded age, would otherwise be classified as unworthy of notice.

No doubt some will look for antecedents to this book but consideration of them merely emphasizes the unique quality of Healy's account. Beside it, a book like Orwell's *Down and Out in Paris and London* seems a rather inaccurate tourist guide. Even Bukowski's journeys through alcohol and Los Angeles take place in a world for which the grass arena is still the other side of the tracks. Bukowski's protagonist still moves from bar to rented room, never leaving a sparse network of social relations, never ceasing to write. The only book that begins to evoke a real comparison in English is William Burroughs's *Junkie*, but Burroughs comes from an educated and wealthy middle class that provides the money and contacts which are an ever-present safety net. It is interesting that Burroughs, deeply versed in literature, made a deliberate decision to write his account of addiction in the hard-boiled cadences of a Hammet detective novel, that most urban of genres. It is the same literary form that can be glimpsed behind Healy's writing – detective fiction was his only reading until chess introduced him to the culture of the middle class. But Burroughs's choice verged on a mannered affectation, Healy's is a visceral decision. Healy's writing rejects totally any of those rhetorical personalities which so much of our culture mistakes for a sense of self. There is no striving after some totalizing consciousness, no pedantic spelling out of the lessons learned from experience, no maudlin grotesque of a self whingeing about its conditions of existence. What we have here is description of the highest order, the eschewing of all levels of morality and psychology in favour of an ethic and aesthetic of accuracy – the determination to record what one human being has observed and experienced. There is no need in this account for the register of either excuse or apology, there is simply the necessity to bear witness to what has occurred.

There can be few who live and work in Central London who have not encountered the inhabitants of *The Grass Arena* and yet I, for one, had never considered the texture of their lives. Indeed, I had assumed it to be so solitary and isolated as to be without substance. Certainly one can see them early in the morning, gathered together on a bench, their movements slightly exaggerated and slow as the first cider bottle of the day begins to release its destructive magic. But the complexity and coherence of the world through which they move – the round of begging, drinking, sleeping, fighting – was something I had never imagined. Nor – and this is one of the most chilling aspects of the book – had I ever considered that invisible social area where these most marginal of people encounter the central power of the State. The casual violence of the police stations and gaols is all the more effectively described because it lacks all trace either of self-pity or of blame. This is the way the world is when the dialectic of need and power is deprived of the social conventions which usually organize its inherent violence.

Although no confession manual, *The Grass Arena* is one of the most important descriptions of addiction I have ever read. In a world where the national and international ravages of both legal and illegal addictions are daily more apparent, one might expect enormous resources to be allocated to research devoted to understanding this phenomenon. The reality is very different. Little is spent on research and any effort merely to state the facts or record the truth is actively discouraged. Addiction, like its political counterpart, terrorism, are crippled Utopianisms whose visions of a better life are so threatening to the normal social order that they must immediately be transformed into illness or crime. But just as the terrorist tries desperately and evilly to search for a more adequate relation between self and State so the addict tries equally to seek a more fulfilling relation between self and body. To think, even briefly, about addiction is to disturb one of the West's crucial constitutive divisions: that between body and mind. The endless question as to whether alcoholism is physical or psychological is, whatever interesting research it may incidentally occasion, fundamentally flawed. In almost all inquiries into addiction it is similar questions which ensure that problem and method pass one another by. What we so desperately need, as in so many other related fields, is a way of conceptualizing body and mind so that they become functions of each other. The power and importance of our mental images of the body and the way they feed back into our very flesh was graphically evident in the hysterical paralysis that was so prominent a form of mental disorder at the end of the nineteenth century. A hysteric's paralysed leg was indeed paralysed, but the leg affected was not the anatomical leg with muscles stretching up into the back but the leg as defined by common sense – the leg as we understand it in everyday speech. The importance of psychoanalysis is that it grew out of the treatment of hysteria and, in particular, the astonishing interchange whereby limbs could be freed from paralysis by the activation of memory in speech. Psychoanalysis, from this perspective, can best be understood as a scientific rediscovery of magic that avoids the crippling division between mind and body. Moreover, the active therapeutic role of the analyst focuses attention on the self as formed in a series of relations with others, which renders that self continuously and constitutively unfinished – identity is always provisional and mistaken. Psychoanalysis should therefore be the area in which one could find the concepts to deal with addiction. But psychoanalysis, through historical circumstances, has had to limit its analysis of the relation between self and others to the very restricted domain of the family. *The Grass Arena* would suggest that the relation to alcohol can only be understood within a wider social panorama.

Alcoholism and addiction in general remain opaque to psychoanalysis. In the twenty-four volumes of the Standard Edition Freud only refers to alcoholism once and that is in a humorous aside when he contrasts the difficulties that confront the fulfilment of the sexual drive with the alcoholic's ease in aligning object and desire. Later psychoanalysts who have addressed the problem are broadly agreed that it is impossible to link alcoholism directly to sexuality. They have emphasized the alcoholic's search for a harmonious relation to the world and have located this search in a fundamentally unsatisfactory relation between the very small infant and its mother. Alcohol, on this account, becomes a fantasy object for the alcoholic, an orally ingested liquid that will re-establish a harmonious relation with the mother.

The emphasis on the desire for harmony between self and world is undoubtedly correct and it would be foolish to deny that every desire and drive is underpinned by our earliest relationships. However, *The Grass Arena* makes clear that, if we are to understand the harmony the alcoholic seeks, we can only understand it in relation to a whole social environment. John Healy's painfully exact description of his youth must rank as one of the most horrendous accounts of a modern urban childhood. The brutalities of the father are duplicated time and again in the environment surrounding the small boy, and the recourse to alcohol can be clearly seen as the construction of a more harmonious world.

One of the amazing strengths of the book is that it manages to convey that the world of the grass arena, a world ready to slip at a moment's notice into the most savage violence, can be seen as preferable to the available alternatives. In the grass arena, social relations are simplified, broken down into a straightforward duality: either you will share the bottle and immediately there is a real sociality, a Utopia besides which all other social relations seem unsatisfactory, or you will steal the bottle and then, equally immediately, there is a direct struggle for power, which has, at least, the virtue of honesty. As you read this remarkable account of a life, it becomes clear how the grass arena, for its inhabitants, comes to be a more satisfactory version of the city that surrounds it.

Beyond the harmony alcohol can produce in a hostile world lies the search for something even more fundamental. No matter how satisfactory any particular set of social or individual relationships may be, this does not mean that the self is not subject to the most fundamental conflict. It is often assumed that the scandal that has always dogged psychoanalysis is its concern with sex. But sex is the common currency of the twentieth century. The real scandal of psychoanalysis, and one that psychoanalysis as an institution has itself found scandalous, is its concern with death. Much ink has been spilled on Freud's early patients' accounts of their sexual abuse as children and whether these accounts should be regarded as fantasy or reality. However, the truly traumatic clinical encounters for Freud were those with soldiers suffering from shell shock. Freud could only explain the endless re-enactment of the terror of battle as tapping a drive even more powerful than the sexual instinct, the drive to extinction. In a Western civilization that defines its psychology and ethics in terms of 'the pursuit of happiness', it is worse than unfashionable to draw attention to the fundamental unhappiness that haunts our very existence. To be introduced to the rhythm of desire and satisfaction is, according to Freud, to be introduced to the possibility that this rhythm will cease. Underlying any particular satisfaction is the possibility of a greater satisfaction, which would release us from the whole cycle of desire and its gratification. The ultimate harmony we seek is that of not-being and this drive towards death is particularly evident in alcoholism. The savage pleasure of the annihilation of self is well captured in Healy's account of his own descent into hell. As the drink takes its hold, time dissolves and Healy's life loses its sequential narrative to become a series of disconnected tableaux, which would finally have been erased, unrecorded and unremembered, if he had not encountered the game of chess.

Chess, unlike alcoholism, has received an inordinate amount of attention from psychoanalysis. While alcoholism, and all associated psychoses, are difficult to explain simply in terms of the family, chess brings us firmly back into a world of limited family relations and their attendant neuroses. Indeed many famous chess players have been analysed as finding in the neurotic structures of chess a way of holding in check psychoses which have finally erupted as they have abandoned the game. Healy comes to chess from the other side, as it were. An ex-addict, he realizes that chess is an addiction but sees its own addictive pattern as a temporary cure. Above all, it enables him to enter the world of 'normal' social relations through the very specific access provided by fellow chess enthusiasts. In his fascinating book on chess, *Idle Passion*, Alexander Cockburn sees the majority of chess players as opting out of a society over which they feel they have no control:

A possibility to be explored is that chess tends to become the overriding passion in social groups that enjoy social power and position but are excluded from the direct exercise of political power. Chess is par excellence the pastime of a disinherited ruling class that continues to crave political dominion but has seen it usurped. Just as, in psychoanalytical terms, chess is a way of sublimating Oedipal conflicts, so, in social terms, it is a device for sublimating political aspirations; the empty omnipotence exercised by the player over his pieces is consolation for lost power. *It is, in general, not a preparation for regaining it.* [my italics]

Whatever the general truth of Cockburn's argument, Healy is a direct counter-example. If, for many chess players, chess is a way out of a society in which they feel powerless, for Healy it was a way in. His final dissatisfaction with it is built into the clarity with which he understands its appeal as a channel for aggression and hostility. What is extraordinary, and would take us once again into that little-understood area where mind and body are effects of one another, is how, after so many years of alcohol abuse, he was able to master this most complex of games.

However, that achievement almost fades into insignificance beside the even more remarkable accomplishment of having written this book. In writing Healy may have finally found a cure that will not in turn become a disease. Writing offers an annihilation of self that will not fix itself in a repetitive channel of addiction. The final experiences that the book records, experiences of religion and love, hold out no hope. But they do offer a perspective on desire and death that leaves both the grass arena and its urban surroundings behind.

To enter this book is, I would imagine for almost any reader and certainly for myself, to enter another world. As one leaves it, as the familiar surroundings reassemble to convince one of the reality and inevitability of one's own existence, that existence should feel both challenged and enriched. Challenged by the existence of lives that one might prefer to ignore, enriched by the record of a life that has compelled attention.

PENGUIN MODERN CLASSICS

A TRANQUIL STAR
PRIMO LEVI

'Works of the highest order of imagination … remind us why Levi is an indispensable writer' *Sunday Telegraph*

Primo Levi was one of the most astonishing voices to emerge from the twentieth century. This landmark selection of seventeen short stories, translated into English for the first time, opens up a world of wonder, love, cruelty and curious twists of fate, where nothing is as it seems. In 'The Fugitive' an office worker composes the most beautiful poem ever with unforeseen consequences, while 'Magic Paint' sees a group of researchers develop a paint that mysteriously protects them from misfortune. 'Gladiators' and 'The Knall' are chilling explorations of mass violence, and in 'The Tranquil Star' a simple story of stargazing becomes a meditation on language, imagination and infinity.

'We are blessed with this collection' *Herald*

PENGUIN MODERN CLASSICS

THE LONELY LONDONERS
SAM SELVON

'Unforgettable … a vernacular comedy of pathos' *Guardian*

At Waterloo Station, hopeful new arrivals from the West Indies step off the boat train, ready to start afresh in 1950s London. There, homesick Moses Aloetta, who has already lived in the city for years, meets Henry 'Sir Galahad' Oliver and shows him the ropes. In this strange, cold and foggy city where the natives can be less than friendly at the sight of a black face, has Galahad met his Waterloo?

But the irrepressible newcomer cannot be cast down. He and all the other lonely new Londoners – from shiftless Cap to Tolroy, whose family has descended on him from Jamaica – must try to create a new life for themselves. As pessimistic 'old veteran' Moses watches their attempts, they gradually learn to survive and come to love the heady excitements of London.

With a new Introduction by Susheila Nasta

PENGUIN MODERN CLASSICS

LIGHT YEARS
JAMES SALTER

'An American master of fiction' *Independent*

Negra and Viri are a couple whose enviable life is centred on civilized pleasures, their children, a variety of friends, and days lived to the utmost, be it skating on a frozen river or summers by the sea. It is a world built on matrimony, and its details – the one moment, one hour, one day – recapture everything.

But fine cracks are beginning to spread through the shimmering surface – flaws that will eventually mar the lovely picture beyond repair. Seductive, witty, tender and resonant, *Light Years* is a ravishing novel of lost lives and the elusiveness of happiness.

'Remarkable ... a moving ode to beautiful lives frayed by time' *Esquire*

*Contemporary ... Provocative ... Outrageous ...
Prophetic ... Groundbreaking ... Funny ... Disturbing ...
Different ... Moving ... Revolutionary ... Inspiring ...
Subversive ... Life-changing ...*

What makes a modern classic?

At Penguin Classics our mission has always been to make the best
books ever written available to everyone. And that also means
constantly redefining and refreshing exactly what makes a 'classic'.
That's where Modern Classics come in. Since 1961 they have been an
organic, ever-growing and ever-evolving list of books from the last
hundred (or so) years that we believe will continue to be read over and
over again.

They could be books that have inspired political dissent, such as
Animal Farm. Some, like *Lolita* or *A Clockwork Orange*, may have
caused shock and outrage. Many have led to great films, from *In Cold
Blood* to *One Flew Over the Cuckoo's Nest*. They have broken down
barriers – whether social, sexual, or, in the case of *Ulysses*, the
boundaries of language itself. And they might – like *Goldfinger* or
Scoop – just be pure classic escapism. Whatever the reason, Penguin
Modern Classics continue to inspire, entertain and enlighten millions
of readers everywhere.

'No publisher has had more influence on reading habits than Penguin'
Independent

'Penguins provided a crash course in world literature'
Guardian

The best books ever written

PENGUIN (P) CLASSICS

SINCE 1946

Find out more at www.penguinclassics.com